# AIKIDO
## THE ART OF
## TRANSFORMATION

"Anyone interested in martial arts, the spiritual path, personal transformation, or the connection between them should read this book. It takes you on the compelling journey of Robert Nadeau Shihan, one of the few Americans who studied personally with Morihei Ueshiba, the founder of Aikido, and then brought his message to the West. This book is an affirmation and testimony of how embodied transformation is possible through a master teacher."

RICHARD STROZZI-HECKLER, 7TH DAN SHIHAN IN AIKIDO, FOUNDER OF TWO ROCK DOJO, COFOUNDER OF TAMALPAIS AIKIDO, AND AUTHOR OF *EMBODYING THE MYSTERY*

"A fascinating tribute to a most unusual, passionate, and influential Western teacher of Aikido, Robert Nadeau. Whether or not you have met Nadeau Sensei, you will be transported by the vivid personal accounts of his students to the ever-challenging, courageous, and deeply transformative training he facilitates. An inspiring resource that will reverberate long into the future."

LINDA HOLIDAY, AIKIDO 7TH DAN AND AUTHOR OF *JOURNEY TO THE HEART OF AIKIDO*

"There is much to learn from Robert. His emphasis on experiential development by deeply understanding and applying powerful principles to life is transforming for everybody."

PETER RALSTON, AUTHOR OF *THE ART OF MASTERY*

"Nadeau Sensei's teachings transformed my life, formed the foundation for my work in conflict resolution, and continue to this day to inform my mediation practice."

ANTONIO PIAZZA, PARTNER AT MEDIATED NEGOTIATIONS

"An extraordinary book for anyone—those who train in Aikido and those who don't—who wants to master their energy system to enhance their performance, well-being, and creativity while elevating their consciousness. When it comes to transformational teachers, Robert Nadeau is the real deal."

AIMEE BERNSTEIN, M.ED., MFCC, PRESIDENT OF
OPEN MIND ADVENTURES AND AUTHOR OF
*STRESS LESS ACHIEVE MORE*

"This exciting book offers Nadeau Sensei's teachings and personal life story together with the experiences of his students. His unique style of expression leads to unexpected insights and upgrades to one's life, on and off the mat."

MARY HEINY, AIKIDO 7TH DAN, NADEAU STUDENT, AND
CO-INSTRUCTOR OF AIKIDO AT THE AIKI SUMMER RETREATS

"If you're interested in the resonance of human systems or imagine it's possible to feel subtle energies and embrace them to move into more aliveness, get this book. With its unique blending of story, testimony, philosophy, and biography, *Aikido: The Art of Transformation* helps every willing reader occupy themselves, their work, and their lives from a place of discovery and rapture. It's a shining testament to the unique, brilliant master teacher Robert Nadeau. It will inspire you to settle, open, and see your life anew."

RENÉE GREGORIO, POET AND AUTHOR OF
*THE WRITER WHO INHABITS YOUR BODY* AND
*ABYSS & BRIDGE*

"It has been a long-standing desire of mine to understand Nadeau's teachings since meeting him many years ago. Now, in one book, his many students have provided an explanation of his teachings on the spirit of Aikido and how to develop it. This book is an important contribution and a must-read for anyone interested in Aikido."

SUSAN PERRY, AIKIDO 6TH DAN AND AUTHOR OF
*THE HIDDEN POWER OF AIKIDO*

# AIKIDO
## THE ART OF
## TRANSFORMATION

*The Life & Teachings of*
## Robert Nadeau

**A Sacred Planet Book**

Teja Bell, Laurin Herr,
Richard Moon, Bob Noha,
Susan Spence, and Elaine Yoder

Park Street Press
Rochester, Vermont

Park Street Press
One Park Street
Rochester, Vermont 05767
www.ParkStPress.com

Text stock is SFI certified

Park Street Press is a division of Inner Traditions International

**Sacred Planet Books** are curated by Richard Grossinger, Inner Traditions editorial board member and cofounder and former publisher of North Atlantic Books. The Sacred Planet collection, published under the umbrella of the Inner Traditions family of imprints, includes works on the themes of consciousness, cosmology, alternative medicine, dreams, climate, permaculture, alchemy, shamanic studies, oracles, astrology, crystals, hyperobjects, locutions, and subtle bodies.

Cataloging-in-Publication Data for this title is available from the Library of Congress

ISBN 979-8-88850-071-2 (print)
ISBN 979-8-88850-072-9 (ebook)

Printed and bound in the United States by Lake Book Manufacturing, LLC
The text stock is SFI certified. The Sustainable Forestry Initiative® program promotes sustainable forest management.

10  9  8  7  6  5  4  3  2  1

Text design and layout by Priscilla Harris Baker
This book was typeset in Garamond Premier Pro with Gill Sans, Meno, and Real Head used as display typefaces

To send correspondence to the author of this book, mail a first-class letter to the author c/o Inner Traditions • Bear & Company, One Park Street, Rochester, VT 05767, and we will forward the communication.

# Contents

Introduction   1

ONE

The Life of Robert Nadeau   7

TWO

Experiences, Memories, and Insights   60

THREE

Teachings of Robert Nadeau   84

FOUR

Recollections and
Reverberations   253

Glossary   288

Notes   292

Bibliography   293

Additional Resources   294

Authors/Editors and Contributors   295

Index   301

# Introduction

There have been many masters and many teachers of a variety of arts over time: fine arts, philosophy, poetry, martial arts, and more. Not all masters are good teachers and not all teachers who command a depth of mastery can transmit to their students the essence at the heart of their chosen art. History has shown us how rare it is for someone to be both a technical master of their art and a gifted teacher. Robert Nadeau, Aikido 8th Dan Shihan (8th degree black belt Master Teacher), is just such an exceptional person.

Nadeau's spiritual journey emerged first as a teenager's questions about the nature of the Universe and the meaning of life. He began searching for answers in judo, yoga, meditation, and bodybuilding. His curiosity set him on a course of lifelong study into the inner dynamics of human development. He was especially drawn to martial arts, showing talent from an early age and enthusiastically studying several, which is how he crossed paths in Tokyo in the early 1960s with the founder of Aikido, the extraordinary Morihei Ueshiba Osensei. ("Osensei" is an honorific title in Japanese meaning "Great Teacher" and is a respectful way to refer to Morihei Ueshiba without always using his full name.)

Nadeau's time with Morihei Ueshiba was life changing. It coalesced the threads of his prior years of seeking and training. It opened him to deeper knowledge through direct experience of the energy, design, and functioning of the Universe. Osensei taught him

Morihei Ueshiba Osensei (1883–1969).

that the true purpose of Aikido is personal transformation, a core precept that the twentysomething Nadeau took to heart. His evolution as a teacher is anchored in a foundation of martial arts. His practice has expanded through his persistent exploration of human nature, higher

Robert Nadeau and Morihei Ueshiba, 1964.

consciousness, and the internal processes of personal growth. He likes to describe himself as a mapmaker and guide on the pathway toward genuine self-discovery, offering universal lessons and practices that apply well beyond Aikido.

Nadeau was not Morihei Ueshiba Osensei's only *deshi* (disciple), nor even the only American to practice directly under him. But he has made uniquely significant contributions to the long-term growth and evolution of Aikido outside of Japan. In particular, his adaptive rephrasing of Osensei's core teachings and reframing of Osensei's esoteric energy practices made them more accessible to modern Western students, and in the process he helped, directly and indirectly, to introduce Osensei's themes to leaders in diverse fields like psychology, somatics, and sports training, as well as into the wider cultural vernacular.

Nadeau's transmission of Osensei's inner art is a rare and precious treasure for students of the Way of Aikido. But his lifelong message has been that these are lessons anyone can use to develop into a better version of themselves, even someone with no background in Aikido or interest in martial arts.

Morihei Ueshiba Osensei inspired Robert Nadeau to explore the inner Aikido of mind/body harmony and personal growth. Nadeau, in turn, has dedicated his life to passing on that spark of inspiration, the living essence of Osensei's Aikido. This, in turn, has now inspired the six of us, all senior students of Nadeau Sensei, to come together to make this book about his remarkable life and quintessential teachings.

As writers and editors, our primary challenge has been to find a way, within the static pages and linear form of a book, to convey Nadeau Sensei's life and teachings in a way that will be meaningful to both students of Aikido and nonstudents alike.

We initially called our project Nadeau Roku, using the Japanese Zen term *roku* for the long tradition of creating such books about important teachers by collecting "stories" about them. We invited a wide community of individuals to contribute their impressions, insights, and recollections about Robert Nadeau. More than eighty people responded, and their writings have been edited together with a selection of photographs, also generously contributed, to form the heart of this book: a written and pictorial record of Nadeau Sensei, told through the voices of his students and friends.

The first chapter is a chronological history of Robert Nadeau's life, how he came to Aikido, and significant milestones during his long life. We drew from our knowledge and history with him, as well as from numerous interviews and books published about him over the years. Nadeau Sensei contributed many historical photographs from his private collection.

The second chapter is a collection of stories contributed by the vital and creative community of students and instructors who have directly experienced Nadeau Sensei's teachings over the decades. They describe his influential role within the Aikido community, what it has been like to train with him, and the relevance of his teachings to their personal development.

The third chapter is our synthesis of Nadeau Sensei's core lessons concerning personal transformation and universal principles. He treats Aikido as much more than a martial art. He presents it as a path toward profound personal and spiritual development. We have done our best to communicate his unique approach to "the Aikido that can't be seen with the human eye." He teaches Aikido from the inside out. His emphasis is always on the importance of direct energetic engagement and full experience as an essential part of Aikido training, and an effective internal process that can be integrated into our daily lives. He encourages everyone to discover finer energetic dimensions for themselves, and our description of his teachings is intended to provide a helpful map and some basic tools for further exploration. To enliven the lessons with a variety of individual recollections and perspectives, we have also woven selected personal stories through this chapter.

The fourth chapter holds more stories contributed by people who have known and trained with Nadeau Sensei at various times and places around the world. They describe their initial encounters with Nadeau, what it has been like to have him as a teacher, and what his teachings have meant to them on a personal level. They recount historical anecdotes, recall vivid experiences, and tell of interactions with Nadeau, on and off the mat, that changed the course of their lives.

Organizing, writing, and illustrating this book has been an opportunity for the six of us to collectively dig more deeply into our understanding of Aikido and of Robert Nadeau—the person and the teacher. The process has become a kind of ongoing training, a part of our continuing Aikido *shugyo* (personal development). We hope that these pages will serve to both acknowledge Nadeau Sensei's lifetime contributions and introduce readers to the inspiring story of his life and the vitality of his teachings.

We offer this book in gratitude to our teacher and friend of many years. He has been very supportive of our efforts, opening his scrapbook, sharing his memories, and giving us critical feedback at several stages of our creative process. We couldn't have done it without him. All errors and omissions are ours.

TEJA BELL, LAURIN HERR, RICHARD MOON,
ROBERT NOHA, SUSAN SPENCE, AND ELAINE YODER

## ONE

# The Life of Robert Nadeau

Robert Edward Nadeau was born March 10, 1937, to Flora (*née* LeBlanc) and Arthur Joseph Nadeau, the youngest of six children in a large Catholic family with French Canadian roots. As a small boy, he lived in the rural town of Fulton, New York, roughly ten miles south of Lake Ontario. During World War II, his family moved to Hartford, Connecticut, where he attended Catholic grammar school. The picture below was taken to commemorate his First Communion.

Robert Nadeau, First Communion, age seven-eight, Hartford, CT.

Cover of *Get Tough* by
W. E. Fairbairn, originally
published 1942.

In 1951, when he was fourteen, he moved to Redwood City, California. His older sister helped him find a weekend job at the local recycling center. There he came across an old copy of *Get Tough*, an early English guide to hand-to-hand fighting based on the practical methods used to train British commandos during World War II. It was his first exposure to martial arts, and he was fascinated.

He entered Sequoia High School in Redwood City, where one of the teachers, Ed DeMello, was a black belt in judo and a former paratrooper in World War II. He offered judo classes and Nadeau jumped in! This was his first formal martial arts training, and according to DeMello, Nadeau "took to it like a duck to water." As a teenager, it was also his first encounter with Eastern philosophy, which attracted him and seemed to hold meaning for him. The local newspaper, reporting on activities at the high school, featured a picture of sixteen-year-old Nadeau in a judo demonstration cleanly throwing his coach with *seoi-nage* (shoulder throw).

In most ways, he was growing up much like all high school boys

Robert Nadeau throwing Sequoia High School Judo coach, age sixteen.

everywhere, getting all dressed up for prom night and stepping out, all smiles, with his steady girlfriend, Margie Fiedler.

With Margie Fiedler, age seventeen.

With Mingo,
age twenty.

Around this same time, Nadeau also began developing himself physically through weight training under Floyd Page, a former Mr. America. During the very early stages of his bodybuilding efforts, still a teenager, he posed with his dog Mingo. He continued bodybuilding for many years, developing a strong muscular physique as he entered adulthood.

But throughout his high school years he recalls feeling, "If the world as I know it is all there is, then I'm not really interested." At the same time, he intensely hoped that there actually was "something more."

Once, one of his high school teachers played light symphonic music in the classroom and asked all the students to write an essay as they listened. Nadeau wrote a spiritual essay. The next morning, his teacher praised his essay and read it aloud in front of everyone, surprising Nadeau. But his classmates were even more surprised when the teacher revealed Nadeau as the author of the exemplary essay because they only thought of him as the black leather jacket "rebel" sitting in the back row. It made teenage Nadeau feel that his fellow students didn't really know him. At the same time, he realized that he hadn't really figured himself out either.

During his senior year in high school, Nadeau enlisted in the Marine Reserves, where, despite his youth, he was assigned to lead self-defense classes because he had more martial arts experience than anyone else in his local reserve unit.

After graduation, he enrolled in his local two-year community college, the College of San Mateo.

Starting in 1955, Nadeau extended his judo training under Yasutoshi "Moon" Watanabe Sensei in Redwood City. Watanabe

In the Marine Reserves, age eighteen.

Sensei had started judo in Hawaii at age eleven, then won the Hawaiian Island Judo Championship at age twenty-three. As a judo teacher in Redwood City, his whole approach focused on mind-body training. A sign in his dojo described the goals of judo as threefold, in this order: mental development, physical development, and proficiency in contests.

At the same time, Nadeau was becoming more and more curious about things like meditation. He tried a variety of approaches. He experimented with what he thought of as "concentration practices," like staring at a candle or sitting outdoors in nothing but swim trunks during a winter rainstorm. He did some Hatha yoga using pictures from a book as reference. But he soon realized that it would be helpful if he had a teacher who could properly guide him.

For a while, he attended a reading group studying the writings of Madame Helena Blavatsky, the founder of Theosophy, a neo-religious movement that draws from both esoteric European philosophies and Asian religions such as Hinduism and Buddhism. The logo for the Theosophical Society, founded by Madame Blavatsky and others in New York City in 1875, brought together various ancient symbols. Theosophy's amalgamation of different traditions was interesting for young Nadeau, and he found the group informative, but all the other members were much older, and he quickly came to feel that reading and

Theosophical Society seal, circa 1875.

talking about Theosophy wasn't enough for him. He wanted something more experiential.

In 1957, Nadeau started more regular meditation and yoga practice under the guidance of Walt Baptiste. Nadeau realized, in retrospect, that Walt Baptiste was ahead of his time in the way he taught bodybuilding for the physical body along with Hatha yoga for developing the energy body and meditation for developing a finer level of self. This training helped Nadeau develop good sitting basics and provided early experiences of "inner work." Nadeau began to feel the effects of this inner work on his judo, and this made him wonder how these practices related to each other.

Around this time, Nadeau read *Autobiography of a Yogi* by Paramahansa Yogananda, which made a strong impression on him. He went so far as to visit an ashram in Southern California. The level and frequency of yoga practice, the cloistered rhythms of monastic discipline, and the ashram's sense of community (*sangha*) all appealed to him, but he realized he was drawn to a more active kind of engagement with the world.

Meanwhile, three years out of high school and looking to serve (and be employed), Nadeau joined the Redwood City Police as a full-time officer in 1958, staying on the force until 1962.

In 1960, aged 21, he married Margie Fiedler, his high school sweetheart.

Wedding of Robert Nadeau and Margie Fiedler, Carmel, CA, 1960.

Working as a Redwood City Police Officer, 1958.

In 1961, Nadeau was introduced to Aikido. There were only two Aikido teachers in the San Francisco Bay area in those days. One was a Buddhist priest named Hara Kusada, and the other was Bob Tann, who had learned Aikido while stationed in Hawaii as a U.S. Marine. The San Francisco dojo was Tann Sensei's first attempt at teaching.

Decades later, Nadeau described his first encounter with Aikido in a 2021 interview with Patrick Cassidy posted on YouTube:

> I had a friend who was Japanese. He knew I was interested in martial arts and told me about Aikido. . . . So, I started looking around to see if I could learn anything about Aikido. . . . One day, I went to San Francisco to visit a judo school, and that day a guy was teach-

ing Aikido. He was new, with just a few white belts on the mat. I watched and felt "something there." Went back with a few training buddies, and the teacher started talking about mind-body harmony. Boom! I was immediately drawn and asked him to build up that class. That was Bob Tann teaching one of his first classes.[1]

Aikido made such a strong impression on twenty-four-year-old Nadeau that he immediately began to study with Tann Sensei, adding Aikido to his cross-training regime. This included his ongoing judo training with Moon Watanabe Sensei, plus his bodybuilding, yoga, and meditation practices, as well as Kenpo Karate classes and training in police tactics as a Redwood City policeman.

Nadeau described the initial attraction of Aikido in the same 2021 interview with Patrick Cassidy:

I really liked Aikido. Got fast results with the ideas I was hearing: keeping one-point, being centered, grounding. Early in my training with Bob Tann in South [San Francisco], Koichi Tohei, the head instructor [at Aikido Hombu Dojo (headquarters) in Tokyo] at the time, visited. He was like, amazing! In the sense of *ki* (vital energy) flow . . . really caught me. I had been training physically for ten years at this point. But doing little things, like centering. Suddenly it was different. My body was different. How it could perform was different. And it was kind of simple. Keep one point. Weight underside. Let energy flow. . . . It was like, WOW. I'd get fast reactions and fast feedback. It was the beginning of magic for me.[2]

In the fall of 1962, Nadeau and his wife Margie decided that he would leave his financially secure job as a police officer in Redwood City and together they would move to Japan so he could pursue his martial arts training and deepen his spiritual development. He boarded a ship in San Francisco and two weeks later landed in Yokohama. She followed a short while later. This was a turning point in their lives. Through personal introductions from friends in California, they were initially hosted by Takeo Nakano, the founding president of JuJu Cosmetics, and his family made them feel welcome in Tokyo.

Nadeau's initial goal was to become a better martial artist and continue his spiritual inquiries. When he first arrived in Japan, he immediately started practicing karate at the Japan Karate Association headquarters, judo at the Kodokan headquarters, and Aikido at Hombu Dojo. He also joined a group of foreigners informally practicing t'ai chi in the park with Wang Shu-chin, a well-known Chinese master living in Japan.

Over time, Nadeau increasingly felt more drawn to Aikido and gradually let go of the other arts. He felt sincerely welcomed by all the people he met through Aikido. Even more importantly,

With Takeo Nakano, his first Japanese host, at the Nakano family home, Tokyo, 1962.

With Margie and the Nakano family, Tokyo, 1963.

1. I will not discontinue the study of Judo without sufficient reason.
2. I will never do anything to disgrace the Kodokan's honor.
3. I will always comply with all regulations of the Kodokan in studying and in teaching Judo

**Kodokan member's oath.**

Kodokan Judo Institute membership card, 1962.

Japan Karate Association membership card, 1962.

Nadeau sensed that on both a personal and universal level, Morihei Ueshiba, the founder of Aikido, embodied the living experience of mind-body harmony that he had been seeking all along. He threw himself into Aikido, while still continuing his personal meditation practice.

In his years at Aikido Hombu Dojo, Nadeau took daily instruction from many senior Aikido teachers including chief instructor Koichi Tohei, Kisaburo Ozawa, Seigo Yamaguchi, Sadateru Arikawa, and Hiroshi Tada. He also attended classes taught by Osensei's son Kisshomaru Ueshiba, and by Morihiro Saito, who would travel from Iwama on Sundays to teach at Hombu.

Morihei Ueshiba Osensei teaching, Tokyo, 1962–64.

Nadeau practiced diligently and came to be accepted into Hombu's tight-knit community of Japanese *deshi* (disciples), who then included: Yoshimitsu Yamada, Seiichi Sugano, Mitsunari Kanai, Yutaka Kurita, Kazuo Chiba, Nobuyoshi Tamura, and Mitsugi Saotome. Mariye Yano was frequently around Osensei in those days, too.

Nadeau at Aikido Hombu Dojo, Tokyo, 1964, with Kisshomaru Ueshiba seated in background.

Nadeau with Koichi Tohei, Aikido Hombu Dojo Chief Instructor, and others, outside Tokyo 1962–64.

Left to right: Roy Suenaka, Morihei Ueshiba,
Seiichi Sugano, Robert Nadeau.

Nadeau did not reside inside Hombu Dojo with the other *uchideshi* (live-in disciples). Instead, he and his wife Margie rented a small apartment just around the corner from the dojo, close enough to easily get to classes or socialize after hours with friends from the dojo. In the hot Japanese summer, they even found time away from the dojo to go for a swim.

But for Nadeau and the other young *uchideshi* in those years, schedules mostly revolved around daily *keiko* (practice). And they were always on call to serve as Osensei's *uke* (attacking/receiving partner), or to travel with him. Sometimes, this meant a group effort, in jacket and tie, ready to accompany Osensei to a public demonstration.

Left to right: Margie Nadeau, Robert Nadeau,
Yoshimitsu Yamada, Eddie Hagihara.

Left to right: Seiichi Sugano, Morihiko Ichihashi,
Robert Nadeau, Shuji Maruyama.

Left to right: Yoshimitsu Yamada, Robert Nadeau, Margie Nadeau.

Other overseas students who were at Hombu Dojo with Nadeau in the early 1960s included Terry Dobson, Bob Frager, Eddie Hagihara from New York City, Henry Kono from Toronto, Virginia Mayhew,

Left to right: Robert Nadeau, Yutaka Kurita, Mitsunari Kanai, Nobuyoshi Tamura.

Left to right: Margie Nadeau, Verell Sugano, Terry Dobson, unknown, Eddie Hagihara.

and Seiichi Sugano's Australian-born wife Verell, as well as a few others from Europe and England. Frank Doran visited for two weeks in 1963 while on leave from his Marine base in Guam, a first meeting that developed into a lifelong friendship.

Nadeau's attraction to Aikido only grew the more he trained with Osensei. In the 2021 interview with Patrick Cassidy, Nadeau recalls the first time he took *ukemi* (art of attacking/rolling/falling) for Osensei:

Left to right: Robert Nadeau, Eddie Hagihara.

Osensei at Aikido Hombu Dojo, Tokyo, 1962–64.

I'd see Osensei bringing his hand up, and people would collapse, stuff like that. Ah, I really wanted to experience that, you know. I know he's not bullshit. I know that people aren't tanking for him. But, God, it looks that way. OK. So, he comes out one morning—when he walks through the dojo, all the students drop and sit, so we're all sitting down as he walks through. And he stops, and he looks at me, and he's six feet in front of me, standing there. And he presents his arm and says, "Nadeau, grab my arm." Oh, I'd been waiting for this for months, right. I'm in good shape. I've got all my California muscles. I'm up like a shot. That hand is right in front of me, and I reach for it. At that moment, I don't know where the hell I'm at. For me, it felt like I'd entered . . . I wasn't in the dojo anymore . . . I'd entered this realm. It felt like a kind of tunnel, kind of dark and long, and kind of rubbery because as I was drawn deeper into that tunnel, the rubber, kind of like a rubber band, tightened. And then I felt myself being flung out, again like a rubber band thing . . . flung out! As I'm being flung out, flying out going down, I hit the ground fairly hard . . . because I went in hard. I did notice that. I went in definite. I wasn't giving him a break. I really went for it. I went in strong and came out strong. When I hit the ground, everyone started laughing because I think my mouth was agape. I was, like, ahhhhh . . . what was THAT? Now you have to understand that somebody else could have had a similar experience in their first week in Aikido, but I'd been around for a while. I'd been thrown by guys, and you'd say, "Whew, this guy is strong," "Whew, this guy is fast," "Whew, this guy tricked me." There'd be something. With Osensei, it was, "What the hell was that?"[3]

Osensei noticed Nadeau's sincere interest in the deeper aspects of Aikido and welcomed his questions. Nadeau used these close encounters as opportunities to also ask Osensei personal questions. He sought guidance and confirmation as he intensified his own inner spiritual quest begun years before when he first started judo, yoga, and meditation back in America.

Osensei with students after practice,
Aikido Hombu Dojo, Tokyo, 1962–64.

Osensei taught Nadeau that the laws of universal functionality and spiritual growth operate together. Nadeau was impressed by how Osensei expressed this through Aikido and, even more directly, through his presence. Osensei emphasized to him how Aikido required more than just intellectual understanding of the concepts, and that authentic inner practice was necessary to grasp the "heart" of Aikido, to be able to manifest Aikido in the real world.

The following quote is drawn from an interview with Nadeau Sensei about Osensei, published by Stan Pranin in *Aikido Journal* in 1999:

I wish I could remember the first question I asked him [Osensei], but I can't recall. Whatever it was, he apparently liked the question and invited me to spend time with him. At first, I got some bad vibes from some of the seniors, but then Osensei kept asking for me, so they relaxed. A lot of it was just to be in his presence and try to absorb something, like osmosis. . . . I would communicate with Osensei by asking questions that I thought were major directions for

Osensei at Aikido
Hombu Dojo,
Tokyo, 1962–64.

my spiritual development that had begun years before in the States. I knew he was very advanced. So, I would say, "Does the Universe work this way?" and explain myself. I would ask him a major directional question. He would confirm or correct it, and then I would work with that information.[4]

Later, Nadeau was asked to take over from Terry Dobson as the editor of the monthly English-language *Aikido* newsletter published by Hombu Dojo, which led to even more frequent interactions with Osensei off the mat.

Osensei in the Aiki Shrine in Iwama, 1962–64.

Robert Nadeau bows to Osensei during a matsuri (festival) ceremony at the Aiki Shrine in Iwama, 1962–64.

Nadeau was inspired by Osensei to dedicate himself to transmitting his teachings to the next generation of students through direct experience. Nadeau Sensei talked about this in *Aikido Today Magazine* in 1993:

> I think he [Osensei] was saying there is a process through which people can realize the "more" of themselves, and so function better. He was trying to get people to realize that they are much more than they are aware of. . . . I would like to see people being Osensei in their own endeavor—to become better artists, musicians, car salesmen, doctors, or whatever. Another George Washington Carver. Now that's something worth going for.[5]

In just two years of dedicated effort, Robert Nadeau earned his Aikido *shodan* (1st degree black belt) in November 1963 and his

Robert Nadeau
at a public
demonstration at
the Tama Aikikai,
1964.

Robert Nadeau
at a public
demonstration,
Tokyo, 1964.

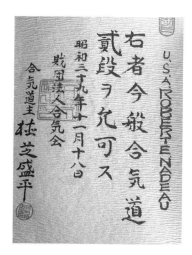

Above: Robert Nadeau's 2nd Dan Certificate, signed and sealed by Morihei Ueshiba.

Right: Robert Nadeau outside Aikido Hombu Dojo holding his 2nd Dan Certificate, 1964.

*nidan* (2nd degree black belt) in November 1964. The latter was a significant enough milestone to warrant a commemorative photo, posing at the front gate of the old Aikido Hombu Dojo. Just before leaving Japan, Nadeau was also given an unusual Certificate of Recognition, automatically affiliating any school where he teaches with Aikido World Headquarters in Tokyo, jointly signed by Morihei Ueshiba and Kisshomaru Ueshiba, with Osensei's personal seal affixed.

In early 1965, Nadeau returned to California and began teaching Aikido at a small school in Menlo Park. He returned to Hombu Dojo in 1966 and again in 1967. A planned trip in 1969 was canceled when Osensei passed away on April 26 of that year.

During his first few years back from Japan, Nadeau was one of only a very few full-time Aikido teachers in the Bay Area of Northern California, and there were not many paying students to start. He made

Certificate of Recognition, 1964.

business cards to better establish himself as a professional teacher while he worked part-time for his brother as an insulation contractor to make ends meet.

One of his early teaching collaborators was Bob Frager, Ph.D., a Harvard-trained psychologist and founder of the Institute of Transpersonal Psychology. Frager had trained under Morihei Ueshiba

Robert Nadeau's business card, early 1970s.

合氣道

Spiritual Development
Art of Aikido
Energy Awareness
Meditation

ROBERT E. NADEAU

Bus: 961-0724
Res: 961-3763

Morihei Ueshiba at home, late 1960s.

Osensei at Hombu Dojo in the early 1960s along with Nadeau. He had also joined the Tempu-Kai in Tokyo and practiced Shinshin Toitsu Do, a system of mind-body integration founded by Japanese martial artist Tempu Nakamura. The innovative cross-pollination between Nadeau and Frager preceded their respective activities in and around the Human Potential Movement and deeply influenced Nadeau's lexicon for teaching Aikido.

In the 1993 *Aikido Today Magazine* interview, Nadeau explained how he came to start teaching in San Francisco as part of the Friends of Esalen:

> I also had some interaction with Bob Frager after we returned from Japan, and he was doing some weird things [at finer dimensional levels] too! He was a member of the Tempu-Kai, so he had his own

training. We did some teaching together, and I got to wondering if we could teach Aikido people—or even non-Aikido people something deeper. We created a workshop situation where we tried to give people—whether Aikido students or not—some of the nitty-gritty aspects of Aikido. There was Dr. Charlie Tart of the University of California at Davis, who was a psychologist and author. He really liked my energy awareness work, so he mentioned it to Michael Murphy, founder of Esalen, and that led to me teaching there.[6]

Whether by coincidence or divine plan, what came to be called the Human Potential Movement emerged around this time, centered in Northern California, right where Nadeau lived after returning from Japan. He was swept up in this historic confluence of people and ideas, interacting with an unusual mix of extraordinary men and women over several years.

Two leaders in the Human Potential Movement, Michael Murphy, cofounder of The Esalen Institute, and George Leonard, a prominent author and later president of Esalen, began taking semi-private classes with Nadeau Sensei in San Francisco. They invited Nadeau to lead workshops at the Esalen Institute on the Big Sur coast, which became a potent ground of interaction between Nadeau and a diverse assortment of influential people who came to Esalen to teach a variety of innovative disciplines, such as Alan Watts (author), John Lilly (psychoanalyst, dolphin researcher, inventor, and author), Jack Kornfield (Buddhist teacher and author), Fritz Perls (developer of Gestalt therapy), Gregory Bateson (anthropologist and cyberneticist), Joseph Campbell (writer on mythology), Aldous Huxley (mystic philosopher and author), Moshe Feldenkrais (somatic movement educator), and Ida Rolf (creator of structural integration), to name a few. Nadeau is pictured at Esalen, atop the Big Sur cliffs overlooking the Pacific Ocean, and speaking with Julian Silverman, resident psychology/spirituality researcher and general manager of Esalen at the time.

George Leonard became a prominent Aikido teacher in his own

At Esalen, Big Sur, 1970s.

Robert Nadeau speaks with Julian Silverman at Esalen, Big Sur, 1970s.

right and wrote about his training with Nadeau Sensei in several best-selling books and influential magazine articles. Here is an excerpt from Leonard's *The Ultimate Athlete*, published in 1975:

> Nadeau's teaching methods run counter to the prevailing direction of most physical education and coaching. The physical education experts continue their work of breaking down every skill into smaller and smaller fragments. Nadeau finds this analysis rather amusing. . . . It can't bring forth the quantum leaps in human functioning he feels are possible. . . . What is more, the principles learned in Aikido should influence the way you play golf, drive, talk to your children, work at your job, make love—the way you live.[7]

Nadeau's approach was also featured in Michael Murphy's 1972 bestselling book *Golf in the Kingdom*, which sold over a million copies and has been translated into nineteen languages. In the book, Murphy shares a passage he copied (in the context of the novel) from the mystic golfer Shivas Irons's journal. In the book, the passage is reproduced in Nadeau Sensei's actual handwriting:

> Walking the course you can learn many things from your new-found friends, the tree rooted deeply to the ground, firm, the upper branches swaying as natural as the breeze flowing through it. So reflect on your stance as you pass the tree. Can you do this, can you see the brook that golfers fear and not fearing but feeling, can you put that flowing water into your swing. The green grass restful to the body, soothing to the soul. Is it so many paces that you put on it or is it a period of rest and calmness between you and the [lie] of your ball. Be the tree rooted, be the brook flowing, be the calmness of the green.[8]

While still in Japan, Nadeau had dreamed of opening a dojo in the Bay Area offering various teaching styles, similar to Hombu Dojo. He carefully planned what it would take to support multiple sensei teaching in one dojo. As his San Francisco classes grew, he invited Frank Doran Sensei to teach, and in 1972 they opened Aikido of San Francisco on Turk Street. They also invited Bill Witt Sensei to teach, bringing even more variety to the dojo instruction team. From time to time, there were also special events when guest instructors, like Terry Dobson Sensei, would join with Doran Sensei and Nadeau Sensei for big demonstrations that helped expose Aikido to a wider community.

Beginning in 1976, the teachers and students of Aikido of San Francisco organized the first Aiki Summer Retreat (ASR) in the Bay Area, a weeklong training led by multiple instructors. It was a big success, growing over the years to attract hundreds of students from around America and the world. The ASR became an annual event and ran continuously for thirty-five years, fostering cross-pollination in the art, cultivating friendships, and nurturing the growing community of Aikido practitioners outside Japan.

In addition to serving together as teachers at Aikido of San Francisco and leaders of the Aiki Summer Retreats, Robert Nadeau and Frank Doran also collaborated with Bill Witt to help establish the Aikido of Northern California Yudansha-kai in 1974, which grew into the Aikido Association of California, which in 2002 morphed into the California Aikido Association (CAA).

In the 1995 book *Aikido in America*, Terry Dobson Sensei described coming to the Aiki Summer Retreat in San Rafael, California for the first time as a guest instructor.

I remember the first time I came to the Bay Area. I was living in New York, and I didn't have any money. Bob Nadeau had invited me to the San Rafael Retreat. He picked me up at the airport and then he took me over and introduced me to the people and said, "Go ahead and teach." I just wanted to watch class; I hadn't thought of teaching it. This was a time when having twelve people on the mat at Bond Street [Dojo in New York City] was rare. Ken Nisson and

Frank Doran at
Aikido of San
Francisco, 1980s

Robert Nadeau
at Aikido of San
Francisco, 1980s.

Terry Dobson
at Aikido of Sa
Francisco, 198(

At the Aiki Summer Retreat, Dominican College, 1981.

I would say to each other, "Jesus, there's twelve people out there! Twelve! Do you realize how many people, twelve! Double digits!" And one of us would say, "Don't worry, you can do it. Don't let it freak you out. Just go out there and do it!" That was where I was coming from. So, Nadeau says go ahead and teach, and there are at least 140 people on the mat. And there are all these black belts. I'd never seen so many black belts except in Japan. And right in the middle is this gorgeous-looking woman and she's smiling at me. I know I know her, but I can't think of her name. It's Joan Baez. And she wasn't the best-looking person in the place by any means. I mean, there were all these gorgeous-looking California people. So, I taught the class and afterwards Nadeau slipped fifty bucks to me. The way he handed me the money was extremely kind. I'll never forget it. I'll always love him for it.[9]

Thanks to the pioneering efforts of Robert Nadeau, Frank Doran, Bob Frager, Bill Witt, Terry Dobson, and many others, Aikido in Northern California took root and thrived, growing organically over many years and blossoming into a diverse community of well-trained Aikido instructors with a wide variety of teaching styles.

Nadeau Sensei himself continued to evolve as well, keeping up with the fashions of the day. He is pictured here standing with his mother, Flora, in the 1980s, and posing impishly in a weight-lifting studio in the 1990s.

With his mother,
Flora, 1980s.

In a weight-lifting gym, 1990s.

Books about, or inspired by, Nadeau.

Nadeau Sensei's seminal influence as a teacher within the greater Aikido community is so diffuse and widespread after many decades as to almost go unnoticed today. He also influenced the broader culture outside Aikido through his teaching, his students, and the many books his students wrote in addition to those by Leonard and Murphy already mentioned.

For example, Aimee Bernstein, another longtime student of

Nadeau Sensei,
1970s.

Nadeau Sensei, wrote in her 2015 business-oriented book, *Stress Less Achieve More*:

> As you will read, I didn't come to this knowledge without help. Instead, I was blessed to find an extraordinary teacher, Robert Nadeau, a seventh [now eighth] dan Aikido master and inner researcher of states of consciousness, whose work has been the subject of numerous books. Today, the work of scientists validates the things he taught over thirty years ago.[10]

Left to right: Francis Takahashi, Frank Doran, Moriteru Ueshiba,
Robert Nadeau, Bay Area, California, mid-1980s.

Even as his approach to Aikido and energy awareness extended into sports, psychology, and business, Nadeau's influence in the Aikido world continued to expand as well. He taught well-attended seminars in major American cities, and overseas in Israel, Russia, New Zealand, Germany, and Switzerland. Many of his early students have become respected Aikido teachers in their own right.

For many years, Nadeau has served as a living bridge connecting California with Osensei's Aikido lineage. When Morihei Ueshiba passed away, Nadeau aligned himself with his son Kisshomaru Ueshiba Doshu and then his grandson, Moriteru Ueshiba, the current Doshu. He was one of the hosts of Kisshomaru Ueshiba Doshu's visit to

America in the spring of 1974, and the first visit of Moriteru Ueshiba Wakasensei (heir apparent, or "young teacher") to Northern California in the mid-1980s.

In November 1998, Nadeau responded to a letter from Kisshomaru Doshu requesting him to come to Japan by organizing a group of students to accompany him to Tokyo so they could train at Hombu Dojo and visit the Aiki Shrine in Iwama. As is often the case in life and training, something unexpected happened. Soon after arriving in Tokyo, Nadeau and a few of his students were invited to visit Kisshomaru Doshu's home next to Hombu Dojo. It was clear that the Doshu was not in good health. There was a hospital bed in an adjoining room, and he had an oxygen tube under his nose, but he sat up and put on a jacket for the visit. Moriteru Ueshiba was also there, in suit and tie. Even Nadeau had gotten dressed up for the meeting. The Doshu welcomed everyone as his wife kindly served tea and sweets.

Much of the audience was taken up with stories and recollections of Nadeau Sensei's time training in Japan in the 1960s. Then

Left to right: Robert Nadeau, Moriteru Ueshiba, and Kisshomaru Ueshiba at the Ueshiba family home, Tokyo, 1998.

Robert Nadeau and students with Morihiro Saito (in kimono at center) at the Aiki Shrine, Iwama, 1998.

Kisshomaru Doshu turned to Nadeau Sensei and thanked him for keeping the spiritual aspect of Aikido alive and said how much he appreciated Nadeau Sensei's sustained focus on Aikido as an art of spiritual growth.

It was clear to all who were present that this was why the Doshu had originally requested Nadeau come to see him. He wanted a face-to-face meeting so he could personally convey his gratitude for Nadeau Sensei's support, his dedication to Osensei's path, and his seminal contributions to the development of Aikido worldwide. Kisshomaru Doshu would pass away fewer than four months later.

On the same trip in 1998, Nadeau Sensei also took his group to Iwama to visit the Aiki Shrine and meet once again with Morihiro Saito Sensei.

In October 2001, Robert Nadeau married for a second time to Katja Simona, a professional Pilates instructor who had started Aikido in her native Switzerland. They settled in San Mateo, a town between

Wedding of Robert
Nadeau and Katja Simona,
Auburn, California, 2001.

Mountain View and San Francisco, where he regularly taught, and close to her Pilates studio.

In February 2002, Robert Nadeau was appointed *shihan* (master teacher) by Aikido Hombu Dojo, receiving this certificate signed by Moriteru Ueshiba Doshu.

Robert Nadeau's Shihan
Certificate from Aikido
Hombu Dojo, 2002.

Nadeau practices with Katja Simona, early 2000s.

Front left to right: Moriteru Ueshiba Doshu, Patricia
Hendricks, Naoko Ueshiba, Danielle Smith, Michael Smith;
back left to right: Frank Doran, Ursula Doran, Robert Nadeau,
Francis Takahashi, unknown, Monterey, California, 2004.

In March 2004, Nadeau Sensei was deeply involved, as one of the
division heads of the California Aikido Association (CAA), in the
group who planned and organized Moriteru Ueshiba Doshu's visit
to Northern California. The Doshu's weekend seminar in Oakland
attracted hundreds of enthusiastic practitioners with an open invitation
for all to participate, regardless of organizational affiliation. Afterward,
the CAA hosts took the Doshu and his wife to the Monterey Peninsula
for a relaxing group excursion.

In 2006, Nadeau again led a large group of his students to Japan to
practice at Hombu Dojo. This time the group dinner was hosted by the
current Doshu, Moriteru Ueshiba, son of Kisshomaru, and Moriteru's

Left to right: Steve Heuseveldt, William Tucker, Scott Sphar, Laurin Herr, Robert Nadeau, Jack Wada, Bob Noha, Tokyo, 2006.

son, Mitsuteru Ueshiba, who is in line to eventually succeed him as the next Doshu.

Despite Tokyo's summer heat, Nadeau Sensei and several of his students found it relaxing to hang out together over coffee at the Shinjuku Starbucks after morning Aikido practice at Hombu Dojo.

Left to right: Mitsuteru Ueshiba, Robert Nadeau, Moriteru Ueshiba, Katja Simona, Tokyo, 2006.

Robert Nadeau with students in front of the Aiki Shrine, Iwama, 2006.

In the Iwama Dojo, 2006.

Sensei again led a big group of his students north of Tokyo by train to visit the Iwama dojo and the Aiki Jinja (Aiki shrine) built by Osensei in the 1940s when he was living, farming, and training there.

During the 1960s, Nadeau accompanied Osensei to Iwama several times and trained in Morihiro Saito Sensei's classes when he came to Hombu from Iwama. Because of this, Nadeau Sensei has a strong personal connection to the place. When the group entered the inner shrine of the Aiki Jinja, he asked for, and was granted, permission to offer the *Su-U-A-O-U-E-Re-E-Gi* chant that Osensei had taught him, his rich tenor voice resonating in this very special space consecrated to the *kami* (deities) of Aikido.

All these years, Nadeau Sensei maintained a busy weekly teaching schedule, dividing his time between multiple dojos in San Francisco, Mountain View, and San Jose, as well as regularly traveling to Europe and New Zealand to lead seminars. He also periodically led what he called "Energy Awareness Workshops" for Aikidoists and non-Aikidoists who gathered in comfortable street clothes to explore the process of personal development and the energy dynamics that can arise in life situations, without reference to martial arts.

Presenting at an Energy Awareness Workshop, 2000s.

Teaching at the Aiki Summer Retreat, Menlo College, Atherton, CA, 2011.

Nadeau Sensei continued organizing the Aiki Summer Retreats in the gymnasium of Menlo College until 2011. His co-instructors over the years included Frank Doran, Mary Heiny, and Jack Wada, as well as Clyde Takeguchi and Hiroshi Ikeda.

With Frank Doran at the Aiki Summer Retreat, 2008.

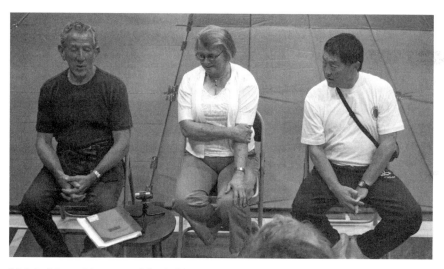

With Mary Heiny and Jack Wada at the Aiki Summer Retreat, 2011.

In 2012, Nadeau Sensei and his students organized the first Osensei Revisited (OSR) workshop at a remote forested campus two hours north of San Francisco. This entailed several days of practice focused on the internal processes of Aikido that Morihei Ueshiba had so strongly

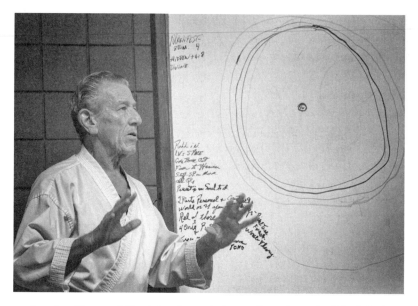

At the Osensei Revisited workshop, Occidental, CA, 2014.

emphasized to Nadeau at Hombu Dojo in the 1960s. These workshops became annual gatherings of Aikido students from the Bay Area and beyond who came to train with Nadeau Sensei and the variety of instructors he invited each year.

For example, during the 2014 OSR, Nadeau Sensei mapped out basic Aikido principles like center/circle and presented Osensei's teachings about dimensionality.

In 2017, Nadeau Sensei was promoted to the rank of Aikido 8th Dan, as was his friend and colleague for fifty years Frank Doran Sensei, seen here sharing a laugh at a joint party organized by their students to celebrate this memorable milestone.

With Frank Doran celebrating their simultaneous promotions to 8th Dan, 2017.

Nadeau Sensei continues to serve as one of the three division heads of the CAA, together with Michael Friedl Sensei and Pat Hendricks Sensei. The three are shown in this 2019 photo making welcoming remarks opening the large public Aikido seminar hosted by the CAA and taught by Moriteru Ueshiba Doshu, which attracted nearly seven hundred students from across America and around the world.

After the 2019 workshop dinner, relaxing around the table with just Nadeau and a small group, Doshu spoke through an interpreter to recount how, nearly fifty years earlier, he had first encountered Nadeau just after

Robert Nadeau with Michael Friedl and Patricia Hendricks, making welcoming remarks at the CAA's Doshu Workshop, 2019.

he had arrived at Hombu. Doshu recalled how Nadeau had patiently helped a twelve-year-old Japanese boy learn his first words in English just as he was entering junior high and beginning to study English at school. Doshu laughingly explained that this had really helped him at the time, and their personal connection had persisted ever since.

In spring of 2020, when COVID-19 forced suspension of all in-person Aikido practice, Nadeau Sensei shifted from on-the-mat classes to weekly sessions in an online "virtual dojo." Improvising, he led

CAA Doshu Workshop, San Mateo, CA, 2019.

Teaching at the Fudoshin Dojo, San Francisco, 2022.

remote attendees in solo physical movements and breathing exercises, explained concepts, drew diagrams on an easel, and sometimes even pressed his wife, Katja Simona, into service as his *uke* when he wanted to physically demonstrate his point.

In the early weeks of the pandemic, with everyone isolated at home and normal routines abruptly paused, Nadeau Sensei emphasized the personal growth potential of accepting "downtime" as a naturally occurring part of life. As weeks turned into months, Nadeau Sensei further refined his teaching approach to better fit a virtual dojo, methodically

Teaching in the virtual dojo, 2020.

leading students through a comprehensive review of Osensei's cosmology and basic principles of spiritual development, attracting students from around the world.

By October 2022, Nadeau Sensei was once again on the mat. He's shown here at a City Aikido seminar held at the Fudoshin Dojo in San Francisco, directly transmitting the essence of Aikido to yet another generation of students, offering them an instantaneous visceral experience of Aikido on the receiving end of an effortlessly smooth *irimi-nage* (entering throw).

As he has done ever since he came back to California from Japan, Nadeau Sensei continues to engage students in dialogue, asking them how they feel and what they sense, encouraging them to access "finer

Teaching at the Fudoshin Dojo, San Francisco, 2022.

energies" on the mat and in their lives, and urging them to never be satisfied with "understanding" without "experiencing" the inner workings of Aikido.

Even after more than seven decades of Aikido, energy awareness, and meditation practice, he continues to explore Osensei's wisdom, and encourages everyone around him to follow this path for developing a truer sense of themselves.

## TWO

# Experiences, Memories, and Insights

 *First Student*

**DAVE LITTLE**
Aikido 1st Dan
Aikido of Mountain View
Corrections Officer (ret.)
Emergency Response Team,
Jail Training Officer

My first recollection of Bob was at Sequoia High School in Redwood City, California, in 1954. He was a BMOC (big man on campus), and I was a 110-pound scrub freshman without a clue.

The next time I was aware of him was about 1960 or '61, when we were both students of Moon Watanabe Sensei at his judo school. Bob was a cop in Redwood City in those days. That was a fun time, and I learned a lot, especially about falling.

In the early '60s, Bob went to Japan to study many different martial arts. He eventually settled on Aikido, which was a stroke of luck, fate, or providence for those of us who would become his students.

On his return from Japan, Bob started teaching in Menlo Park, and I hold the distinction of being his first student. Moon Watanabe also trained with us. Those were heady days for me. I learned some new ways of falling and thinking about self-defense. What fun we had trying things from both judo and Aikido. I remember a day vividly on the lawn at my house when Bob made a point about falling while using a potato cut in half as a prop. I never forgot that, and I learned to fall really well.

All the years I spent with Bob are dear to me. We have a bond that most people never share, nor could they understand: teacher, student, and friend. Doesn't get much better than that. I still use many of the things I learned then. Down, one point, drop your shoulders, and breath. Always breath.

In later years I became a correctional officer for Santa Clara. I went through the academy at fifty years old, and believe me, those precepts I learned from Bob helped on more than one occasion. For example, two of my classmates couldn't qualify for the pistol or shotgun. I had noticed that both of them held their shoulders almost in their ears when shooting. When they came to me, a few times practicing dropping shoulders down, relaxing, breathing, and "thinking down" was all it took. Both qualified the next time out.

My first instinct when working in the Santa Clara county jails was not to go hands on, but stuff happens. So, my training with Bob came to the fore often enough. Surprising how easy defusing tense situations became just by using down shoulders, one point, and breath.

We all make mistakes in life, and believe me, I've made my share. It's my fortune to have learned a few things that, when I was smart enough to use them, helped me out. Thanks to my Aikido training with Bob, many times bad things were made better.

Thanks Bob, for being my teacher, but most of all for being my friend. Love ya man!

## ⟁ *Robert Nadeau—Peaceful Warrior* ⟁

DAN MILLMAN
Author: *Way of the Peaceful Warrior*,
Public Speaker

In 1969 or 1970, during my tenure as gymnastics coach at Stanford University—more than a decade after I'd practiced judo, karate, and Okinawa-te in high school—I decided to try my hand at the flowing art of Aikido. I looked in the Yellow Pages and found a local school in Mountain View, California, a fifteen-minute drive from my home.

When I called to inquire, a gruff voice on the other end said, "Nadeau here." I expressed my interest in taking an introductory class. Then, since I'd been accustomed to Japanese instructors in my youth, and "Nadeau" sounded French, I asked him if he was an experienced Aikido instructor. (I may have put it, "Are you any good at Aikido?") He answered matter-of-factly, without a trace of self-importance, that he'd studied in Japan with the Founder. Satisfied, I began my twice-weekly training at the Mountain View dojo, where I met Bill Witt and other fine practitioners.

Early on, Bob Nadeau impressed me as a man who lived with his head in the clouds and his feet on the ground. For me, Bob Nadeau—how and what he taught—*was* Aikido. I imagined that all instructors taught about centering and energy awareness. Only later, after sampling the style of numerous other Aikido sensei, did I gain perspective about Nadeau Sensei's unique approach, influenced by his connection to Esalen. This time at Esalen enriched his teaching of Aikido as a way to work energetically, and as a means of personal evolution. From what I had read of Osensei, Nadeau's holistic, energetic teaching may have resonated most deeply with the Founder.

Given that I'd practiced gymnastics for a decade, which emphasized strength and explosive power, I had a particularly challenging time at first learning to relax when facing a daunting *uke*. In much the same way a coach tells a novice golfer to "let the weight of the clubhead do the work" and "stop trying so hard to hit the ball," Nadeau reminded me often to "relax" and "flow" and "extend *ki* (vital energy)," which I found frustrating and then liberating. This struggle to unlearn old habits revealed that *everything is difficult until it becomes easy.* This valuable training enabled me to practice *ki* in daily life and flow, breathe, and relax my way through each day.

One day, as Nadeau and I practiced—I was still pretty much a rank beginner—I asked him, "Sensei, can Aikido really work as an effective form of self-defense on the street?" I still remember his terse response: "If you're looking for self-defense, get a piece [a gun]." Then, on my next attack, he evaded and body-slammed me to the mat, perhaps making a point.

Years later, Nadeau's student, author George Leonard, would earn a *shodan* (first degree black belt) and begin teaching L.E.T. (Leonard Energy Training). But the shoulders on which he stood were clearly Robert Nadeau's. George had mastered the throws and rolls—the physical techniques—so his L.E.T. style transcended yet included the combative aspects of Aikido, moving into an energetic way of living and moving—personal mastery through Aikido. Under Nadeau Sensei's guidance, Aikido truly became a way or path. Students like George Leonard extended Robert Nadeau's lineage and legacy.

I later moved to Ohio and taught in the physical education department at Oberlin College. I helped sponsor the Oberlin Aikido Club where Frank Hreha served as our capable instructor. I continued my practice at Oberlin but stayed in touch, on and off, with Nadeau Sensei, who set the bar and standard for the kind of Aikido I most appreciated. He will always have a special place among the various martial arts teachers I've known.

## ▣ *The Magician* ▣

### ROLAND SPITZBARTH
Aikido 6th Dan
Silversmith

The first time I walked up the long stairway to the Turk Street dojo in San Francisco, I felt energy unlike anything I'd known before. It was a mixture of warm acceptance and power, and I felt challenged to open up to the unknown. I wanted to know more about this and went to all of the classes. This was February 1976.

Three 4th Dans (fourth degree black belts) were teaching: Bill Witt, the nuts-and-bolts man; Frank Doran, the twirling dervish; and Robert Nadeau, the magician. They looked completely different, and yet they were all teaching Aikido. I was timid, self-righteous, and klutzy; nevertheless, I felt accepted gracefully by each one of the three in his own way. As a result, I grew up with a multifaceted view of that vibrating thing: Aikido.

Summer camp (Aiki Summer Retreat) was a revelation. Bob's evening meditation sittings opened up new dimensions for me. This dazzling, frightening, esoteric new world of Northern California Aikido that I had started to explore still seemed separate from what I knew as normal reality. However, Bob's presentation of Aikido to the nuns of the Dominican College, where the event was hosted, changed that. I watched him transform from the god-like, aloof presence I had experienced on the mat into an everyday person the nuns could relate to. He slipped into the Catholic mindset with ease, and I started to realize that there are applications of Aikido to life far beyond self-defense.

Jump to 2001. Saito Sensei had just passed away. He had supported my independent Zurich dojo for the past two decades, and now I had lost my connection to the Aikikai (Aikikai Foundation headquartered in Tokyo). It so happened that this was the summer all three of my old teachers from Aikido of San Francisco came through Zurich. Bob was the one who told me: I'll take care of you. So I joined his division and came home to the Aikido Association of Northern California, which later became the California Aikido Association.

During the '80s and '90s, many direct students of Osensei were still teaching. I tried to catch as many of them as I could. I was fascinated by a common quality they all seemed to have, beyond great personal differences and different presentations of the art: unconditional love. Bob is one of them.

His unique approach to focus directly on the personal development of his students and to provide a road map for that has helped me through some difficult personal times, as well as given me the tools to be helpful for others. Open, settle, drop your center. Do it again. 1-2-3, play the game, use the process. Feel, don't think. The tools are always with me when I'm losing my footing on a slippery steep mountain slope or when I help to find common ground in a difficult discussion. Thank you, Sensei!

## ⟐ *Authentically Unpredictable* ⟐

RICHARD STROZZI-HECKLER
Aikido 7th Dan Shihan
Dojo-cho, Two Rock Dojo
Cofounder, Aikido of Tamalpais
Founder, Strozzi Institute, Center for Leadership & Mastery
Advisor to Supreme Allied Commander of Europe &
U.S. National Security Advisor, 2003–2006.
Designed and Implemented the
Marine Corps Martial Art Program (MCMAP)
Author: *Embodying the Mystery*

I began my Aikido training in a rusty Quonset hut in 1972 on the island of Kauai in the Hawaiian Islands. When I decided to move back to the mainland, I was encouraged to write a letter to the dojo-cho in San Francisco asking permission to train at their dojo. Since I had some background in judo, karate, and Chinese arts, this kind of formal request didn't seem out of the ordinary.

Now it seems like something out of a Greek drama.

I even included in my letter a note from my Hawaii sensei attesting to my sincerity and commitment. I sent them off in the mail and continued training. Shortly after, I received a warm reply from Nadeau Sensei confirming I was most welcome, and he was looking forward to meeting me.

When I arrived at the Turk Street dojo in San Francisco (I remember being something like the thirty-sixth student who signed up), I introduced myself to Nadeau Sensei. I handed him the letter he had written to me and the letter from my teacher in Kauai, expecting him to remember our correspondence. I waited for him to inform me of anything I should know about protocols in the newly formed Aikido of San Francisco. Instead, he barely glanced at the letter, side-eyed me, and nodded to the dressing room, "You can change in there." That was it—a different welcome than I had expected from the tone of his earlier letter.

I tell this story because it illustrates something I learned about Nadeau Sensei from this first meeting with him. He is authentically unpredictable. This is a quality that consistently shows up in the context of his teaching.

By authentic, I mean he tries to be informed and moved by an inner listening that can seem initially unpredictable but is an allegiance to a much larger perspective gleaned from his time with Osensei.

For example, there was the moment at the old Aiki Summer Retreat at Dominican College, when he called me out to be *uke*, then unexpectedly slapped me hard on the face as I reached for his wrist. I immediately went off on the rush, balling up my fists, ready to fight. He held up his finger and said something like, "That! That's what's to learn." This was a seminal moment for me when I could see up close and personal my reaction to threat, imagined or real, and the imprint was something I work with to this day.

Or when a small group of us were preparing for our *shodan* (first degree black belt) exams, and he ignored me in the three-month lead-up, to the point of not even having my name on the list of candidates though I had been one of his primary *uke* for the past three years. This was very difficult for me. It felt like I had been put into some kind of infectious disease quarantine. It was effective ego reduction at the time, but it also opened up for me an important new vista in my internal work. These kinds of unpredictable but innovative moves made Nadeau Sensei an exceptionally creative teacher.

The other thing that stands out about Nadeau Sensei's uniqueness and mastery is his capacity to see a person's patterns and character by observing their energy. I remember, for example, he told me (and this happened with several students) that I was ahead of myself, and another time that I wasn't fully committed to the attack as an *uke*. What was extraordinary about those moments was that I also received similar feedback—ahead of myself and not fully committed—in my personal and professional life. He was instrumental in showing many of us how to read energy practically and profoundly.

While Nadeau Sensei had exemplary *waza* (techniques), he used the art as a portal to teach how to contact the deeper energy source of Aiki.

He architected his classes so we could learn how to pass through this portal ourselves. He was a master of listening to, and responding from, a space much larger than one's individual personality or just trying to perfect a technique. He embodied this "state" in his throws, which were very powerful and gentle at the same time. It was as if you were being lifted by a potent, vast billowing of air that had both substance and emptiness.

His contribution to the art is considerable, and I am grateful to have trained under him.

##  *Ukemi*

JOHN MENARD O'CONNELL JR.
Aikido 3rd Dan
Co-founder and former dojo-cho of Aikido of Noe Valley
Management Consultant for Team Building & Conflict Resolution
Co-director, Chief of Training, New Games Foundation
Co-author: *The New Games Book*
Co-author: *Learning Leadership Skills by Facilitating Fun,*
*Games, Play and Positive Interaction*

I have been fortunate and privileged in my Aikido career to serve as *uke* for quite a few exceptional Aikidoists. Of course, it probably helps to be bigger than any of them (except maybe Terry Dobson)! It makes it a lot more impressive when you go flying.

I like to think my *ukemi* (art of attacking/falling/rolling) was pretty decent, too.

Some sensei were extremely smooth, some did long flowing beautiful blends, some nailed you before you even made contact, some kind of played with you a little bit before issuing the coup de grace. A few were excellent technically, but you always felt there was muscle involved. Some could be harsh and not very forgiving, so you had to be focused on keeping all your parts connected in the right places. There's a spot of arthritis on my right wrist that reminds me forty years later of one particular sensei's *kote-gaeshi* (wrist-twist techniques) nearly separating my hand from my arm. Not quite fast enough, or maybe it was a message.

I never had any such experience with Nadeau Sensei. From the first time I took *ukemi* for him, through my best days and even a bit past my prime, I always felt like he knew exactly what I was capable of, what I was giving, and matched it perfectly. And I always tried to give him the best attack I could—straight, solid, genuine, and strong.

He was demanding because he always wanted an honest attack and the precise one for the technique or principle he was presenting. If someone came in with a "mushy" punch or off-target, he might step away, and say, "What's that supposed to be?" or "What do you think you are doing?" It would usually prompt a mini-lecture, or at the least an aside to the rest of us, explaining the point of *ukemi*. Someone grabbing inappropriately for the technique, pulling instead of pushing, or vice versa usually drew some irritation and the mini-lecture.

It was also interesting to me that usually, when the attack involved a grab of some sort, I got a hold of him. But just when I did, there wasn't any resistance. Before I could do anything with the grab, he was gone, and I was on the ground. He had some favorite moves, where just as you were about to get him, it felt like the floor dropped out from under you, or the rug got pulled, or a big hole opened up. Those were fun.

Probably my favorite experience was at the old City Aikido Dojo on Oak Street in San Francisco. Bob always wore these kinds of old-fashioned, heavy 1950s-type glasses. For whatever reason, this one day I decided: "I'm going to nail him this time if I can." I came in pretty hot with a *shomen-uchi* (frontal strike to the forehead), and I thought I had him. The blade edge of my hand was about a half inch from the bridge of those glasses. I could see it clearly and was sure I was about to hit him when I realized that my hand wasn't getting any closer, at which point I realized I was upside down, still trying to strike up, but I couldn't reach any farther, and I started laughing in mid-flight. I hadn't even noticed that my feet had left the ground.

It wasn't a hard throw, very smooth, and I rolled out of the high fall easily, just as Nadeau Sensei turned to the class and said, "You know when it's good, they laugh!"

I'm not sure how obvious the whole thing was to outside observers, but I'm sure he and I felt the same thing and knew exactly what had happened. It definitely felt great.

It may have been Bob, Terry Dobson, or Saito Sensei, or maybe all of them, who talked about how Osensei felt it was a privilege for students to take *ukemi* from him. He felt that they received transmission (teaching) from experiencing his throws. Maybe a bit of *ki* (vital energy) passed to them in a way that they absorbed.

I feel I've learned and absorbed a tremendous amount of what I know of Aikido, taking *ukemi* from Nadeau Sensei. I'm pretty sure some *ki* was involved. It was definitely a privilege.

And I got to laugh a lot.

## ◬ *Aikido and the Human Potential Movement* ◬

JOOP DELAHAYE
Aikido 2nd Dan
Aikido of San Francisco
Physical Therapist (ret.)
Bird-Watcher, Beach Volunteer

My awareness of Robert Nadeau far preceded my meeting and training with him. In 1971 or '72, I was a student at Laney College in Oakland, completing prerequisite coursework to enter the architecture degree program at UC Berkeley. A friend in one of my classes was doing Aikido on campus. He kept pestering me to check it out and even introduced me to one of his teachers, Tom Everett, when he passed by in the college quad. I finally did start training a few weeks later.

Tom Everett was a brown belt then, and a very engaging, interesting teacher who brought us all these weird energy exercises, done while moving and/or while meditating. These included energy circle, the concept/experience of *hara* (lower abdomen source of *ki*/heart/mind), unbendable arm and other *ki* energy exercises, sensing with newly discovered senses, etc. All these activities came from Tom's studies with Robert Nadeau, who was teaching at the Unitarian Church in San Francisco at the time.

Tom also tried to put into words the experience of being thrown by Nadeau. I listened but had no idea what he was talking about.

My Aikido studies continued in fits and starts from that point on, and eventually, I moved to San Francisco and went to the Turk Street dojo. I still remember my member number at the dojo: 184.

The incredible vitality of the '70s Human Potential Movement was easily felt on the mat at Turk Street. First generation students of Feldenkrais, teachers at Anna Halprin's Dancer's Workshop, Lomi School founders, and famous folk singers mingled, trained, and blended together.

My primary teacher then was Bill Witt. I also attended Frank Doran's classes until it was time to seriously get ready for my *shodan* test, which I took at the San Jose Dojo in February 1977. My test preparations included going to all the Turk Street dojo classes, including, of course, Bob's class.

The varied and sometimes challenging students who were then Bob's *deshi* (disciples) taught me so much. I recall Letty Pang, a small woman, presumably physically weaker than me, who could stop me in my tracks. Super frustrating! This is when I met Richard Moon and Steven Samuels, both of whom took it upon themselves to help me in my *shodan* preparations, although neither of them had taken their own tests yet.

Once I passed my *shodan* test, my attendance at classes led by other sensei gradually dropped away. Nadeau Sensei became my primary teacher and eventually I became one of Bob's preferred *uke*. Finally, what Tom Everett had said years earlier about Nadeau's throws became a reality for me.

Nadeau helped me access the deeper lessons of Aikido, the beyond-technique presence and awareness that he learned from Osensei. I do not believe I could have learned this from any other teacher.

As I focused my attention on my career, my attendance at Aikido classes dropped off. I did not have the "fire in the belly" to make a living teaching martial arts. However, I loved being on the mat and interacting with fellow *deshi*. The lessons I absorbed in Bob's classes stayed with me and sustained me in the coming years of professional and personal challenges.

A story that I have often told friends, not just Aikido friends, is when I dropped into a Nadeau class in the early '90s. I had not trained with any consistency for years. Classes then were on Oak Street, just off Van Ness. That particular night a lot of Bob's old *deshi* showed up. I remember John O'Connell, and I believe Elaine Yoder was there, too. Harvey Moskovitz, and Bob Noha were there, I think. I cannot remember everyone, but it was a wonderful night of training.

And it was made more wonderful when Bob stopped in the middle of class and introduced us older *deshi* to his present students. That touched me so much, that he loved us all and honored us in this way. The next morning my body felt like I had been hit by a truck!

I carry a deep affection for Bob and have great respect for his commitment to the vision of a transformative Aikido. One that facilitates change.

## △ *Nadeau's Anecdotes* △

NANCY VAYHINGER
Aikido 3rd Dan
Aikido of Petaluma

Nadeau Sensei's instruction is most often laced with humorous personal references and anecdotes, adding inimitable personality and color to his deeper message—without which it just wouldn't be Nadeau. Here's one simple vignette, which I heard firsthand from him.

Nadeau said that he had found a book about hypnosis as a young teenager, and he talked a school friend into a hypnosis session in his bedroom after school. Nadeau reported that the hypnosis was very effective—to the point that he worried whether he could get his friend or himself out of their trances, though he ultimately was successful.

This speaks to Nadeau's lifelong interest in states of consciousness in a humorous and touching story.

 *Recollections*

MARY HEINY
Aikido 7th Dan

I first met Nadeau Sensei in 1974. I had just returned from Japan and started teaching Aikido at the University of California, Santa Cruz. A friend and colleague from Shingu, Japan, Jack Wada, insisted that I go to one of Nadeau Sensei's classes. I believe he was teaching on the second floor. I had brought my *gi* (practice uniform) and was embarrassed to be arriving late. Jack Wada said it was ok, so we went in. The class was already in session, but no one was wearing a *gi*.

In fact, they seemed to be lying on their backs.

Nadeau Sensei was asking them to answer some questions I couldn't comprehend. I thought to myself, "What the *&!!?"

I too lay down, and he asked us to imagine what came before Creation. I thought, "What the *&!!?" but tried to imagine a time/state/process/situation/place before Creation. At the moment I could not, but the question remained in my brain for years. Then, many years later, I had a sensation of "yin first birthing yang," and my technique changed.

Denise Barry Sensei once asked me to co-teach with Nadeau Sensei at her dojo. I told her I could teach if she translated, because I could not understand his vocabulary when he taught. I had a great time that weekend, and I learned an important lesson from Nadeau Sensei. We were sitting around on the mat after class, and Nadeau and

I were sharing a cushion. Nadeau Sensei seemed to move slightly over in my direction. So, being a good *kohai* (the junior in a relationship), I moved aside to accommodate him. Then, on the third shift, I fell off the cushion. I looked up, surprised, and he said, "Hold your seat."

That was important for me to look into, and my technique changed again.

Another time, Denise told me Nadeau Sensei was hosting Henry Kono Sensei who would teach a class and translate a tape from the 1960s of Osensei talking to the two of them back in Tokyo. I was very excited to hear the translation. I knew Kono Sensei from Canada. All the while Kono Sensei was teaching, I waited impatiently for when he would translate the tape. Finally, the tape was set up and it played beautifully. Hearing Osensei's voice was very moving. After a few minutes, Nadeau Sensei asked Henry to translate. Kono Sensei said he couldn't understand a word. There was an awkward silence. My memory is poor, but I think Denise pushed me forward and said I could translate it. Again, I thought, "What the *&!!?" I sat down and concentrated. Finally, I could translate somewhat. After I spoke, Nadeau Sensei gave his thoughts on what Osensei had expressed. I was startled that he seemed to be in harmony with what I had just heard Osensei say, despite the fact that I knew he did not know much Japanese.

We alternated like this for a while. I realized that Nadeau Sensei had more than a devotion to Osensei—he had a deep connection. I was moved and have always paid attention to Nadeau's teachings. Occasionally, I still need a translation.

Nadeau Sensei has been vital for the spread of Aikido in the Bay Area and other places in the world. He consistently maintains the essential teachings of Osensei and the importance of studying Aikido as a mind/body process, not just a collection of techniques to "get." I hope he continues to do so for a long time.

## ⟐ *What's Most Important* ⟐

ANDREI KARKAR
Aikido 2nd Dan
City Aikido of San Francisco, Fudoshin Dojo

Nadeau Sensei always brings us back to what's most important in ourselves at a given point in time, or in relation to a timeless universal level. He teaches with absolute emphasis on principles: those which are most important, and in the appropriate order. His message points to truth and freedom. His methodology leads to an ability for functioning transcendence.

Nadeau Sensei's approach has helped me shed qualities that don't serve me and strengthen those that do. Training with him has made me a healthier and more complete person that can more effectively give and receive in the world around me.

The lessons received from Nadeau Sensei have allowed me to manifest a deep intention, which has helped me find my mission in life and a vehicle to creatively and meaningfully apply my still-developing abilities for good. I now find myself in an influential corporate position with the potential to affect the world socially, economically, and environmentally at the highest levels.

The principles of Aikido work. Nadeau Sensei's teachings work. They have enhanced every facet of my life with a moral and creative resonance only beginning to unfold, for which I am eternally grateful.

## ⟳ *Gratitude for New Perspectives* ⟳

LINDA HOLIDAY
Aikido 7th Dan
Chief Instructor, Aikido of Santa Cruz
Author and Translator: *Journey to the Heart of Aikido:*
*The Teachings of Motomichi Anno Sensei*

It must have been 1971 when I first met Robert Nadeau Sensei. At the time, he was one of a very few teachers of Aikido in Northern California. I had begun the mystifying, exciting study of Aikido the previous year as a first-year student at the University of California, Santa Cruz (UCSC). My teachers there were Robert Frager Sensei and Frank Doran Sensei, who worked together to support us fledgling Aikido students at UCSC.

Nadeau Sensei had an actual dojo nearby in Mountain View. Although I wasn't a personal student of his, I am profoundly grateful for the many vivid lessons he imparted to us.

We were especially lucky that these pioneering teachers worked together to develop Aikido in California. Aikido was a new art then—an import from Japan. As a result, everything our teachers taught us was imbued with a sense of mystery and discovery. It was as if a door suddenly opened in a wall where previously no door had been visible.

The intensive workshops that Nadeau Sensei and Frager Sensei co-taught made a big impression on me. I would ride with other Santa Cruz Aikido students to Mountain View, walk up a flight of stairs, and emerge into a different world: the mat in Nadeau Sensei's dojo where anything was possible. He and Frager Sensei would lead us through exercise after creative exercise, inviting us into new experiences of mind-body unity: meditating, breathing, visualizing . . . walking up and down the length of the mat, creating the sensation of being carried along by a powerful river, practicing Aikido techniques while releasing the ego, letting a larger intelligence conduct the techniques.

These simple words can't convey the depth of the experiences that they fostered, and which led me, as a young person, to step forward eagerly on the path of Aikido. I am forever grateful to Nadeau Sensei and the others who pointed the way and led with a smile.

When I returned from training in Japan in 1977 and assumed the leadership of the Aikido club in Santa Cruz, Nadeau Sensei and other teachers warmly welcomed me back and supported me as a young instructor. Attending Nadeau Sensei's classes over the years has both inspired me as a student and strengthened me as a teacher.

I'll never forget the seminar in which he asked all of us to articulate what we were currently struggling with within our practice. "That's your future strength," he told us in a startling reframe, "just starting to show itself on the horizon." I was so struck by this wonderful new perspective that I immediately brought it back to my dojo in Santa Cruz. What a positive approach! Ever since, I've given feedback to students in terms of "strengths" and "future strengths."

I appreciate Nadeau Sensei's sincere respect and love for Osensei, always bringing him closer for those of us who did not have the opportunity to meet the Founder in person. I am moved by how faithfully and how consistently Nadeau Sensei has conveyed the essence of what he experienced directly with Osensei.

I have deep gratitude to Nadeau Sensei for a lifetime of dedicated Aikido practice, search, and teaching. It has opened the way for so many of us and will continue to reverberate into the future.

## ⟁ *Precious Moments* ⟁

PATRICIA ANNE HENDRICKS
Aikido 7th Dan Shihan
Dojo-cho, Aikido of San Leandro
California Aikido Association, Division I Head
U.S. Representative, International Aikido Federation

There is no way to sum up the life and dreams of a master, but I aim to highlight some of the precious moments I have experienced with Nadeau Shihan.

I believe the first time I saw him teach and demonstrate Aikido was over forty-five years ago when I was still a white belt. His attention to his partner's spirit and energetic direction was something to behold. His teaching method was uncompromising, and his continuous references to Osensei and his gifts caught my eye and soul.

When I was *uchideshi* (live-in disciple) to Stanley Pranin Sensei, I got to go to the Christmas dinner with Nadeau Sensei and Doran Sensei. It was daunting to me to attend an event and listen to all the stories.

Years passed, and I started augmenting my training by attending noon classes in the dojo then called Aikido of San Francisco. Not a class went by that didn't pique my curiosity.

After returning from Japan where I had lived in what had been Osensei's house in Iwama, I couldn't help thinking about what it was like for Nadeau Sensei to have actually trained with Osensei in person. I have always felt that he understood the subtle intricacies of Osensei's ability to transcend space and time.

For the last twenty years, I have had the honor of helping to host various Japanese sensei, Doshu, and many CAA holiday dinners and get-togethers with Nadeau Sensei. I cannot imagine the CAA without his passion for energy and *ki* (vital energy). He is a treasure for all of us and the entire Aikido world.

## △ *What I Owe Bob* △

### MARK HOUSLEY
Aikido 1st Dan
Aikido of Mountain View

On the mat in my first class with Nadeau Sensei, I felt like what I imagined the Tin Man in Frank Baum's *The Wizard of Oz* had experienced in his opening scene: rusting in a field, unable to speak, unable to move, and most important of all, unable to feel what was going on around him. It wasn't that I was out of shape, that Sensei was abstruse, or the *uke* (attacking/receiving partner) that day was unhelpful. No, it was as if my head, hands, and heart were rusted in place and disconnected. By the end of the class, my brain was sure that whatever it was that Sensei was teaching, I was unlikely to learn it: the necessary wiring just wasn't there.

But I had paid fifty-five dollars for an entire month of lessons, bought a mis-sized *gi* (practice uniform), learned to tie my new white belt, and wanted some return on my investment. In my third or fourth class, Sensei called me up, as *uke*, to demonstrate some variation of *nikkyo* (second-teaching techniques). In my first and only out-of-body experience, I watched myself plunging straight down to my knees, while thinking this is what being struck by lightning must feel like, ending up face down on the mat and, very oddly, laughing. How was that possible? What the hell just happened? Was some of the wiring there after all? I wanted to find out.

I'm not sure I ever found out. But trying changed me. Today, Sensei seems like Baum's Wizard, who confused me when I first watched the film as a little kid, but made sense to me as I got older. While Nadeau Sensei's words often didn't make much sense to me, his process, actions, integrity, example, and presence helped me unstick some of my rusted parts. His classes, full of students, each with their own big or little piece of the puzzle, infused me, or better, transfused me with little bits of Sensei, generating my own process that connected head, hands, and heart into a whole system. At least part of the time. To steal Sensei's metaphor, most of the time on the mat I was just Mark. But occasionally, as I trained, Mr. Housley appeared. And that made it all worthwhile.

Most importantly, that experience, watching it surface and develop in other students, took some of the cynical rust out of my heart and replaced it with hope and joy. And for that, I owe Bob deeply.

# THREE

# Teachings of Robert Nadeau

Robert Nadeau has been an inspiring teacher for generations of students interested in self-discovery and inner development. He mixes verbal explanations with active practices designed to introduce students to new experiences that guide them toward a better sense of who they truly are as people and how they can potentially live more balanced and harmonious lives. He addresses core questions faced by anyone seeking a way to develop themselves into all that they can become, whatever their art, profession, or calling.

As described elsewhere in this book, in the 1960s, Robert Nadeau was a direct disciple of the founder of Aikido, Morihei Ueshiba Osensei, training under him and other senior instructors at Hombu Dojo in Tokyo as a young man. Before he went to Tokyo, Nadeau had already been searching for answers in judo, yoga, meditation, and bodybuilding, all of which have informed his subsequent development. But Morihei Ueshiba Osensei was a profoundly inspirational presence and Nadeau acknowledges him as his seminal teacher.

As such, there are many references in these pages to Morihei Ueshiba Osensei and Aikido, the modern nonviolent *budo* (way of the warrior) he founded in Japan in the mid-1920s. Osensei was literally and figuratively a Great Teacher.

Aikido, written right to left, signed and sealed by Morihei Ueshiba.

Aikido can be translated as *The Way of Spiritual Harmony*. It is written using three Japanese characters: *ai* (harmony/union), *ki* (energy/life force), *do* (way/path), composed vertically top to bottom, horizontally left to right, or horizontally right to left as in this rendition from the Founder's brush.

Osensei's approach to teaching Aikido was naturally rooted in his own spiritual journey and his own training in various arts and traditions. He lived and taught within the cultural and historical context of the Japan of his day. He readily demonstrated techniques but rarely taught them in detail. He explained Aikido at length, but then told students they had to experience Aikido firsthand if they wanted to understand it in its full depth. By all reports, Osensei's explanatory diagrams were a complex amalgam of esoteric symbols and arcane language. His lectures were famously difficult to understand, even by his Japanese students.

In Nadeau Sensei's quest to come up with teachable English language expressions that adequately transmit the authentic essence of Osensei's process to modern students, he mixes Osensei's original vocabulary with the language and concepts of Western psychology, the modern Human Potential Movement, and his own personal experiences, creating a teaching *patois* uniquely his own. His diagrams during class famously tend toward stick figures and line drawings. His lectures can be challenging to follow at times, even for his longtime students. But somehow he always comes up with an effective approach to transmit the inner teachings of Aikido as a Way, beyond technique, beyond mere form.

On the Aikido mat, he can demonstrate powerful, fluid technique honed over decades of training and refinement. He teaches these techniques as a way to explore fundamentals like base, center, alignment, posture, attitude, connection, and energy flow. He often contrasts the appearance, feeling, and effectiveness of someone "doing" a technique versus "allowing" it to unfold naturally. He urges students to intuitively sense the appropriate timing and spacing, and move without the filter of thinking to allow a fuller experience of the dynamics between *nage* and *uke* (the throwing partner and the attacking/receiving partner in Aikido pairs practice). He encourages everyone to practice harmoniously. While his core themes have been consistent over the years, his language has continued to evolve as he experiments with various ways to present essential elements. At his Mountain View dojo, he expresses his approach to Aikido this way:

"Don't ask me how I did this.
Ask me who I have to be where this is possible."

Nadeau Sensei's teachings touch on universal themes. The lessons go beyond Aikido. The inner practices can be done by anyone without any knowledge of Aikido or background in martial arts. Because the practices focus on an experiential process in service of self-discovery and self-improvement, individuals in the arts, education, sports, or business may find them useful and relevant. It's all about human relationships and universal energy!

## Beginning Basics

Nadeau Sensei encourages new students to begin where they are. As Osensei told him, you don't need to go anywhere special to practice Aikido. It is here and now.

The first step is getting Present. This means being Present in your body and mind. One way to get Present is to settle into your experience. You might begin by naming the elements of your felt experience in real time, letting go of judgment without trying to change what you are experiencing. This can be as easy as labeling your sensations, feelings, moods, or surroundings. Listening more deeply in this way, we can begin to let go of preconditioned thoughts and habits and develop the inner spaciousness needed for new growth—spiritually, mentally, emotionally, and energetically. Feeling the rhythms and sensations of your breath can also be a powerful way of bringing your attention to the present.

With this orientation to practice, you naturally release tension. Letting go helps to shift the focus from thinking to deeper feeling and sensing, from cognitive understanding to embodied experience. Whatever the approach, being Present in the here and now is a good way to start practice, according to Sensei.

## ◲ *Easy the I, Open and Allow* ◲

MIKE ASHWELL
Aikido 6th Dan
Riai Aikido, Ponsonby, New Zealand
Aikido Teacher and IT Consultant

Living in New Zealand, I have seen Nadeau Sensei once every year or two over the past nearly thirty years. It was always clear when Sensei demonstrated that his *uke*'s balance was compromised from the moment he engaged. I have always believed that there was much more to Aikido than the physical techniques. Seeing what Nadeau Sensei was doing sparked my curiosity, and that spark continues to burn.

I often acted as Nadeau Sensei's chaperone when he came to New Zealand, so I spent a lot of time with him on his visits. This allowed me to see him as a whole person and not just a sensei. I got to see the transformation he underwent when he stepped onto the mat, no matter how he felt when we traveled. In more recent times, I saw how exhausted he was after the training had finished. Most importantly, I saw how much he cared about what he presented and how much he wanted us all to "get it."

When I walked up crowded streets with him in the early days, I expected the people coming toward us to part and go around him, but they didn't. He was no longer "Nadeau Sensei." In that situation, he was just regular old "Bob."

His smoking used to annoy and upset me, but I understand that it's part of who he is. He stayed in my home a couple of times when he came to New Zealand, and he got to know my son. They would smoke and chat outside on the deck. The next time he visited, he brought a loaf of sourdough bread with him because he had remembered that my son loved sourdough from San Francisco. This small example was another side of him that I appreciated. Of course, if New Zealand customs officers had stopped him, he would have been in trouble because you cannot bring fresh food into the country.

I have come to believe six words, "Easy the I, Open and Allow," are at the heart of Nadeau Sensei's teachings. He used these words the first time he visited New Zealand, and every time since. Over the years, these six words have continued to bug me. I have felt that while I understood the words, the picture was still incomplete. Along the way, I have developed a deep understanding of Sensei's process. I have experienced their effects and changes in my body. However, it is only recently that I fully understood these words need to be directly experienced and felt. It was not enough to know and understand them. I needed to feel and then sense what was beyond the words with my body rather than my head.

Sensei's practice of settling and opening to the correct lineage in order to undertake whatever is needed at the moment has been especially invaluable. For example, my home is split between a garage and a barn. To get between the buildings, I have to climb a set of stairs several times a day. Every time I approach them, it is a challenge. I know that I need to settle, center, and adopt the "stair climber" lineage. I can climb the stairs with virtually no pain when fully doing this. However, if I don't, the pain stops me, and I lose my balance. Naturally, this means that I must prepare myself more fully for the rest of the steps.

Listening with my body and not just my ears is one of the benefits that Sensei's teachings has provided me. Listening without judgment or challenge is so vital in successful communication. After all, that is really what Aikido is about.

My knees have given me problems for a lot of years. Eventually, I needed surgery. The convalescence period took a long time. My new knee did not like any direct contact with the ground and had very limited movement. From an Aikido perspective, I could no longer do *shikko* (knee walking) or *ukemi* (art of attacking/falling/rolling), leaving me feeling like I was no longer a complete person and, therefore, not a proper teacher. However, my love for the art kept me from giving up and made me focus on what I *could* do.

Nadeau Sensei's ongoing teachings of "Easy the I, Open and Allow" became my focus and have guided me on a journey to explore the inner art, the unseen Aikido. This has been a great gift, changing my understanding of Aikido and its value and purpose completely, allowing me to realize that I still can be a good teacher and student with much to offer. Those six words have helped me rediscover my joy in the art.

## ⬓ Don't Apologize for Being Here ⬓

CAROL SANOFF
Aikido 2nd Dan
San Francisco Aikido

Sitting at my part-time technical-writer desk job one day early in 1979, a clear, unfamiliar voice in my head said, "Go watch an Aikido class." I had seen a couple of Aikido demonstrations years before. I had studied t'ai chi. I had been a rower in college. I looked up "Aikido" in the White Pages, left work early, and got myself to the Turk Street dojo in San Francisco.

The steep stairway from the front door up to the second floor was long and had a bend toward the top; nothing could be seen but endless stairs. Rounding the bend, there was a counter to the left, and behind the counter was a man in a slick polyester shirt smoking a cigarette. Clearly, he owned the place.

I entered a large room full of mats and took a seat on a bench at the side. Then, after a while, people began to drift in, wearing white suits, some in long black skirts, stretching, chatting. Finally, just before seven o'clock they quieted and aligned as if a magnet had been drawn across the floor, and the smoker, now likewise clad, emerged from the back, strode to the front, and knelt down in one fluid gesture. The class had begun.

It was a melee. People were gliding, grabbing, circling, flying through the air, landing with thuds and slaps. I was definitely in the wrong place.

And then, during an instructional break, the teacher said to the class, "Don't apologize for being here." In that moment, I realized that I had spent much of my life in subliminal apology, and that something crucially important had just been uttered within my hearing. I needed to keep listening.

I signed up as a new Aikido student on my way out. I scuttled my half-baked idea of going traveling indefinitely. Instead, I aimed my Tuesdays and Thursdays toward these classes and this teacher even if, as I said to myself, "I'll never be able to do that fancy stuff *they're* doing."

I was ungainly and slow to catch on to the most basic elements ("the *other* right foot"), but began to find my sense of center and ground and extension. Gradually the impossible became possible. After many a back-flop, my body learned to fly through the air and land with a satisfying thud. *Ukemi* became my great love, and I would practically quiver at the edge of the mat, hoping to be one of the lucky ones beckoned forth. I was *hungry*.

The clarity of that first invitational exhortation led to a commitment such as I had never made before. It was the start of a life that bent itself toward deeper personal responsibility, embodied joy, and came with a litter of treasured playmates, each on her own learning curve. We were all gathered and woven into some high energetic mass, night after night, by the presence of master teacher and craftsman Robert Nadeau. You will have heard of him. You probably trained with him. He is vivid, authentic, one-of-a-kind, and completely faithful to his lineage. All attempts at description fall short.

That was the luckiest day, and those were some of the best years of my life.

# Open and Settle

Another way Nadeau Sensei encourages students to be more present is a process he calls Open and Settle. To open to the experience of finer energies may involve breathing and feeling more freely or opening one's gaze to see more widely. And, at the same time, to settle into one's body, both physically and energetically, for a more direct experience of whatever is present.

Open and Settle is one of Sensei's most accessible exercises for beginners and advanced students alike. He often uses it as a kind of energetic warm-up, a familiar foundation for further explorations. For example, he might follow Open and Settle by asking students to more fully receive the invisible support emanating upward from the ground beneath their feet. He will guide students to feel the soles of their feet, then to sense the surface of the mat that supports them, and then to feel the floor beneath the mat, and the earth beneath the floor.

Opening and Settling is accelerated by appreciating these natural forces and aligning with gravity. Practicing this way cultivates a fuller sense of grounded presence.

Nadeau Sensei's emphasis on being grounded with a stable base reflects his lifelong training in judo, meditation, yoga, and Aikido. Training with Osensei at Hombu Dojo, Nadeau recounts, included classes with long sessions of *suwari-waza* (seated techniques done on the knees) and lots of *seiza* (formal seated posture on the floor), which he believes Osensei emphasized to settle everyone in their lower bodies and bring them down to earth for a more direct experience of the ground.

The practices of being Present and Open and Settle are designed to gently guide students to feel more completely and realistically what is happening in their lives in real time.

## Becoming a Calmer Person

NICOLA FITZWATER
Aikido 2nd Dan
Aikido Oamaru, New Zealand

My children can evoke strong feelings of frustration and anger like no other human being can. Yet, I can remain calmer by practicing Nadeau Sensei's grounding, settling, and centering process.

For example: I asked my daughter one evening if she wanted her hair plaited or in a ponytail—her response was a major tantrum. Instead of getting drawn into her world or sending her to time-out in her room, I settled, grounded, opened, comforted her, and asked what was going on. It turned out she was having trouble with one of her classmates. I was able to resolve the situation with my daughter. This outcome would not have been possible if I hadn't taken a moment to ground and settle.

Another example: During one of the seminars in New Zealand, we were practicing an energy exercise where Sensei said to imagine there were "nozzles" on the ends of our hands where energy flows through and out. So, I visualized energy coming from beneath the ground, passing through my body and shooting out of my hands to take down my *uke*. It must have been pretty good because Sensei could "see" it and asked me to demonstrate in front of the class. When I did this, Sensei could again sense the energy I was shooting out because he asked the class, "Can you SEE that?!"

I thought that was cool.

## Allowing

Nadeau Sensei also highlights the importance of what he calls Allowing to bring a fuller experience to any part of these internal practices. To allow something is to accept it as it is as it unfolds. Sensei says, "Allow yourself to open more," "Allow yourself to settle more," "Allow more base," or "Allow more space."

Open and Settle, and Allowing, require practice and repetition before changes gradually become apparent. However, the shift from thinking to feeling and deeper sensing can be faster once the process becomes familiar.

As illustrated in diagram 1, he speaks about three different levels at which a person may respond to the energies of a given situation: "Think, Feel, and Sense." Thinking is a normal and necessary response to a new situation. However, Sensei describes overreliance on thinking as being up in our heads and largely oblivious to our inner feelings and body sensations.

He teaches that we are all capable of feeling and sensing deeper dimensions of ourselves and connecting with finer and finer energies. Gradually we can integrate upper-level awareness with deeper-level experience. We practice this internal work ourselves to actualize the pro-

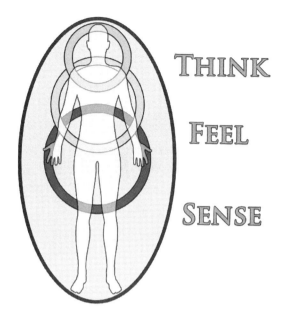

Diagram 1. Think, Feel, Sense.

cess. Reading these paragraphs and understanding the concepts is not enough. According to Sensei, sustained practice approached honestly is essential for a self-driven process of inner change.

## △ *Allowing Gratitude* △

MOLLY HALE
Aikido 5th Dan
Aikido West
Dojo-cho, Aikido of Penn Valley
Co-director, Ability Production, a non-profit hosting three projects:
Spinal Cord Injury (SCI) support; Aikido;
and the Malawi Project supporting food security

I've been giving a lot of thought to my thirty-six-year relationship with Nadeau Sensei. I have had the great fortune of training with many dynamic Aikido teachers, and Nadeau Sensei has been a crucial influence in my training. Every time I've been on the mat with him, I have come away with new language, expanding perceptions, and deepening respect and gratitude for the interconnectedness that Osensei brought to the martial world. I have grown with Nadeau Sensei's growing. If there is one word that is always with me, it is the word "allowing," which he dropped into my consciousness many years ago.

Off the mat, Nadeau Sensei and I have become "eye-rolling buddies." He sees me coming toward him, rolls his eyes, and says something to the effect of, "Here comes trouble." It is a tender, joyful aspect of our encounters, complete with the touch of an embrace. I treasure these moments. Looking into his face, I have said, "You realize, of course, that I love you."

One year, there was a very late evening at the Aiki Summer Retreat in San Rafael. I was sitting in the lounge tossing a balloon back and forth with another woman. Sensei strolled in. Sat down. And for the next half hour the three of us tossed that balloon back and forth in total silence. Then, finally, there was a point when there was an acknowledged completion, and we all went our separate ways. Something profound was transmitted in that encounter, though I couldn't tell you what it was exactly. It seemed a heart thing. A love thing.

I am grateful that Robert Nadeau Shihan has offered his wisdom, his movement, and his perspective on this Aikido life and held true to the gifts he received from Osensei.

On the land where I live, there is a large container of black bamboo. These plants grew from a small pot his students collectively brought me back in 1995 when I was laid up for two months in Stanford Hospital after breaking my neck. I have fondly named my thriving, flexible, growing stand of bamboo "Robert."

## Easy the I

Nadeau Sensei counters the human tendency to overemphasize thinking relative to feeling and sensing with a process he calls "Easy the I." The **I** in this context is an individual's experience of who they are at the moment they start practice. **I** is a natural part of who we are as human beings, but it is not *all* we are.

Easy the I is a way to shift from overthinking to a more direct experience by letting go of our preconceptions about who we are, what we are capable of, and how the world works.

A helpful way to start the process is to come into your best alignment with gravity, standing or sitting. Then, simply let things be as they are. Allow the thinking mind that typically filters and interprets our life experiences to take a break from its normal habits of constantly prioritizing understanding, doing, and controlling. As the I eases, a sense of inner spaciousness and calmness naturally emerges, offering its own transformational potential.

There is no need to make up anything or figure anything out when practicing Easy the I. Just allow your body and mind to naturally unwind and be present in feeling—not holding on or pushing away any experience. Be open to experiencing whatever arises in this moment of ease. I doesn't have to do anything. It just has to relax and let go. That's it!

#  *Why I Train with Robert Nadeau*

ROSS MADDEN
Aikido 6th Dan
Instructor, City Aikido of San Francisco.
Author: *The Three Poisons: A Buddhist Guide to Resolving Conflict*

In 1980, my then-wife Maia wrote a graduate thesis on George Leonard Sensei, who taught at Aikido of Tamalpais. When she interviewed him at the dojo, she said she had had a vision of me (who had never trained Aikido) in the dojo in a *gi* and *hakama* (practice uniform and traditional divided skirt) throwing people around. When she told George of that vision, he said the best person to train with was a fellow named Robert Nadeau, who had trained with Osensei, had a dojo in San Francisco, and had been George's teacher as well. So, I decided to watch a noon class at the Turk Street dojo and saw Nadeau Sensei do *shiho-nage* (four-direction throw), which seemed utterly beautiful and fascinating. After that, I was hooked and signed up, and have been at his dojo ever since.

In other words, Robert Nadeau has been my sensei for more than forty years, and my Aikido spiritual home has always been at his dojo, through several location changes since Turk Street.

It's unusual to train with someone for more than forty years, so I have to ask myself: WHY?

First and foremost, because Robert Nadeau charismatically embodies for me the presence and mystery of Aikido, as well as the earnest diligence that needs to be applied to live it. He has a great deal of natural presence. He continually explores the nuances of spiritual growth and ways to teach his students how to approach and experience it in their own lives (even if he is sometimes short-tempered at their dunderheadedness).

He taught me that *ki* (vital energy) is not a theoretical construct but a vibrant, living energy that pervades us all, if we let it. My first inkling was when, as a white belt, he had me *uke* for him on an *ushiro katate-dori sankyo* (third-teaching technique from rear one-handed grab), during which I felt an energy vortex course upward through my body. Having had that experience, I thenceforth understood that we were indeed working in the energy realm and that it would be through that realm that we best connect with others.

Concomitant to my early awareness of actual *ki*, I was deeply impressed by Nadeau's insistence that technique—while important—is developed and perfected in the service of *ki* and universal harmony, and thus not an end in itself. Bob told us the story of the *Aikidoka* (Aikido practitioner) who "trained ugly" for twenty or thirty years to improve his *kote-gaeshi* (wrist-twist technique). His throw certainly got better, but at the end of those years he was still a jerk, and thus it was all for naught. On the other hand, Robert's teachings have to do with process and personal transformation. His dojo has always existed to explore the deeper nature and purpose of Aikido.

Finally, he taught me to "Easy the I," which is a long and challenging path for most students. Partly because our perceptions of ourselves and others are seen through the screen or filter of our little "I," we don't experience things purely until we can reduce the impact of all those delusional feelings and ideations. In addition, because Aikido operates as a sort of bio-feedback loop, the mere fact that we work with another person means we will have to confront the limitations of our energetic presence in every technique. By learning to "Easy the I," we can get a proper take on how to redefine our energy presence without ratcheting up our small selves to try to excuse the perceived limitations in our techniques.

Ultimately, Nadeau Sensei deepened my understanding of being an honest, present human being. I am very thankful for having been able to learn from him.

## △ *Medicine for a Sick World* △

### JUSTIN NEWMAN
Aikido 4th Dan
Aikispirit South Miami Aikido Dojo
Doctor of Functional and Holistic Medicine

I began my Aikido training a few decades ago while still a pre-med student at the University of Miami, several years before meeting Robert Nadeau Shihan.

On first meeting him, he said something that immediately caught my attention and has stuck with me ever since.

"We don't need more Aikido teachers. We need Aikido doctors, Aikido lawyers, and Aikido homemakers. Let's take this developmental process off the mat."

The developmental process of Aikido that Nadeau Shihan was referring to provides actual evidence through direct personal experience. For example, we spent a lot of time in the first part of that workshop simply walking back and forth across the mat. However, we would periodically stop moving, settle down, open up, and connect with a clearer, more available version of ourselves. Then a more functional version of ourselves would resume walking.

During that initial workshop, Nadeau Shihan would repeat and affirm, "Clear, I am." This mantra helped us settle down and soften the mind and ego to sustain that functioning more easily.

Gradually, a "body allowed," as he often said, would naturally walk more comfortably. The rest of our mind and self would be more easily engaged, fully present, within the walking body. Experiencing how this process can be implemented in ordinary ways would help us to distinguish between the *idea* of walking and the *actual* walking.

I hadn't noticed before that I had been spending way too much time *thinking* about what I was doing rather than *being* in the actual experience of the activity!

Experiencing this multidimensional developmental process and the possibilities it offered, I wanted to gain firsthand insight by practicing the inner workings of Osensei's Aikido. This led me to spend twenty-five years training with master teacher Robert Nadeau.

In my earlier years of training, I had spent some time with other students of Morihei Ueshiba Osensei, the Founder of Aikido, including Mary Heiny Sensei, Mitsugi Saotome Sensei, Henry Kono Sensei, and Ed Baker Sensei. All of them were absolutely fantastic in their own ways. But none of them presented Aikido as a tool that could lead to development on such a grand scale as Bob Nadeau.

Around the time of our first meeting, I had just begun my holistic and functional medicine practice and was also the father of two small children. The experiences I had while training Aikido with Nadeau Shihan, both on and off the mat, were illuminating. For me, they amplified the words of the Founder when he described Aikido as a system for building bridges, a medicine for a sick world.

During the years that followed, I invited Nadeau Shihan to come to Miami for a few additional workshops. And he invited me to continue coming out to the San Francisco Bay Area for training each year, which I have done with gusto!

My training on the mat began to change completely. My focus departed from technique to process. Whether it was solo training, working with a partner or multiple partners, or weapons training, it was all being processed through the lens of personal development. As a result, I could increase my capacity and root myself more deeply while under pressure. This, and many other aspects of Osensei's process, became much more easily translated into my daily life.

Working with this process, on the mat and in my day-to-day personal and professional life, has given me abundant evidence that a simple, convenient, and relatively ordinary framework can help people become potentially like superheroes in their personal worlds. As a physician, I have been inspired by the development and transformations manifested in many of my medical clients when I've shared Osensei's methodology with them. A relatively small-time cook who became the director of food services for a major university. A budding young scientist who became a senior researcher and advisor to a multinational board of directors. Weekend warriors who quickly outshined their competition. Government officials, nonprofit community developers, and householders have all benefited from the process that Nadeau Shihan has been sharing with us all these years.

On a more personal note, I have immensely enjoyed the time spent with Bob Nadeau. I especially recall a memorable road trip down the Sonoma Coast. We stopped briefly at an overlook, with the majestic coastline below us, and discussed the manifest, hidden, and divine aspects of Creation, the world of our being, our true self and how it engages within characters and roles that we play, our lineage and mission in life, and so much more. Of course, we had a lot of laughs too, not to take ourselves too seriously.

Whether in private discussions, road trips, or even spending time on many occasions late at night channeling the living spirit of Osensei into dialogue with us, there has certainly been no shortage of opportunities for me to expand into finer versions of myself, to learn and grow through our relationship.

Bob has always encouraged me to "know yourself," much as Socrates once said. Not through concepts or words, but through experience. Remain diligent, consistent, and available to a practical, applicable developmental process. Work with it on a day-to-day basis.

I have been saying to my clients for quite some time that within all of the challenges we face are the nutrients that are needed for our growth and development. Pure energies are like nutrients. They are all around us, helping us reenergize and recalibrate. The possibilities are truly limitless!

With profound gratitude, I will always hold Robert Nadeau Shihan in my heart and in the depths of my being. Words cannot truly express my love and appreciation for him and all he has done.

## Awareness and Experience

A recurring theme in Nadeau Sensei's teachings is the distinction between Awareness and Experience. He uses the word Awareness to broadly describe our mental understanding, thoughts, concepts, and ideas. He uses the word Experience equally broadly to describe our first-person involvement with the sensations, emotions, and energies arising in the here and now. Awareness can be used to map the landscape of life and to understand the world around us. Experience is visceral, immedi-ate, and direct. Awareness is no substitute for experience, nor vice versa. Awareness and Experience are complementary. Both are important in a balanced life.

Sensei observes that many people tend to overemphasize their Awareness of the world around them while underemphasizing their Experience of inner energies and feelings that arise within them when encountering new or challenging situations in life.

Some people may respond initially by formulating ideas about the dynamics at play. They consider their options, weighing the pros and cons of various reactions to calculate their best approach.

In diagram 2, Sensei illustrates that powerful supportive energies

Diagram 2. Awareness Experience.

Diagram 3. Awareness Experience Interact.

operate at a deeper level of existence. The curved lines and sparkles in the lower half of the diagram represent energy and intelligence that is always present and available to everyone directly through Experience.

Diagram 3 shows how Awareness and Experience can complement and feed into each other to stimulate further activation. Recognizing this bidirectional mutuality can contribute to cultivating better harmony between mind and body that energizes and supports us in life.

Sensei teaches that in Aikido, as in life, consistently effective functional performance depends on the balanced development of both Awareness and Experience.

For example, a beginning Aikido student may have an idea about how an Aikido technique works and try their best to mimic their teacher's demonstrated movements. But the student cannot perform the technique smoothly. Then, as they continue to train, through trial and error and perseverance, their movements become more coordinated, their performance improves, and their practice deepens as Awareness is supplemented by Experience.

Sensei emphasizes that Awareness without Experience is incomplete. To bring this lesson to life, he sometimes uses the example of a hot soak in a Japanese *ofuro* (bath). A person might have an idea about bathing in an *ofuro* from pictures in a book about Japan. If they walk close to an *ofuro*, they can see steam rising from the water and feel its moist warmth on their face. But until they actually climb into the *ofuro* they cannot possibly appreciate the full experience of soaking in very very hot water up to their chin.

Sensei often ends this lesson by encouraging students to be open to new experiences and, if a new experience presents itself, be courageous enough to climb into their metaphorical *ofuro*, at least to "check it out." He further encourages them, once immersed in their new situation, to allow whatever energies arise to play themselves out thoroughly and to take the time to soak in the experience of those energies.

# 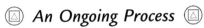 *An Ongoing Process*

AMY SHIPLEY
Aikido 2nd Dan
City Aikido of San Francisco
University Instructor, Personal Trainer
Wildlife Hospital Clinic Supervisor

I started training Aikido in 1992 with Bob Noha Sensei, then left California in 1995 to live and work in Japan. I returned in 1997–98 and began training again with Noha Sensei, who would take groups of students to Robert Nadeau Sensei's classes in San Francisco on Tuesdays, which is how I came to meet him.

What struck me immediately about Nadeau Sensei was the power he emitted. This energy seemed to carry over to the students in the class. Everyone was smiling and having fun and getting thrown about in ways that were astounding to me.

By 1999, I was 3rd Kyu in Aikido. When I moved to San Francisco, I made City Aikido my home dojo to train with Nadeau Sensei.

One particular day, Sensei called me out. It was the first time I ever really felt what his technique was like. I was always scared of being *uke* (attacking/receiving partner) because: (1) he'd make people fly; and, (2) I was afraid of getting hurt. However, the technique he did with me was amazing. I think it was a *kokyu-nage* (breath throw). He slid to the floor, and I flew over him. One second I was standing, and the next second I was on the floor. I wasn't hurt. It didn't hurt. I landed like the mat was a cushioned mattress. I don't remember anything that happened in between except that I just flew across a void. When I turned to look at him, astonished by what just happened, he had this big smile.

I understood that this "power" flowed through him and his *uke*. So, it wasn't just a technique but a blending of some natural force that occurred in the connection of *uke* and *nage* (throwing partner). And the power of that was invigorating! It didn't break me down. It lifted me, and I wanted to feel that again.

One of the stories he told that had a profound impact on me very early on was about a little boy who was afraid to jump off a high dive. Nadeau heard the boy's father say, "Oh, you are afraid." Sensei was disappointed with that response because, from his perspective, the father could have said, and should have said, "Oh, that's just energy to help you to do the dive." I found truth in that story. While I still have fears, I try to open up and accept whatever happens, trying not to force an action but to flow with it and accept the result that follows.

There isn't a day that goes by where I don't apply lessons learned from Nadeau Sensei in my life. One day I needed to go to a currency exchange bank. I carried $1,000 in my purse and walked to the MacArthur BART station in Oakland, a notoriously dangerous station. My senses were on high alert, but I was also trying to remain calm and casual. I remember another woman on the street in front of me, and I was moving closer to her. Suddenly, I sensed that someone was focusing on me. I noticed a man pass the woman and start to reach for me. I wasn't looking specifically at him, but I felt him. I did a perfect *tenkan* (turning blend) and was about to grab this fellow's arm when I realized it was my boyfriend. All was well. I have no doubt that it was my training with Nadeau that helped me tune in to these energies and respond in a way that harmonized with the situation I encountered.

Nadeau Sensei has helped me realize that there is always more to uncover. Aikido is more than just technique. It's a process of self-discovery. It's a way to understand yourself. It's a process that is always ongoing, always growing, always changing. Training is a way to check in with that process and play with energies. On the mat, you get an opportunity to experience your reaction to a specific type of energy. You can give yourself a chance to access your greater self in response to that energy. In real life, you may not get any time to respond, so I appreciate on-the-mat practice because I feel better able to slow down to whatever is thrown at me and respond in a way that is beneficial to me, regardless of whoever or whatever I'm dealing with.

Because Nadeau Sensei had (and has) a direct connection with Osensei, I feel that I have received a near-direct transmission of Osensei's teachings. Nadeau Sensei's passion and love for the Founder have helped me more fully experience the great depth of Osensei's teachings and his vision of the world.

## ⟨△⟩ *Lifetime of Training* ⟨△⟩

### BOB NOHA
#### Aikido 6th Dan
#### Chief Instructor, Aikido of Petaluma

I vividly remember my first experience with Nadeau Sensei. It was late in 1966, and I was sixteen years old. I had previously studied Western boxing and Kenpo Karate and was greatly enjoying practicing Aikido in Mountain View with Ed Riggs Sensei and Sig Kufferath Sensei, who had started the dojo. Nadeau Sensei had just returned from Japan and assumed the position of Chief Aikido Instructor at the dojo.

In my first class with Nadeau Sensei, we practiced *shomen-uchi ikkyo* (first-teaching technique for a frontal strike to the forehead).

I can still remember the *experience* of the first technique he did on me. There was a smoothness and flow to it that has remained a vivid experience after more than fifty years. Through the fog of my sixteen-year-old brain, I realized that this was something special. I knew from that first experience, on a mainly unconscious level, that Aikido was a much bigger practice than I had imagined. I dedicated myself to following this path.

I continued to practice and eventually teach Aikido in the Bay Area during the next ten years. During this period I went to college, served in the U.S. Air Force, got married, and started a family.

In the summer of 1975, our family moved to the Buffalo, New York area to be near my wife's family. The unemployment rate in the area was about 18 percent, and my only job skills were from service in the Air Force.

One day, I was walking along one of the main streets in downtown Buffalo, feeling the weight of needing to find work and care for my family, when I experienced a presence of mind and body that I knew with certainty came from Nadeau Sensei's training. It was almost as if he were walking along beside me. It lifted my sense of discouragement, and this allowed me to do well in a job interview later that day, which helped me obtain a trainee position with an insurance company, which opened the door for me to a successful forty-two-year career in the insurance industry.

One of Sensei's core teachings is dimensionality. We are multilevel beings who can grow and develop through progressive levels of increasing fullness and functionality. I benefited from this process as I moved up the corporate hierarchy to higher and higher levels in the insurance industry, eventually reaching the number two position in a profitable $300 million division of my company. Along the way, his teachings helped me craft for myself a business character capable of succeeding in a business environment for which I had no previous experience or training.

Osensei embodied a map of the universe and its functionality. Outside of Aikido, he expressed his vision in Shinto terminology that was challenging for both Japanese and non-Japanese students alike to grasp. Nadeau Sensei somehow absorbed Osensei's profound teachings more deeply than many. For those of us who became his students, Nadeau's *waza* (techniques) and Nadeau's words have opened a sense of direct connection to Osensei's Aikido. To my ears, Nadeau was able to express Osensei's teachings in a form that was not only understandable but *practicable*. It is difficult to overestimate the value of Nadeau's contribution in this area, as many people in Aikido have said that Osensei's teachings could not be understood, and therefore we shouldn't even try. This would have been a huge tragedy because it would have ignored the best and most profound part of Osensei's teachings.

Nadeau Sensei's approach to Aikido has helped me on the mat—both as student and instructor—by always keeping the size and scope of Osensei's vision as a major focus of training. He consistently emphasized the inner process of Aikido in its many forms over a technique-only practice. His process-oriented practice also helped me develop myself off the mat. My business character developed differently from my on-the-mat Aikido character. Both are yet again different from my family character. Nadeau teaches that the process of character development— the alchemy—is the same, but the chemical ingredients, the energies, are naturally different in different environments. This is a crucial point that has been enormously beneficial navigating my life.

Nadeau Sensei once quoted Seigo Yamaguchi Sensei from Hombu Dojo, who said to him, "Behind every technique, there is an epic poem." I like Nadeau Sensei's version of this even better,

"Behind every technique is an epic experience." It is our job to stay open and pay attention!

## ◬ *Walk Like a Human Being* ◬

### ANDREAS PEFANIS
City Aikido of San Francisco

It was my second class with Nadeau Sensei, and he called me up for *ukemi* (art of attacking/falling/rolling). I was still in a fighting mindset, so when Sensei said, "Here, grab my wrist," I launched toward him, having no doubt that I was about to get him. But no matter which way I went, although his wrist was right there in front of me and so close, I would lose it and keep chasing until everything disappeared. Finally, I landed on the mat, and heard Sensei's voice behind me: "Do you want to try again?"

Of course, I thought to myself. And yes, I had already devised a plan, and right away I put it into action. When he would offer his wrist, I would launch my attack and then immediately turn 180 degrees, and get him for sure. I thought he wouldn't expect that.

I proceeded with my attack and my plan. But, once again, as soon as I made my turn, Sensei disappeared, and then I slammed into an invisible ethereal wall. I felt transformed into a dreamlike state, bouncing off the walls inside the dojo, and finally landing on the ceiling in the corner, looking down. It felt as if I was split into two, with my conscious self being a spectator to all that was occurring below, being able to see myself on the mat rolling away from Sensei with the rest of my classmates watching. I had no idea what was happening, nor was I able to comprehend or explain what took place and how it was possible.

Over a decade has passed since that day.

If I could summarize what Nadeau Sensei's teaching means to me, it would be words he once said to me: "Walk like a human being . . . keep your integrity."

## Standing Practice

Another way Nadeau Sensei introduces students to the benefits of aligning Awareness and Experience is with a simple Standing Practice. He asks students to begin in a seated position with the affirmation, "I want to stand better." The next step is to allow the energies available for standing to flow, and then to stand up from the chair.

During the first attempt or two, the students will likely have a partial experience of the energies and still feel the need to make some effort as they stand. But, as they continue to practice sitting, standing, and back, after a few cycles, they begin to sense what it means to stand better.

The Standing Practice guides students to draw on energies that better support the movement of rising from a chair. This includes aligning the physical structure of the body to be in harmony with gravity and opening energetically between the seated and standing postures. Gradually the experience of sitting and standing becomes more fluid compared to initial attempts, revealing to the student the difference between an idea of a task and the experience of doing it. This simple practice can be used with any physical activity, such as climbing stairs or chopping wood, that benefits from improved alignment between body and mind working together.

## ⌂ *A Natural, Never-Ending Process* ⌂

### OLIVER THORNE
### Aikido 3rd Dan
### International Teacher and Coach

When I first met Robert Nadeau Shihan in 2004, I knew little about him and even less about Aikido. Since my late teens, I'd been training in a few different martial arts. I was twenty-four years old, and I had been dabbling with karate for a few months when I came across John Stevens's translation of Osensei's *The Art of Peace*. It's fair to say this book changed my life—as six months later, I found myself training as an *uchideshi* (live-in disciple) with Patrick Cassidy Sensei in Switzerland.

*Uchideshi* was the kind of martial arts practice I had always dreamed of, albeit with misty mountain temples in Asia, not lakeside dojos in Switzerland. So here I was, living in Switzerland, six months into my Aikido training, and about to attend a weekend seminar with Robert Nadeau Shihan. I still recall the exact moment when we met. He had a certain expansive presence about him, which was transmitted even through a simple greeting. I knew it was going to be a big weekend after that handshake.

I didn't know at the time, but a part of Nadeau Shihan's teaching involves calling people up in front of everyone so he can take *ukemi* (art of attacking/falling/rolling) and "check you out." At the first opportunity, I jumped up to be checked. We had been practicing an old favorite of his, *ikkyo-nage* (first-teaching throw), with a receptive opening and an entering step through to throw. As we went through this together several times, he talked it through, with the group of around sixty or so people looking on. He kept encouraging me to "go again," and after several rounds, he said something like, "I like something here, try one more time. . . . Ahh, I get a sense of deep listening." I was profoundly touched. He was deeply listening to my deep listening. In that moment, I felt a silent resonance between us along with the spoken affirmation. Afterward, I sat back down, not thinking much of it (apart from feeling charged), but my close friends, fellow *uchideshi*, and *Aikidoka* (Aikido practitioners) from our dojo were leaning over and smiling and saying nice things, and I felt a glow throughout my body.

There was another characteristic moment that day, where Nadeau Sensei hit me in the forehead while telling me to "keep my head up." I appreciated his "old school" methods. I rode home along the lakeside in the backseat of the car after that first day of training. It was a clear summer night, and you could see the stars. I can still vividly recall this drive home as I was completely silent, without thought, just soaking in the world as it was happening.

That weekend changed my life. There is no doubt in my mind that Aikido has been the backbone of my life ever since my time as an *uchideshi*.

I can recall the next meeting with Nadeau Sensei a few years later when I was a *shodan* (first degree black belt). This time, I had the opportunity to take *ukemi* for Sensei throughout the weekend. I always sat close by and was ready to dive into action. My only memory from that weekend is the sense of grabbing a force of nature, something like grabbing the branch of a tree, which is deeply rooted and powerful; a very natural feeling, and yet, simultaneously, mysterious.

Over the next ten years, I practiced Aikido all around the world. I often came back to the basics I'd learned from Nadeau Sensei: presence, grounding, back and under, center-circle, and two forces. I was fascinated by the simple body movements he used to increase a sense of ground, to balance out the front and back, left and right, up and down, the repetition of "body, body, body," and of course, the "one by, two by, three by" exercise.

I dreamed of traveling to train in San Francisco since those early Aikido days. However, for several years I had no contact with Nadeau Shihan. Then, about 2016, it hit me with a sense of urgency: I needed to go to connect personally with Sensei. During my training, I had long had a sense of dimensional shifts and hints of what we might think of as "the magic" of Aikido. I'd been meditating for years, practicing yoga daily, and training Aikido pretty much full time, but I knew something more was possible in my practice and daily life. I felt I was missing nuances of the practice, important "tricks" to move along, simple misunderstandings that stopped the process, and some fundamentals I needed to understand. I had a sense of needing to go to the next level, which brought me to the City Aikido dojo in San Francisco.

It isn't easy to describe my experience training in San Francisco. I had never established a personal relationship with Nadeau Shihan; he didn't know who I was or why I was there. I began my journey with three questions for Sensei, and he answered two of them in the first lesson of the first training on a Sunday morning. He has a strange knack for knowing what's being asked for before it is even asked! After that first Sunday morning training session, everyone went for coffee. There was some discussion about class and some of the finer training points. I was sitting on the periphery listening, feeling a combination of jet lag and post-training energy. After a while, he turned to me and asked, "So, what are you doing here?" It's a directness I appreciate. He wanted to know where I was coming from in practice and process. My answer was simple, as it was my third unanswered question, "How do I go to the next level?" With this, we were set for three weeks of intensive training and coffee drinking. It was like an injection of his life's teachings in condensed form.

Since that first visit, I've traveled to San Francisco to train several times and maintained my connection with Sensei, calling him often to discuss the process. Nadeau Sensei sometimes calls himself a "one-trick pony" because what he teaches is so deceptively simple. There is a presence-ing, a settling and opening, a grounding, and a deeper feeling, which is at the root of everything he is doing. In the simplicity, there is depth. Working through those depths, experience and guidance are invaluable.

Over time, my training and communication with Sensei has clarified much of the process for me. The main points are the importance of core, character, clearing, downtime, the relationship between experience and awareness, the situation/world, as well as lineage, and most of all, dimensionality. This last one probably captures everything Sensei is doing, but then each thing he does is a doorway into dimensionality, ultimately leading to Self. It is difficult to explain these ideas in words, and impossible to describe the experience of the process in words.

These days if I were to emphasize something in the process, it would be the naturalness of what we are doing. The human condition seems to be strung out between experience and awareness, so clarifying this relationship through our own experience is fundamental. Still, it is naturally going on already. We just have to take time to settle down and notice it.

Likewise, there are rhythms in life. Downtime is one of the most natural of these rhythms. On the personal scale, we do it every night when we go to sleep and then wake in the morning.

On a seasonal scale, when winter months approach, downtime can feel like slowing down, drawing inside, and needing to sleep more, stay warm, and do less. Catching that natural inclination to hibernate and noticing the energetic rhythm of drawing-in on a seasonal scale helps me gather energy and stops me from pushing myself to do more during winter when it is naturally a time to return to myself and do less.

We move in and out of downtime all the time, in almost everything we do, in endless cycles, naturally. We can sense our natural downtime rhythm, attune to the situation and to the world we are in. Downtime facilitates a process that leads to renewed energy, and often a dimensional shift. For every down, there's an up.

For me, a major missing piece, and one I still struggle to get a handle on, is "character." Character has been the focus of my practice in the last five years, as it was the answer to the second of my questions to Sensei (one of the questions he answered without me having to ask). Understanding and experiencing the centralizing function of character, that we are always being some sort of a character, that we can clear and shift through characters as appropriate for ever-changing situations, is a natural process. Character is a natural part of being human. Just growing older is a character shift. Who I am today is not who I was at fifteen. But much more than this, character is a sort of functional unit that can quickly consolidate itself for better or for worse. We sometimes need to be reminded how to kick-start the process of shifting characters, to change into a more appropriate character for the situation. When I'm going to teach a class, I take a minute to feel the ground, my body-self. I breathe, and clear, being present. The character I am as "teacher" will come to the fore, ready to teach, naturally. It takes some practice, but this is possible for anything and everybody.

This leads me to a final point, which is that anything and

everything can be an opportunity to process, to "pump the pump" as Sensei might say. Sitting down and standing up. Raising and lowering our arm. Walking three steps forward and three steps back. Breathing in and breathing out. All are simple natural activities, and with a slight focus-shift inward, the pump begins to pump and energy flows. These days, hiking up hills, jogging along the river, lifting a few weights, speaking together with my partner, riding a motorcycle, cooking a meal, and teaching an English class are all possibilities to be more present, more grounded, more myself—which, paradoxically, means a fluidity of characters with a certain mixture of qualities for the situation at hand.

These processes are natural and ongoing all the time. Nadeau Sensei brings us back to them in his unique way, for us to each find our own unique way. And there's always more. That's the beauty of Nadeau's process work—it's never-ending.

# Center

Sensei teaches practices like being Present, Open and Settle, Allowing, Easy the I, and Standing can help cultivate a better balance between awareness and experience. And this, in turn, can lead students to an enhanced sense of their Center.

He explains that Center is often described as one internal point below the navel. However, it can also be experienced as an energy flow running vertically through the body's core, like a pillar or a conduit that extends above and below physical boundaries, as shown in diagram 4. The right and left spirals represent natural energies constantly flowing upward and downward around our center.

Exploration of the Center can start by relaxing the mind and experiencing the body. For example, take a broad stable stance and allow the body to better align with its natural center of gravity while settling into the *hara* (lower abdomen source of *ki*/heart/mind.) Aligning with gravity provides an essential foundation for cultivating and refining our sense of spiritual alignment with the Universe. Sensei encourages utilizing Centering as an energy practice, not just a physical exercise.

## Energy

As we Open and Settle into our Experience, we may begin to feel and sense finer Energy. Sensei invites us to Experience the subtler dimensions

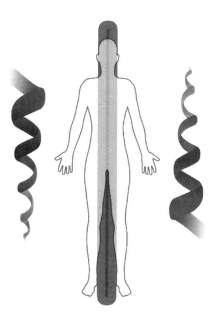

Diagram 4. Standing Center with Up/Down Energies.

of Energy and play with them, staying Centered and grounded. He teaches that our internal Energy system is an essential source of our innate natural intelligence. He encourages students to trust the system's self-organizing capabilities and inherent harmony with the underlying principles of the Universe.

To describe this Energy, Nadeau Sensei prefers American vernacular like "vitality," "juice," and "aliveness," instead of the Japanese word *ki*, as in Aikido, the Chinese word *qi*, or the Sanskrit word *prana*, used in yoga. He does this to avoid giving the impression to his primarily Western students that the intrinsic life energy is so esoteric as to be inaccessible to regular folks or only understandable in a foreign language. He likes to say that whatever words we choose to name the energetic life force of the Universe, it is there for us to experience, expressed in both the manifest dimension of our visible reality and in the more hidden dimensions of unseen forces that invisibly support and motivate our physical actions.

The new Energy we encounter through Centering may initially feel unfamiliar. For example, when facing a challenging situation, our physical posture might be pushed "up and forward." On the other hand, by opening and settling "down and back," we can reconnect with the ground and better align with the new energy flows we are experiencing. The new Energy may initially feel uncomfortable, or it may feel pleasant. Either way, he teaches that the Energy we sense is always there to support us.

Once, one of Nadeau Sensei's students was working with a difficult client in a customer service situation. The customer was highly resistant to the suggested solution to the issue. Rather than making further attempts to convince her, the student shifted his focus to his own Center and allowed a moment of quiet. As his Experience of Center continued to deepen, the atmosphere began to relax and clear. In the clearer space that emerged, the customer, on her own, began to talk about her real problem. As she continued to talk, she allowed that the suggested solution was actually a pretty good one. Rather than trying to further her acceptance, the student continued to focus on the Experience of Center and the customer accepted the solution without further prompting. Afterward, another employee said they had never seen anyone deal with such an irate customer in such an effective manner and asked, "How did you do it?"

## ⊡ *Coming Home to Universal Energy* ⊡

WENDY PALMER
Aikido 7th Dan
Co-Founder, Aikido of Tamalpais
Founder of Leadership Embodiment
Author and Speaker

The first time I saw Nadeau Sensei was at the Unitarian Church in San Francisco. I felt a deep sense of coming home as I experienced Nadeau Sensei executing the movements of Aikido. Grace, beauty, and power flowed around the room as he threw students. Later, at the Turk Street dojo, I was inspired by his continuous references to universal energy—which he usually referred to as "IT." He was talking about tapping into the universal flow, and he said, "IT is always Deeper, Wider, and Finer." That has stayed with me and continues to be part of my life's inquiry and spiritual journey. I am deeply grateful for what I learned from Nadeau Sensei.

#  *Essence of the Art of Aikido*

RICHARD MOON
Aikido 6th Dan
Dojo-cho, Aikido of Marin
City Aikido of San Francisco
Musician, Composer, Cosmic Explorer

In late 1971 I began training in the art of Aikido with Robert Nadeau. Some students follow Japanese tradition and call him Sensei, meaning teacher, or Shihan, meaning professor. He said we are Americans, so we called him Bob.

Bob was a personal student of Morihei Ueshiba Osensei, the Founder of Aikido, who famously said, "True *budo* (way of the warrior) is the loving protection of all beings with a spirit of reconciliation." His *budo*, Aikido, embodied a transformative relationship to *ki*, the rush of universal energy.

Since I first started studying Aikido with him, Bob has taught the essence of the art this way:

"When you are faced with a situation, the energy system responds to handle the situation."

Our life force, the positive or creative energy of our lives, responds to the need or demands of a situation. Harmonizing (*ai*) with this energy (*ki*) is the fundamental principle, the "way" (*do*) of Aikido.

Osensei said, "I feel what you feel, that you call fear, but I call it a summons to action." Bob translated that into, "Fear is the harbinger of power."

Bob taught that how we respond to the energy of any situation can transform how we experience ourselves. There's you being affected by changing energy. This can be thought of as adrenaline or an electrochemical hormonal reaction. I like to talk about it differently, as a "rush of energy." Any stimulation caused by this rush of energy activates our response. The reactions that follow are an aftereffect. Normally, or habitually, our identity will allow only a controlled amount of energy into our systems, so we can "handle it," or so we are comfortable.

Bob described "opening and settling" as the basic practice that allows harmonizing with an increasing flow of energy. Working with the energy in that way increases our capability, our power to function in harmony with the energy's original intention. Bob describes this as a shift in identity or shift of dimensions. It can change our character.

When we open to it, this energy can be empowering. It can enhance our capability, sometimes with an exhilarating rush, like a "runner's high." We sometimes label this positive rush of energy as exciting, fun, thrilling, alive.

However, when we resist the energies, our reactions (reactivity) can show up as fear or aggression. It can even make us freeze, like a "deer in headlights." Often, we try to resist or stop the flow of negative energy through our system and label it as anxiety, tension, stress, fear, anger, depression, etc.

Whether the energy is labeled positive or negative, we often attribute our emotional reactions to the stimulus of the energy rush (the situation), rather than recognizing that it is the energy itself that is primary, and our reactivity is a secondary aftereffect of the energy. Recognizing this distinction and adapting to it effectively is a learned skill. Allowing the energy to flow through us, without labeling it "good" or "bad," engenders a dimensional shift. This essential insight characterizes Bob's transmission of Osensei's art.

Bob often uses numbers to describe and practice dimensional shifting. For example, we can practice moving from a 1x1 to a 2x2, with increasing numbers representing a better space (size), sense of self, level, or dimension. The concept continues through additional dimensional shifts: 3x3, 4x4, and so on. The numbers used are somewhat arbitrary. They represent a process of step-by-step "squaring away" that can help us get to know who we are at a better level. If we are resistant, or fail to step up to change in the face of more energy, there can be a sense of increasing pressure on us. A 1x1 person cannot comfortably handle the energy of a 2x2 situation. Conversely, a 3x3 person is not upset by the energies of a 2x2 crisis.

Bob has said many times that Osensei wanted people to experience the empowerment of energy as a creative force, and that Osensei's teachings were intended to enable everyone to harmonize with the energies around us in life, enhancing our abilities in whatever we do, not just martial arts.

Bob has always focused on the "inner practice" of Aikido. He has repeatedly explained, demonstrated, and taught us how we can each begin to make that shift of identity through the art of Aikido by practicing centering, grounding, flowing, and blending. By doing so over many decades, touching so many students in the process, I believe Bob has served his "bestowed mission" as one of the most important channels in the world for the direct transmission of the essence of the art of Aikido from Osensei to the next generation.

##  His Many Visits

HENRY LYNCH
Aikido 6th Dan
Chief Instructor, Riai Aikido
Riai Aikido Learning Centre, Auckland, New Zealand
Founder and Director, Faraday

I first met Bob Nadeau Shihan when he and Richard Moon Sensei traveled to New Zealand in the 1980s to teach at an early one of the Riai Aikido's National Friendship Festivals we host throughout New Zealand every year. That particular Festival was in Rotorua, on the North Island.

To this day, I can clearly remember one of the sessions Nadeau Sensei led, in which he spoke about going from one stage to another by utilizing energy flow. He illustrated this by moving from the white mat to the blue mats placed around the edge of the practice space, demonstrating how different platforms, and different approaches to utilizing energy and flow, can influence our Aikido and our lives.

The benefits that Nadeau Sensei has given to the Aikido community in New Zealand cannot be underestimated. First, by his gracious attendance over many years. We are a long way from California, and he has visited more than ten times. Also, by his explanations of the application of the art in daily life. And finally, by his vivid description of Osensei's teachings. Nadeau Sensei has also contributed to the development of Aikido in New Zealand through his students who have accompanied him on his visits over the years, thus adding another fantastic dimension to the whole experience.

##  *Meeting the Challenges of Daily Life*

SASUN TORIKIAN
Aikido 5th Dan
Aikido of Petaluma

I remember my first time training with Nadeau at a seminar in San Francisco. It was not an Aikido seminar but an energy seminar, which is part of why I started training in Aikido to begin with. I was not so much interested in learning self-defense as in learning more about myself.

I have come to have a deep appreciation for Nadeau Sensei's goal—his life's work—of remembering, understanding, and embodying Osensei's teachings rather than just teaching a martial art.

The greatest personal challenge I have had to meet was my wife's serious illness. This situation lasted for six years, and she is better now. Meeting the challenge of being her care and support is something I could not have done without my training. My daily practice of opening up to the challenges and allowing the energies was essential to being there for her and supporting me. During the times she was hospitalized, I practiced the lessons I learned on the mat while walking to and from her room during my daily visits.

Thank you for the teachings, Nadeau Sensei!

##  *Blending Together*

ELLEN STAPENHORST
Aikido 1st Dan
Songwriter, Musician, Speaker, Performer
AikiWorks Workshop Facilitator

I first met Robert Nadeau Sensei in 1983 when Bob Noha Sensei took me to San Francisco for a class. From the first time I saw him step on the mat, I was struck by how his energy seemed to coil from his feet through and around his body to his hands and arms and on upward and outward. His words were intriguing and usually made sense to me, and what didn't make sense showed up in other ways. I felt like I was in the presence of a controlled, wild, brilliant animal—a little scary and like a magnet, attracting and repelling.

I got to train with him many times over the years. Aikido was the main vehicle, but it was the extracurricular "arm-flapping" sessions that really sank in and changed me. We spent time experiencing and attempting to describe different energies around us and running through us (not easily verbalized), and then equalizing with them.

This has been part of me ever since. It is marvelously helpful to me in many ways, especially as a musician and performer. . . . I connect energetically with the audience and the situation before stepping onto the stage. It's there in daily life in any situation, especially challenging ones. I am grateful to both Nadeau and Noha for being able to deeply explore and experience different ways of showing up with energy.

In retrospect, I see that Nadeau was committed to continuing the exploration that led Osensei to Aikido, a way to reconcile the world.

It was a rich time in the Bay Area for Aikido, and I was lucky to be able to study with many excellent teachers. I'm glad that the atmosphere was open, not jealously guarding one way over another, but appreciating the different approaches that showed up. These approaches blended together, and Nadeau Sensei was a central hub. I began to see that there is much more to the world than I can understand, but I can still accept and even embrace. Although I haven't trained in the art of Aikido for many years, it is with me every day. It's a mystery to continue to delve into, a way to reconcile the world.

## ◢ *Win, Place, Show* ◣

### STEPHEN SAMUELS
### Aikido 3rd Dan
### Artist and Craftsman

When I first met Bob Nadeau, he was teaching a class in energy awareness at the Unitarian Church in San Francisco. It was not exactly a real Aikido class. There were no mats and no dress code. It was just people wearing street clothes in a big room. A sort of "come as you are" party.

At that time, I was still a long-haired, bearded "hippie" who had been through years of psychedelics, 24-7 weed therapy, yoga, meditation, living in remote nature, and so on.

I had experienced "energy" in many ways, including Kundalini and out-of-body adventures. I was definitely part of what was by then an emerging and growing movement of long-haired spiritual explorers.

Bob was a super straight-looking, ex-Marine, ex-cop with well-groomed, slicked-back hair. He certainly looked like he was one of the "other guys" who couldn't possibly know about the mystical experiences that people of my world had stumbled into.

What was I going to learn from this guy?

Bob started working with us with various "sensing" energy practices such as extending a flow of energy longer than one's arm, settling into the body, centering, etc. I didn't know what this stuff was, but it did seem to be a continuation of some of the yoga I already knew about, and I was intrigued. Eventually, these first classes evolved. Portable mats were brought in, people started wearing *gi* (practice uniforms), and it became sort of an Aikido class. We learned to roll, to blend with a partner, etc., but all the while, the emphasis was on "you with you" and energy. I still had no idea what this stuff really was, but it was clear to me that something important was going on because I always felt better after each class, and that condition lingered and grew.

After many months of these classes, I moved to Kauai in the Hawaiian Islands. I knew there were Aikido classes there also and thought, "How great that one could find this stuff all over the world." Little did I know!

I did go to a dojo on Kauai run by teachers of the Koichi Tohei lineage of Aikido, but after a couple of months I dropped out.

Something was wrong.

When I had trained with Bob, I always left feeling more enlivened and feeling better than when I came. When I left the

Kauai dojo, I felt worse. Clearly worse. It took a while for me to really understand why, but it was a question that pestered me.

Once day I had a conversation with myself about this. It dawned on me that whatever it was that Bob was teaching was something I wanted to learn regardless of the reason. It was not going to happen in Kauai, and I could not rely on him being available forever and if I really wanted it, I'd better do it now.

By the time I got back to San Francisco, Bob's classes had moved from the church to a new, full-fledged Aikido dojo on Turk Street. Real mats, a formal *shomen* (ceremonial front of dojo), people wore *gi* (practice uniforms), and classes were conducted in a more formal Aikido manner.

There were also monthly dues required, which I did not have since I was essentially broke and homeless; however, this got resolved by me becoming the janitor for the dojo. I would arrive early in the morning, vacuum the mats, clean the restrooms, changing rooms, office, and stairs, and be ready for the start of noon class. After that, I would hang out with and be available for whatever Bob wanted to do, which was usually eat lunch and sometimes be driven places. I became his driver, so I got to tag along on whatever the adventure of the day might bring.

After those excursions, we'd get back to the dojo to start the beginner and evening classes. Kind of long days, but for me, great times!

During some of the after-class coffee shop times, I often heard him say something strange: "I'm not really an Aikido teacher. I'm really a meditation teacher."

Strange to me because he certainly looked like an Aikido teacher! I also knew he had a small, ongoing meditation group at his home; however, at this time, I had no idea what they were doing there.

This went on for a few years, and somewhere during that era, Bob had become rather famous on the newly evolving Human Potential circuit, teaching at places such as the Esalen Institute and the like. He was suddenly earning much more.

He began sporting a gold neck chain, had paid off his home mortgage, and had extra cash to play with.

Our afternoon travels took a new twist somewhere within this section of time. Instead of going right to lunch, he would direct my driving to one of the local horse-racing tracks. I'd stay in the car, and he would dash in, and after a while, come back to the car, and then, maybe, we'd still have time for lunch.

Upon returning to the car, his mood would vary, but mostly I could tell he was not pleased. For most of this time, I had no idea about the what or why of whatever was going on. But eventually, he began to explain what it was.

The meditation group had been picking horses for the daily 2:00 p.m. races.

They would choose three horses for win, place, and show. If you pick all three correctly, it's a big winner. And they were picking close, but something was wrong. They might get the three horse names correctly, but the win, place, and show order of them would be wrong. Or they might get only some of the names, etc. So back to the group and try again—but sadly, with similar results. Overall, there were losses rather than the expected big wins. I have no idea how bad the losses eventually became, but I did notice some of the gold jewelry vanished along the way.

Bob had a total belief in the meditation group and the information they were getting but couldn't deny something was amiss. He speculated that since what the group was "seeing" was the future, that that future was subject to change with even a small variable added.

One such variable could be the very act of him placing a bet on the race. They kept trying, but it never really did work out well, as far as I know.

While this all seemed a little odd to me at the time, I did learn a few things from Bob because of it. One of those was if you think you have a good idea, then you have to really put your butt on the line and be willing to risk whatever it takes to try it out. Another aspect of that is much like what Osensei says about training as if it is a life-and-death situation. If you hold something back, you'll never really know: win, lose, or draw. The only way is to go for it and learn, regardless of what anyone else might think.

Now, of course, over many years with Bob, I've learned his energy practices and his teachings about what Aikido can be. For that, I will be eternally appreciative and grateful.

I've never encountered another sensei who even comes close. And still, there are these little extra experiences I would never have had except for him. Thank you, Bob!

## Situation and Character

Nadeau Sensei uses the term Situation to describe the energies arising in our present circumstances. For example, in Aikido, a partner's attack represents a Situation. The attack has distinctive dynamics that activate additional Energies in the person responding to the attack. As the attacker and responder engage, they are both present in a space that itself has energy. In Aikido, we train to resolve conflicts harmoniously by cultivating our sensitivity to the Energies of a Situation so that we can intuitively gauge timing and distance to resolve the attack peacefully.

The same principles apply to the challenges of personal character development. In Sensei's lexicon, our Character is forged through our individual experience of the energies that arise in the situations we face in life. Character is responsive to the specific Energies that make up a particular Situation, regardless of whether the Situation is one we intentionally seek or one in which we find ourselves due to external circumstances beyond our control.

Nadeau Sensei says that every Situation we encounter in life—not just doing Aikido on the mat—presents us with the creative Energies to mix up an effectively functioning Character for that particular Situation if we can allow ourselves to Experience the Energy of the moment fully. The better the mixing and Remixing of Character Energy with Situation Energy, the finer and more functional the expression of Character becomes. When Character and Situation harmonize, there is a blending together, a sense of oneness that naturally emerges.

As such, one of the primary goals of Aikido, according to Nadeau Sensei, is to train ourselves to become capable of fully expressing the personal qualities of our Character appropriately for different Situations, combined with the ability to quickly let go of one Character for another as circumstances change.

## The Gift

DANNY MCINTYRE
Aikido 5th Dan
Dojo-cho, Riai Learning Centre, Auckland, New Zealand
Director, Interior Construction Company

Five or six years ago, Bob visited New Zealand and stayed at our home. All seminars were over, and we (Bob, Richard Moon, me, and a few others) were in the local village having coffee late one evening.

Bob got up from his seat and gestured to me to follow. "You better see this," said Bob, as he stumbled toward the florist shop ahead of me. Sensei walked through the shop, seemingly hunting for something, and finally took hold of an orchid. "How much?" The lady florist told him the price, and Bob went into a charade of how old he is, protesting she was trying to break his bank and his back. I was somewhat shocked. However, the florist kept her composure and told him he would surely love the orchid, and that she too had a back, and a bank. Nadeau just smiled, gave her the money, and waved happily to her as we left the store.

Bob handed the precious orchid to me and told me to protect it on the drive home, to make sure to hand it back in perfect order so he could pass his gift on. Arriving home, he gave the orchid to my wife, Jenny.

Describing Nadeau's teachings with one-liners (open and settle, etc.) doesn't quite do it for me. So, my wife Jenny suggested I try expressing my sense of things with this haiku, as a gift in return.

> easy, I, easy
> open, allow, recognize
> settle, underground
> center to circle
> feel, partake, feel, sense, feel
> circle to center
> two forces merge
> to each other, surrender
> character forms

## Feldenkrais and the Zone of Resonance

JEFFREY S. HALLER, Ph.D.
Aikido 2nd Dan
Feldenkrais Method Trainer & Practitioner
Functional Movement Consultant

There is not a day that goes by that I don't use something I learned from Nadeau Sensei in my professional practice as a Feldenkrais Practitioner. While I have not been on the Aikido mat for years, I practice Aikido daily with my clients. To me, Aikido and the Feldenkrais Method® are essentially the same. They both hold that a person has infinite potential for refinement and expression beyond the image established for them in their conditioned experience.

In Aikido the enactment of self-expression is found within Aikido practice as passed down in the legacy of Osensei. In my Feldenkrais practice, I am primarily working with people who have suffered some significant injury or loss of functionality that impacts their physical integrity and/or their emotional dignity in ways that would interfere with their ability to be comfortable on the mat. I have to establish an environment, a relationship where the questions I ask of my clients with my hands are answered from within my clients themselves. Therefore, I practice Aikido with them on a microlevel by interacting to find the most productive self-organization and internal support they need to recover their capacity to meet everyday life.

It is a principle of both Aikido and the Feldenkrais Method® to be able to meet each moment with unlimited creativity. An Aikidoist in the Nadeau tradition is trained to spontaneously meet any emerging situation in the never-ending now moment. The secret is to sustain this capacity to meet life's challenges. The consciousness we tap into will emerge, and we will play in the zone of resonance.

Thank you, Bob, for all you gifted me.

# Frame and Flow

Sensei uses the terms Frame and Flow to describe the relationship between structure and Energy. In Aikido, Frame is the arrangement of the body posture, in stillness and motion, while Flow is the movement of energies (*ki*) through that frame. He teaches that all Aikido techniques naturally have both Frame and Flow.

He urges students to feel the energy flowing between themselves and their training partners and to adapt their physical structure (stance, alignment, position, movement) as needed to experience Flow fully. Through sustained practice over time, we can all learn to cultivate the proper structural alignment of our body so that physical Form does not interfere with energetic Flow. The relationship between Frame and Flow in Aikido is dynamic and alive in the moment. Movement, breath, and energy are the Flow that passes through the Frame. When allowed to develop without too much thinking about how or why, Frame and Flow will naturally align with each other, synchronizing and integrating to operate harmoniously.

More generally, Nadeau Sensei teaches that the principle of Frame and Flow offers an approach to dealing with many situations outside the dojo whenever we feel overwhelmed or under pressure. Frame and Flow can improve our capacity to experience more profound levels of finer Energy no matter what we are doing.

For example, athletes talk about being "in the zone" when they intuitively know what to do in response to the dynamics of a situation. The way their Frame harmonizes with the Flow in these moments can reveal the beauty of human excellence.

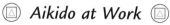

## Aikido at Work

### OLIVE
#### City Aikido of San Francisco

My work required representing my department during hearings at city hall. The public could file formal complaints if they believed the department was withholding public documents. As custodian of records, I would appear before the commission to ensure government transparency through open records.

These hearings could be intense. The setting was formal: eight commissioners sat elevated on a dais in a semicircle. It looked like a courtroom, except there were eight "judges" peering down at a lone department representative.

Whenever my agenda item was called, I would approach the table in front of the commissioners. The complainant was always to my left. Members of the audience, sometimes numbering in the hundreds, sat behind. Being questioned in this setting, surrounded by the imposing commissioners, the aggrieved complainant, and the skeptical public could be overwhelming.

But I found that my training in Aikido with Nadeau Sensei prepared me for just this kind of challenge. One of his key lessons was "under pressure, let things flow." I would imagine the commissioners' pointed questions, the complainant's anger, and the public's curiosity and doubt all becoming one flow entering through my head and then out through my feet. I didn't let all this energy get stuck in me; instead, the circulating energy grounded me and gave me more energy and confidence. I don't recall ever using this lesson before I held this position at work, but I required something extra to get me through these hearings. Nadeau Sensei's "under pressure, let things flow" was just the insight I needed.

## ⧌ *Presence and Self-Development* ⧌

### LAURENCE BIANCHINI
#### Aikido 3rd Dan
#### City Aikido of San Francisco, Aikido of San Leandro

When I think about my experience taking Nadeau Sensei's classes and asking questions to understand what Osensei taught him and what he teaches, I mostly remember stories and quotes. Some are mysterious and intriguing, some illuminating, and some extremely confusing.

"I taught you everything I can. I did my best. Now you have to listen to your system. The system will teach you."

This is the daunting task Nadeau Sensei is leaving his students with. He also would say:

"I am teaching you a process. So, I expect you to be good at everything you do."

I have thought a lot about these words, as well as many other phrases Nadeau Sensei has uttered to the class, or to me directly, and I have to admit that they sometimes scare me. The scariest one is:

"Imagine Osensei appears to you for ten seconds, to show you one technique. Would you be ready? Would you be present? Would you catch it?"

Unfortunately, my reaction is still, "No, I wouldn't!"

Nadeau Sensei's gift to his students is the trust that we can all become great. But the path he pushes us on is very hard. Nadeau Sensei not only teaches techniques, but also basic moves and principles (flow, ground). He tries multiple tricks to put us on a path of self-development, self-exploration, which he calls a "process." And because he is trying to teach us this process based on his own experience, he tells us stories to get us to exercise our imaginations.

I remember how puzzled I was during the first Nadeau class I attended. I had been encouraged to go to the class by Joe Shelley Sensei, who was teaching at Fudoshin Dojo in San Francisco. I was left with two contradictory feelings: one that rejected this approach, and another that was full of curiosity and a feeling that there might also be something very deeply buried in these esoteric words that resonated with me. I especially liked Nadeau's use of imagination to expand the efficiency of the technique and our body's performance, an approach that reminded me of a trick I had as a kid that would make me run really fast.

Nadeau Sensei would frequently stop the class after repeating a movement multiple times and ask: "What does it feel and look like?"

He expected students to come up with some visualization that represented the driving force and the power behind a technique. Is it a tree, is it a pole, a pillar? He would ask: "What color is it? What material? Is it wood, concrete, metal?"

We practiced an exercise where you squat and your partner pushes on your shoulders to keep you closer to the ground. You needed to push up using the image of a hydraulic press rising through deep-water pressure. Nothing can stop a hydraulic press, so nothing should stop you.

Sensei didn't teach much about the physical dimension. But he talked a lot about different levels of perception and the need to elevate oneself, the way you'd do it through therapy or meditation, to access new potential, which he called "levels." Honestly, I struggled with many of these images and concepts— like the land of the roots, where the energies lie in the ground, and you can tap into them. I had never experienced someone teach Aikido that way.

So, I thought there was something for me there, and I stuck around, attending most classes for three or four years. I made no progress for a couple of years, feeling as dumb and confused as I was in the beginning, until it started clicking. I am not necessarily one to seek approval from others, but when I saw approval in Nadeau Sensei's eye, not just once but repeatedly, I felt like I had climbed Mount Everest on my knees.

I consider myself very privileged to have attended Nadeau Sensei's classes. I'm only sad I don't have another ten or twenty years to grasp the depth of his teachings. I cling onto the sentences that he repeats over and over again.

Because it's all about being present, developing self-awareness, and tricking your mind and body into functioning better, Nadeau Sensei's teaching goes beyond what we practice in a dojo. Flow, for example, is a huge thing that took me years to grasp. We all know how to use flow to drive cars on the highway, bike, swim, and ski. He asked us to think of the wind, and suddenly I could visualize it. I could feel when it was there and when it wasn't, which was a huge "Aha" moment.

Sensei mentioned that when he was in Japan, he would practice balance and flow in the subway. So I did the same, on BART, riding from San Francisco to the East Bay, trying to feel that invisible energy created by the train's motion, in the turns to the right or the left, in the accelerations and decelerations. For example, I'd ask: What's pushing my upper body forward when I sit back and the train starts? It was fascinating and fun!

Osensei's teachings are still very obscure to me, although I am grateful to have approached them and gotten closer via Nadeau Sensei. It is confusing to understand so little after so many years, but it is also the beauty of Osensei's Aikido: an infinite exploration of the self and the art.

I have had great times with Nadeau Sensei! I enjoyed going for drinks after class, interacting with fellow students and *sempai* (senior students) to try to make sense of it all. I also liked going to the woods in Occidental for the annual Osensei Revisited workshops, especially the Sunday morning coffees with everyone all together.

Nadeau Sensei has dedicated his life to training in the art. His deepest desire is to teach the process and help every student grow. As adults we are not always so good at understanding deep teachings. So, Nadeau Sensei tells us stories: the woman who would unbutton her shirt every night without noticing, breeding dogs, etc. Extreme patience, consistency, repetition, using the same exact words or completely different words until something clicks inside and there's a little "Aha" moment. So much effort and intent to bring a student to that exact moment of revelation, for which I am so grateful.

# The Two Beats of Creation

Practicing Aikido or doing any of these internal processes, we may begin to feel the energetic dynamics of up/down, in/out, or expansion/contraction patterns. These patterns are expressions of what Nadeau Sensei calls the Two Beats of Creation, fundamental forces in the Universe that consistently present themselves as pairs of complementary opposites that naturally balance and activate each other. There are many ways to represent them in different cultures, including the well-known Yin/Yang symbol shown in diagram 5.

Osensei variously referred to the Two Beats of Creation as the workings of the Shinto deities Izanagi (male-who-invites) and Izanami (female-who-invites), or the interactions of fire and water, or heaven and earth.

Nadeau Sensei uses Osensei's terminology, as well as his own vocabulary for the Two Beats in different teaching situations: Yin/Yang, male/female, positive/negative, assertive/receptive, up/down, in/out. He teaches that whatever we wish to name them, the two beats operate universally. These opposite-but-complementary forces are always alive within us. Acknowledging this truth can help us realize the underlying unity of the Universe.

For example, a person might be unbalanced by an unexpected or threatening situation that leaves them feeling distraught or out of sorts. On the other hand, when the Two Beats come into balance the same person might feel like something inside "just clicks" and they can rise to the occasion with additional creative energy.

Diagram 5. Two Beats of Creation.

# Remixing

Nadeau Sensei puts the principles of the Two Beats of Creation into practice in a process he calls Remixing, by which he means mixing-up a better Character with finer Energies.

As in many other practices, he starts with a broad stance, opens his arms, bends his knees, and settles into his body. Then he asks students to imagine their right hand holds their Yin energies while their left hand holds their Yang energies. He asks them to feel both hands, both energies fully. Then to sweep their hands in a large circle and bring them together in front of their waists with a clap. This is an opportunity for Yin and Yang to unify, to give birth to a new and improved "you," to Remix a Character capable of more fully expressing your innate human potential.

Remixing like this is a kind of instantaneous internal alchemy that Osensei taught as an essential part of Aikido. The choice of Energies to Remix, the words used to represent the forces of the Two Beats of Creation, can vary from moment to moment and person to person. But the principles are always the same. Balancing the complementary polarities of our nature is a way to refine and improve ourselves, in practice and not just in theory.

Nadeau Sensei teaches that the benefits of Remixing are not limited to Aikido. And the form of the practice is quite flexible. It can be done with or without clapping, standing in a different posture, or even sitting, as long as there is a process that unifies your own personal Two Beats of Creation.

Nadeau remixing during an Energy Awareness Workshop.

#  *Alchemy*

### JADE DARDINE
Aikido 1st Dan
Kuma Kai Aikido
**Physician (Hospitalist and Hospice Director)**

I first met Nadeau on his sixty-third birthday in the year 2000. I was twenty years old. I had begun my Aikido practice as a child but, after a long hiatus, had recently returned to Aikido and somehow found myself invited to a private party in his honor in an apartment in San Francisco. Eventually, I found myself face to face with Nadeau, who began to talk to me about alchemy. "Do you know what that means?" he asked me. I was as confused about this question as any twenty-year-old whose familiarity with the word came from reading *The Alchemist* as a teenager. For me, there was only one sensible response at that moment. I nodded my head furiously, suspecting that I was about to receive an important teaching. Seduced by Nadeau's invitation to join him outside on the fire escape, we surreptitiously ducked out into the night's darkness, the glow of his cigarette brightening and then dimming repeatedly as he waxed on about feminine and masculine, Izanami and Izanagi, yin and yang . . . blending together to become something new. As I listened, I felt I was experiencing this exact paradigm, at that moment.

This experience was a defining event in my life and continues to drive my curiosity about life and being.

Experiences like this are intimate gifts. In my case, they affected how I approached serving as Nadeau Sensei's Aikido *uke* (attacking/receiving partner). Entering his energy field as *uke* typically results in being spun, flipped, twisted, and pounded. All the while going through complete discombobulation combined with complete presence in time and space. And landing softly in the exact position necessary to meet the mat in such a way it feels like landing on a cloud. Being Nadeau Sensei's *uke* is not like anything else I have ever experienced.

Nadeau's resources for communicating seem to be infinite. But by far, my favorite is when he holds my hand in his and I can feel waves pulsing through his palms that seem like pure love, a knowingness that seems celestial.

Today, in my interactions with patients, my family, and my world, I strive to always consider the objective data in front of me and to allow the less obvious, invisible wisdom to inform my perception. When called upon to be a bigger version of myself, I can.

I will be forever grateful for the time I have been able to spend with Nadeau. My relationship with him has been life altering. He has helped me taste a small bit of the vastness of existence, the interconnectedness of the Universe, and the power that this connection contains.

## ◬ *The Rippling Effects of Lessons Learned* ◬

SONJA SUTHERLAND
Aikido 1st Dan
City Aikido of San Francisco
Feldenkrais Practitioner, Feldenkrais Assistant Trainer

I began training Aikido over twenty-five years ago while doing a four-year training in the Feldenkrais Method. Many Feldenkrais teachers train Aikido, so I, too, wanted to experience how Aikido might inform my own Feldenkrais practice. I started training Aikido at a dojo near where I lived, and after I had taken my first test, a fellow Feldenkrais *Aikidoka* (Aikido practitioner) invited me to an Aikido workshop. Robert Nadeau Sensei was teaching.

We all bowed in for training, and instead of starting right away with basic techniques, Nadeau Sensei talked about how Aikido isn't just about mastering martial techniques but about transforming ourselves as we engage with the world. I already began to sense how this approach resonated with my Feldenkrais practice.

Nadeau Sensei began deepening and widening his stance while making big, sweeping arm gestures around himself as he talked about how we can practice tapping into universal forces that flow all around us and within us. These are forces from the earth and from the heavens that we can access, channel, and mix to provide a foundation for how we train, who we are as we train, and how we live our lives on and off the mat.

Nadeau Sensei encouraged us to stand up, and we practiced with him as he gestured up and down his midline, opening his arms and whole self to the depths and height of heaven and earth. Then Nadeau Sensei called up an *uke* and demonstrated an Aikido technique that I had seen others do before, yet it had a very different feel to it.

As his *uke* came in forcefully, Nadeau Sensei moved swiftly and fully, shifting the dynamic space between them. Before his *uke* had even touched Nadeau Sensei, the *uke* was already falling, and in one fell swoop, without an inkling of resistance, he flew through the air and landed on the ground with a big grin on his face. Something amazing had just happened. Within the blink of an eye, all that conflicting, fighting energy that the *uke* had come in with was transformed.

I could feel in myself that I had found what I didn't know I was looking for. This was the kind of Aikido training that I wanted to develop. This was the kind of Aikido that would go hand in hand with my profession as a Feldenkrais practitioner helping people to resolve and dissolve their conflicting movement patterns, to coordinate their actions, and to move through their lives.

Nadeau Sensei then demonstrated a basic technique for us all to practice. As we bowed and began to train, another rookie *Aikidoka* and I paired up. Unfortunately, we got all tangled up in our efforts to "do" the technique. It wasn't working so well. Nadeau Sensei came over, watched us for a minute, and then said to me, "Here, grab my wrist." I latched onto his wrist with all my might. Unfazed, he looked at me and said calmly, "Look, I can connect with you in such a way that your elbow moves"— he moved, and my elbow turned out. "Or I can move in a way that affects your shoulder," he said, as my right shoulder went up to my right ear and raised me onto my toes. I was notably impressed that he already had my balance with such ease, and then he dropped me back down onto my feet. "Or," he continued, "I can tap into the river that runs beneath you, in which your past, your present, and your future flows, and move from there."

And suddenly, with no effort or ache, I was down on the ground with a huge grin on my face. I could barely contain my delight and awe. It was as if I had always wanted to fall down that way but didn't know how to fall so gracefully and effortlessly. Nadeau Sensei had scooped me up—all of me: who I was, where I was coming from, and where I was headed. And at that moment, I knew where I was headed in my life had just changed.

Instead of training at the dojo five minutes from where I lived, I decided to drive half an hour into San Francisco four to six times a week in order to train with Nadeau Sensei and his community of dedicated *Aikidoka*, and I did so for the next ten years.

I still remember the first time I ventured to San Francisco to train at Nadeau Sensei's dojo. Nadeau Sensei was teaching. As I experienced on that first day and many more times on subsequent days, he was sweeping his arms in big gestures while deepening and widening his stance as he talked about how training Aikido gives us the opportunity to practice dealing with forces and pressures all around us, and the opportunity to develop our ability to transform ourselves and how we meet the forces as we form our path forward.

As Nadeau continued his process and practice, he called up a seasoned *uke*. The *uke* came in powerfully, and with a huge swoosh he flew through the air effortlessly. Witnessing their interaction was like being close to a very powerful wave in the ocean—majestic, awe-inspiring, and commanding respect.

As I sat in *seiza* (formal seated posture on the floor) on the edge of the mat taking in this experience, Nadeau Sensei suddenly came over to me with his powerful presence and extended his hand as an invitation for me to stand up and *uke* for him. In front of everyone, I just sat there with a wide-eyed gaze and shook my head "no." It was my knee-jerk reaction. Without missing a beat, Nadeau continued on his way, teaching the class without any sign of insult or disappointment. But I was horrified. I felt embarrassed and angry at myself for being disrespectful toward Nadeau Sensei. After class, I went to apologize to him. However, before I could say anything, he looked at me and said, "You will get there. Give yourself time." I bowed and got off the mat with tears in my eyes. It was as if Nadeau Sensei had seen me coming his way, with my angry, judgmental attitude toward myself, and he shifted my inner narrative—he took the fight right out of my internal dialogue with myself. It was a small moment that had such a significant impact. It was then that I realized how training with Nadeau Sensei would be transformative for me on many levels in my life.

With Nadeau Sensei, I learned how to tame my inner critic and make room for possibilities yet unknown. I learned how to transform my fearful reactions and befriend powerful forces. And

I developed my ability to not shrink or deflate in the face of a challenge but rather to remain full and present under pressure. I have applied these abilities to many pressure-filled moments in my life, both on and off the Aikido mat. Not only to the pressures that other people and the world around me create, but also the pressures I put on myself.

In writing these words, I realize that I cannot possibly convey the profound effect Nadeau Sensei and his teachings have had on me. The powerful impact of Nadeau Sensei and his teachings come from years of practice with him that touch every aspect of my life. And how could this not be the case? The rippling effects are endless when you empower someone to transform who they are.

## Center and Circle

Nadeau Sensei presents the combination of Center and Circle (or, Center Circle) as another expression of complementary partners that mutually activate and balance each other in our human system. He teaches that experiencing the subtle resonances of Center and Circle can lead to better physical, emotional, and energetic integration on the path of mind/body harmony.

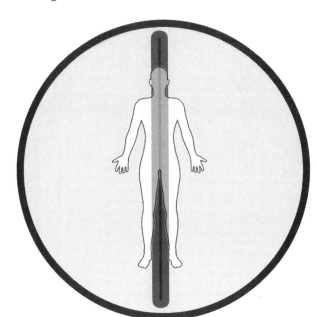

Diagram 6. Standing Center Circle.

To enhance our sense of Center and heighten our experience of Circle, Sensei offers a multistep process involving breath and chanting that he learned directly from Osensei as an Aikido training process, which can be practiced by anyone.

Standing with legs a little more than shoulder-width apart, knees slightly bent, open and settle to begin. Do several cycles of Centering practice with up/down energy flows while slowly raising and lowering both arms combined with deep breathing. Up/down and inhale/exhale are both primal expressions of the Two Beats of Creation. Let them synchronize naturally.

As illustrated in diagram 6, this process will gradually activate the Center, which might be felt as subtle changes in posture, alignment, attitude, or vitality. First, slowly open both arms wider and wider, letting the energy of the Center expand outward in every direction until it reaches its natural limit, creating a sense of a Circle around you. Then, gradually lower your arms and let the energy of the Circle flow inward until it is absorbed back into the Center. Repeat several cycles, allowing

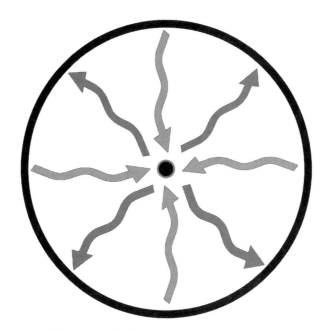

Diagram 7. Center Circle Energy Flows.

yourself to ride the natural rhythm of the process until you internally feel the balancing of energies.

Center and Circle practice activates Two Beats of creative energy, as illustrated in diagram 7. One beat naturally flows outward from one's center toward the circle, and the other beat naturally flows inward from the circle toward one's center, creating a beneficial cycle of reciprocal energy flows that naturally activate and reinforce each other.

Next, add your voice to the ongoing cycles of arm movements and breath. The first chant he teaches uses two syllables, "Ahhh" and "Ohhh." Let the sound "Ahhh" expand outward from your Center until it reverberates all around you and reaches its farthest limit. Inhale, then voice the sound "Ohhh" flowing inward toward your Center until it subsides of its own accord.

As the cycle continues, a sense of operational stability and a feeling of pulsing balance will gradually emerge, reverberating between "Ahhh" and "Ohhh," between the outward flows and inward flows, between a fuller Center and an increasingly revealed Circle.

The Circle/Center chanting of "Ahhh" and "Ohhh" can be followed by another sequence using different sounds: "Ma-mi-mu-me-mo" and "Ya-yi-yu-ye-yo."

This is still a Two-Beat process, but the multisyllabic chants can generate subtly different experiences. He tells students: "Play with it!" Allow the sounds to resonate through your body. Feel the harmonics as they vibrate within and without. Sense the effect on your Center. Experience the dimensionality of the Circle and its inherent connection to the Center.

Osensei taught that people are intrinsically oriented by their inner nature toward either Center or Circle as their preferred starting place. Therefore, the sound you start with or the syllable you chant is a matter of personal preference, as long as your Energy flows into and out from your Center. Students should start with what feels most natural to them, and stick with it consistently at first. Eventually, though, everyone should complement their initial preference by experiencing both Center and Circle.

By way of example, Nadeau Sensei describes himself as primarily a Center person who is naturally attracted to the power of up/down Energy flows and has had to work over the years on being more of a Circle person in terms of maintaining harmonious social relationships with the people around him. But he recognizes another person with more circular proclivities might not be as drawn to up/down exercises like bodybuilding with weights the way he was as a younger man. Instead, they might prefer walking in the woods where they feel energized and refreshed by the sense of space and aliveness all around them in the forest. But then they would find themselves needing to balance this with an improved capacity to stand up to pressure and get down to business when faced with deadlines, for example.

Ideally, a primarily Center person will develop the Circular qualities of their Character enough to find inner balance. Likewise, a primarily Circle person will develop the Center attributes of their Character sufficiently to find their inner balance.

When the up/down Energies of the Centered person are uni-
fied with the in/out Energies of the Circular person, one may feel a
"doubling-up" of Energies being added and amplified. This incremental increase in the experience of Energies flowing through us is to be
expected as a natural by-product of Circle/Center harmonization. But
doubling-up can sometimes feel overwhelming, pushing even experienced students out of their bodies and into their heads where they
think about the concept of surging Energies rather than experiencing
them directly. Nadeau Sensei urges people not to be afraid when such
doubling occurs. Instead, they should allow themselves to feel the qualities of the underlying Energies while continuing to Open and Settle
even more to stay deeply rooted. As always, he teaches the importance
of being Present while allowing things to unfold in their own time.

As an illustrative example of Center and Circle development,
Nadeau Sensei describes how Morihei Ueshiba worked initially on
strengthening his Center, beginning as a teenager who wanted to
become physically stronger doing sumo exercises on the beach of his
hometown of Tanabe, Japan. His experiences in the Japanese Imperial
Army during the Russo-Japanese war when he was in his twenties
developed him as a centered character, physically strong, depend-
able under pressure, and a natural leader. After the war, he went to
Hokkaido with a group from Tanabe to carve the new village of
Shirataki from the northern island's vast forests, where he faced many
new challenges that further strengthened his core. In Hokkaido,
Morihei Ueshiba met Sokaku Takeda, master of Daito-ryu Jiujitsu,
and further refined his Center through the rigorous practices of this
traditional fighting art.

Later, he met the charismatic Onisaburo Deguchi, the artistically
creative and extraordinarily gifted spiritual leader of Omoto-kyo, a new
Japanese religion rooted in Shinto. Onisaburo recognized Morihei's
strongly centered character but urged him to develop the more circular aspects of his nature to cultivate a finer balance within himself.
Onisaburo made such a strong impression that Morihei decided to live

and train within the Omoto-kyo compound in the small town of Ayabe (near Kyoto) from 1922 to 1925.

Decades later, Osensei confided to Nadeau that during his time in Ayabe, Onisaburo was constantly "on his case" to more fully feel, sense, and experience Circle, and it was only when he did so that his extraordinary capabilities as Osensei—Great Teacher of Aikido—truly emerged.

## △ *Importance of Trust* △

SUSAN SPENCE
Aikido 3rd Dan
**Aikido of Mountain View**
**Physical Therapist**

I started training in Aikido in 1984 with Robert Nadeau by a lucky coincidence. The pool where I swam laps every day happened to be across the street from his Mountain View dojo. I had trained for a couple months in judo two years previously and was interested in more martial art training but knew next to nothing about Aikido. So, I watched a Friday evening class. I was immediately enthralled with the energy aspects of Aikido and started training with Nadeau Sensei six or seven days a week. I quickly understood that he was teaching more than martial art techniques. He was teaching principles applicable to life.

Personal inner development is the foundation of Nadeau's style of teaching, and I left each class feeling changed, enlightened, and always enhanced. He was the first teacher in my life who validated energies that I felt but had no words to express. As a recent graduate in physical therapy, I was already well trained in the mechanical aspects of the body, but began to understand the body on an energy level. Training with Nadeau helped me physically ground and introduced me to the spiritual aspects of his work and his determined pursuit to understand the greater intelligence of creation.

I would occasionally travel to train Aikido at the San Francisco dojo, and on one of those nights Nadeau asked me to test for my blue belt. I had not trained for the test and barely knew the names of techniques. My *uke* had to whisper the name of an alternative technique after I got stuck repeating only one response to *tsuki* (straight thrusting punch). I would not have pushed myself to test at that point in time, but I trusted his request, passed the test, and in the process discovered that my training in Aikido had built within me a capacity for responding to pressure that I had never before experienced or thought possible. This ability to respond under pressure by opening to a better level of myself and accepting the available energies has helped me in countless difficult work and life situations.

In the many years I have known Nadeau, I have trained with him both on and off the mat. I have not always been the most consistent student, but I continue to explore and use the principles learned every day. Whenever I attend a class with Nadeau Sensei, I know he will challenge me to achieve a deeper level of presence and open up to more of who I can be.

I have seen Sensei teaching basic attacks many times, emphasizing that *uke*'s physical attack is visible, but the intent, and what came before the intent, is not so visible. This is a principle I use every day as a healer. As I settle to a better level and open to the bigger story behind the patient's presenting problem, the diagnosis and treatment become apparent. I have had colleagues and patients ask: "How did you know to ask that question?" I didn't "know." I used a process I have learned through training with Nadeau that helps me open to the "intelligence of the situation." Being more deeply centered in the situation to facilitate that wisdom is a process that I continue to refine as I keep working with Nadeau.

Perhaps the most important lesson that runs through most everything I have learned with Nadeau is to trust in his process. I enjoyed *ukemi* (the art of attacking/falling/rolling) and found it a tremendous privilege to *uke* for Nadeau. I learned to trust my process of aligning myself to the job of *ukemi*, of aligning to him as *nage* (throwing partner), and of aligning to the specific situation. I also learned that when I didn't align myself effectively, Nadeau was always quick to correct me.

The process of aligning as *uke* has helped me align and center better in my job as a healer. I am able to be more deeply present with my pediatric patients and their families. Over time I have come to trust my own alignment, and that has helped me successfully work with many complex patients. Nadeau gave me many tips along the way: center, center-circle, depth, roots, squared away, balance. I use all of these. I have learned to trust that the process of transformation always works. I trust that by settling to a deeper, bigger level of myself, I will function from a better place. I trust that the intelligence of the system will be available from this better place.

Although the COVID-19 pandemic limited training at the dojo, it created a unique opportunity for Nadeau to reach many students across the country and around the world through weekly Zoom classes. I was impressed with his ability to transition to a new teaching style and grateful for all I learned while unable to physically train on the mat. I continue to be challenged by Nadeau to be more, to go beyond the obvious, and always to go deeper. I would not be who I am without the support, guidance, and encouragement Nadeau Sensei has provided over many years.

## 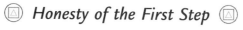 *Honesty of the First Step*

### STEVE FLEISHMAN
Retired Math Teacher
Songwriter
Adult Player/Manager, Los Angeles Baseball League

In June of 1972, in La Habra, California, I was part of a personal growth group meeting that used a vast array of eclectic exercises for consciousness-raising. This was an age of exploration and guru-shopping. Someone in the group knew about Robert Nadeau and invited him to do a workshop.

The first thing I couldn't help but notice was the contrast between Bob and the leader of the growth group, who had the appearance of a lean, cerebral Berkeley professor. Bob had an unmistakable presence, inhabiting his body fully, and speaking without formality or airy-fairy spirituality. I wanted more of this, though there was a period of testing: was he for real, did he have hidden motives? All my doubts have fallen away, and I have embraced the truth of Bob's work at an ever-deepening level.

Over the years, I have gone from an overly mental head tripper to a much more grounded person, living in my body much more than in my head. Before Bob, my condition was best described in a poem I wrote:

> *I'm thinking too much*
> *And sinking out of touch*
> *By shrinking into the clutches*
> *Of thinking as such*

Although I did give Aikido a try in Northern California and in Los Angeles, it was not a draw for me. Knowing that the physical activity that really speaks to me is baseball, Bob has consistently recognized that sport as a physical practice for me, easily translating energy work to suit a baseball player instead of a martial artist. It has helped me to play adult baseball into my mid-seventies.

I had been a food abuser (a compulsive overeater) for many years. In 1983, I hit rock bottom with my food binging and joined Overeaters Anonymous. The twelve-step program has been invaluable. But I know that without the work I'd done with Bob over the years, I would never have had such a miraculous recovery. Addictions always start in the mind, and what I have learned in processing has allowed me to transcend the compulsions of the conscious mind. The twelve steps of recovery have worked naturally with the things I have learned from Bob. This starts with the honesty of the first-step admission of our condition, which fits with the initial alignment to "what is" in Bob's process. Surrendering to a higher power in the twelve steps easily aligns with Bob's approach to moving from awareness to experience.

I am incredibly grateful for the teachings and friendship from Bob over the years. The confidence, sense of being, ability, and personal tools I developed with him have helped me handle whatever comes my way and have been invaluable in my journey.

## Dimensionality

Practicing Aikido and transformational work with Nadeau Sensei helps us become more present, whole, and balanced. We learn to trust our system's innate wisdom and naturally *become* more centered and grounded. We begin to experience previously unfamiliar forces. We are introduced to the multiple levels of consciousness and energy in the Universe and, therefore, within each of us. This is what he calls Dimensionality.

He uses Osensei's terminology, represented in diagram 8, showing three concentric circles as dimensions or layers of energy. The Manifest Dimension comprises generally observable physical matter and energies. These are the concrete manifestations of reality. The Hidden Dimension contains subtler energies that are less obvious and tangible, but that powerfully motivate and support our actions in the Manifest Dimension. Finally, what is called the Divine Dimension contains the finest energetic expressions of universal principles and archetypes of the primordial Original Source of Creation.

Diagram 8. Dimensionality: Manifest, Hidden, and Divine.

Nadeau Sensei teaches that these energetic dimensions coexist in the same space-time continuum, and that permeable energetic membranes are all that separate the dimensions. Each dimension has multiple gradients. Through intentional investigation and practice, subtler energies become more accessible. With proper training, anyone can pass through these membranes to experience aspects of ever-finer dimensions.

## ◻ *Master of the Hidden Realm* ◻

### DAVE GOLDBERG
Aikido 6th Dan
Founder and Director, Aikido of San Diego
Embodiment Teacher & Improv Artist

Immense gratitude with a dash of reverence pretty much sums up my feelings for Robert Nadeau. I consider him a living treasure for the art of Aikido and a mentor who's shown me nothing but generosity with his time and energy.

Before aligning with Nadeau Sensei, I trained under several of Osensei's disciples while living in Japan. Much of my time there was dedicated to discovering the Founder's Aikido—the "Aikido that isn't seen by the human eye." I still think it's funny, or at least ironic, that I needed to return to California to get closer to it. Of course, I didn't realize that when I left Japan in 1993, but that's what happened.

I am more authentically me, and so is my expression of Aikido, because of Robert Nadeau. Osensei's Aikido—made accessible through Nadeau Sensei's work—"in the flavor of ME." I know there are many other *Aikidoka* (Aikido practitioners) who can say the same.

What's fascinating about Nadeau Sensei's legacy is how it transcends Aikido. How many people can say that Robert Nadeau affected their lives off the mat? Whether it's a new level of teacher, husband, wife, boss, parent, student, or whatever, how many can say Robert Nadeau's work left a positive and lasting effect? Multiply by the number of years he's been at it, and it boggles the mind.

Osensei described the three realms of the Manifest, Hidden, and Divine. Among Aikido's first generation of Osensei's disciples, Robert Nadeau, I believe, is THE master of the Hidden realm. If you're not sure what that means, looking into it would be a great exploration.

Let Robert Nadeau's legacy be an everlasting reminder that Aikido is a dimensional art. Let it be a reminder that I/you/we are dimensional beings, and who the hell knows what the limits of that are? Finally, and most importantly, at this juncture, let his work inform and touch a new generation of human beings in process. (Amen.)

I am overwhelmed with gratitude for the time, energy, and interest Nadeau Sensei has extended to me over the years. I'm sure many people feel the same. So let's pay it forward. Thank you, Sensei.

## ◬ *The Dimensional Mapper* ◬

JEFF ADAMS
Aikido 4th Dan
Aikido of Mountain View

I met Bob in January of 1976 and am still under his tutelage. Of the many gifts to be found in his training, perhaps the most significant is the practice he has named "The Process." The Process is a physical set of movements that assist you in embodying a real physical understanding of the effects of your psycho-emotional state on any given activity/expression you are doing.

In one of his explanations of The Process, he uses the analogy of a person capable of lifting 10, 20, 30, or 40 pounds. A person capable of lifting only 10 pounds cannot be expected to lift and sustain a workout with 40 pounds. Maybe they can lift 40 pounds once or twice, but they will not be able to sustain the workout using 40-pound weights. This example applies aptly to the psycho-emotional state in all of us. We all need to be in touch with our mental and physical being, to know and acknowledge truthfully to ourselves where we are at any given moment.

When asked how I would describe Bob as a teacher, I coined a *nom de plume*: "The Dimensional Mapper." Bob's life work has been to assist us in comprehending the different phases, the "dimensions," of ability and understanding that one goes through in any undertaking; to be OK with and allow each phase to build upon itself. This is much like a coral reef adding layer upon layer to grow.

When asked why I still study under Bob, I say it's for the possibilities that await me. He is quick to point out when I am in a zone and just as quick to point out my self-delusion. Under his watchful eye and physical training, he allows me to actively pursue my version of The Process.

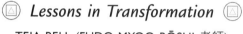

## *Lessons in Transformation*

### TEJA BELL (FUDO MYOO RŌSHI 老師)
Aikido 6th Dan
Lineage Dharma/Qigong Teacher

In the early 1980s, San Francisco Aikido, also known as the Turk Street dojo, was an alchemical chamber. Transformation and awakening potential were the engaging themes of the times. Aikido was a full-spectrum, mind-body vehicle for realizing this potential. My fellow students and I were on fire for Aikido. That fire was lit by Robert Nadeau Sensei. Enthusiasm is too mild a word to use to describe our love of Aikido or the passion and depth in how and what Nadeau Sensei was teaching. Each day in the dojo was another opportunity for self-discovery, the embodiment of skills, self-empowerment, and learning about the Universe—experiencing firsthand the workings and the principles of the Universe through our bodies.

That was the nature of Aikido practice in those days, full of joy and wonder, breakthroughs with body and heart, and mind-opening experiences. That was also the nature of Nadeau Sensei's teaching. It embraced the dynamics of harmony within ourselves and in relationship with others; the principles of centering, spiraling, and fluid balance; and the experience of connection inside and out. It was about more than technique. We were getting a taste of Osensei's "art of peace."

Robert Nadeau is a first-generation, direct-lineage student of Morihei Ueshiba Osensei, the Founder of Aikido. He carries the flame of Osensei's "inner art of Aikido" and its broad scope of meaning and purpose. That is not something you can communicate in words, but it is something that Nadeau Sensei transmits through his teachings and his expression of Aikido. Nadeau Sensei always draws the line back to the teachings of Morihei Ueshiba Osensei. Even as a teacher, he is always a humble and grateful student. That is the nature of his living connection with Aikido through Osensei. This is a vital lineage.

Friendships made in those times continue to this day. We also benefited from the excellent teachings of Frank Doran Sensei and Bill Witt Sensei at the Turk Street dojo.

Traveling from Marin County, where I lived, to San Francisco for Aikido class meant a big part of my days were devoted to Aikido. There was class time on the mat, practice before and after class in the dojo, and sometimes time spent after class at a restaurant or coffee shop for the "secret teachings." Nadeau Sensei explored the pathway of Aikido techniques to understand and embody the principles of Aikido, which included feeling and moving from the center, harmony in relationships, blending, staying connected, ki musubi (energy connection), zanshin (sustained energetic connection), and more.

After regular class, some of us hung out and did "process" work with Nadeau. One evening our investigation was on lineage and, more specifically, knowing and recognizing our unique lineage characteristics and qualities. My time in the process circle revealed that "creating beauty" was a primary lineage for me. Standing in the presence of my "beauty" lineage, Nadeau invited me to feel and experience the fullness of this lineage. As I did so, I became overwhelmed by the flush of the experience and said, "It's too beautiful!" At this point, Nadeau stopped for a moment and said, "How can someone in the lineage of

Creativity and Beauty be overwhelmed by too much beauty?"

He said it with a smile. He pointed out that my experience of "too much beauty" was based on a small self-identity that could not hold the fuller dimensions of my lineage. If this was indeed my lineage, I must inherently have the capacity to know and experience myself in its greater fullness. Anyone in any lineage can open up to a deeper, finer level of themselves to expand the appreciation of, and connection to, the resources of their lineage.

The next step in the process was to let go of that level of my confined self-identity that experienced "too beautiful" into the next level of myself that could hold the added energy of a more direct and deeper experience of my creative artistic lineage. This revelation has continued to inform my understanding of myself and the nature of human "self" perception.

So often, our shared human conditioning limits our growth and potential, causing us to hold on to an identity that cannot see beyond its current habituated set of boundaries. Yes, human beings have many possible "levels." Using Nadeau's "map," I have come to know our ability to move between levels or dimensions of ourselves. The process also helps clarify the nature of our perceptions, how they can limit us, and the possibility of moving through those limitations into greater freedom.

##  *Fearless Dimensionality*

CHIP FORMAN
Aikido 3rd Dan
City Aikido of San Francisco
Business Owner

Nadeau Sensei is fearless in bringing his unique and profound perspective about Aikido and Osensei's "Dimensional Process" to his students and the world. What initially seemed like a strange esoteric philosophy over time became an embodied revelation of a practice that opens the soul and manifests such amazing experience and understanding. Nadeau Sensei's "process" and presence touched me deeply about twenty years ago, and I never let go. I would be at the dojo religiously every Tuesday to engage and soak in the experience. It was always new and, at the same time, familiar. Something was revealed slowly and in stages. After being deconstructed and freed of "spiritual ideas," the natural unfolding and trust in the experiential process became a grounding and deep opening, where energies and experiences were happening on multiple levels.

I was fortunate to take a lot of *ukemi* (art of attacking/falling/rolling) from Sensei, and in a lot of ways it was overwhelming and profound to feel how effortless and powerful Aikido could be. Aikido was life changing for me. All was exposed, and all was revealed. He is a remarkable teacher who can be so patient and persistent with us, even while demanding we deepen and clarify the actual bodily experience of this dimensional practice of the spirit.

One time it was just a few of us in class. I was game, and Sensei guided me on a journey into our dimensional being, pushing me to touch new ground that became available, providing the insistence that I needed. I continued processing the class for several days. I felt I had been moved into new territory and embraced a new sense of being. One never forgets, and I was not the same after that. Thank you, Nadeau Sensei, for the gift of your teaching.

## From Mattresses to Dimensionality

ROY JOHNSTON
Aikido 6th Dan
City Aikido of San Francisco

Exploration is a good way to describe the experience of being in Nadeau Sensei's classes. Certainly, he teaches the martial aspect of Aikido, but his deeper focus always seems to be something much more than that. He leads in a way whereby we explore together, himself included, how we work, and how the Universe works. We are all connected. We just have to get out of our own way. In hindsight, thirty-four years after I started, it is not as easy as it sounds. Luckily for us, he is a phenomenal teacher and has some "tricks of the trade" to share, along with a process that sometimes best reveals itself off the mat.

At one time, Nadeau Sensei's City Aikido dojo was located on the second floor of a building at the corner of Eddy Street and Van Ness Avenue. It was a pretty nice location with lots of windows overlooking the street. We moved there after our long-term location on Oak Street was transformed into the San Francisco Conservatory of Music. We'd been on Eddy Street a few years when the landlord informed us that the vacant storefront downstairs below the dojo was being rented out as a restaurant. Apparently, there was significant concern from the incoming tenant about the noise level downstairs caused by students above landing on the mats. A brief *koshi-nage* (hip throw) test from upstairs sent the restaurant owner reeling. The sonic booms he heard were a deal-breaker for him, and so our month-to-month dojo lease was about to be terminated. I suspect the street-level restaurant space was worth a whole lot more to the landlord than an Aikido dojo upstairs. We were on the chopping block.

In an effort to come up with a solution, Nadeau Sensei called a meeting with our black belts. Rents being what they are in San Francisco and with a nice central location, nobody wanted to move. Many ideas came up, such as banning *koshi-nage*, only soft rolling, and various quiet training practices. Just when it seemed inevitable that, of course, we would have to relocate, somebody came up with the idea of getting a bunch of mattresses and putting them down underneath the mats to dampen the sound. This idea was getting some serious consideration from Nadeau Sensei, so much so that some rough calculations began about how many mattresses would be needed. All told, it was going to be something like seventy-two twin-size mattresses. Dojo finances being what they were, of course, the idea was to get them for free.

The whole time this idea was being floated, I had kept my mouth shut. In my humble opinion, this was a crazy idea. I didn't even bother to offer any of my myriad reasons why I thought this would never work. It just seemed way too outlandish to me, and I dismissed it outright, sure it would simply die out as cooler heads prevailed, and Nadeau Sensei thought better of it. The evening ended, and it seemed inevitable that we would have to move the dojo as scouts were assigned to scour the city for a possible new location.

After class the following Tuesday night, Nadeau Sensei motioned for me to talk to him. He cryptically held out his closed hand, silently indicating he was passing something along to me. I opened my hand and found myself now in possession of a hundred-dollar bill. I must have looked puzzled because he went on to explain that he had a little project for me and wanted to buy some of my time. He knew I wasn't working at the moment. I knew that sometimes Nadeau Sensei would ask students who were short on cash to help him with his estate cleanout service or some odd job if he needed extra hands. Anyway, I looked at him, like, OK, what do you want me to do?

He said he'd been giving more thought to the mattress idea to save the dojo, and he wanted to buy a few hours of my time making calls to see what I could come up with. I must say, I was dumbfounded. I thought the idea had already been dropped due to the craziness of the whole plan. But, I figured, one of our more wild-eyed black belts had probably caught Nadeau Sensei's ear and was nurturing this wacky idea. So, now, here I was, holding his hundred-dollar bill, and I knew there was no way he would take it back. I was trapped in an impossible project, advancing an idea I felt was stupid, crazy, and doomed. At that moment, I wondered what I had done to insult the gods to deserve such a fate.

In an instant, my mind raced through multiple ideas of how I might get out of this, all the while knowing I could not. There and then, I vowed silently to myself that I would go through the motions, spend the next few days on the phone making calls to who knows who, and at the end acknowledge my defeat. I settled on a plan to humbly apologize and return the money to him at the end of the week. I had no intention of keeping his money, but I knew I had to do what he had asked. After all, this was my sensei asking. While I could not fully accept my misfortune, I could take comfort in my upcoming apology plan.

So that week I got on the phone and started making some calls. Now you have to realize that I was somewhat of a phone guy. Over the years, I'd had a number of somewhat shady sales jobs that required dialing-for-dollars cold calling. I'm talking phone banks hawking advertising specialties with questionable prizes: radio advertising time, toner for printers, etc. This was all well before cell phones and caller ID, at a time when people actually picked up the phone to answer when someone called. It's worth appreciating, though, that it was an art, or a hustle, depending on how you looked at it, to connect with a stranger over the phone in a matter of moments and in the end have them buy something from you that they really weren't looking for or needed. But still, dialing for seventy-two free mattresses? This seemed a bit far-fetched even for my blood.

Nevertheless, this was my assignment, my fate, and I was determined to do the best I could. I wanted to be able to look Sensei in the eye at the end of the week and say I did my best when I gave him his money back. As my calling got underway, I started to hone in on motels, hotels, and summer camps, thinking that they might be the only ones who would even have that many mattresses. Perhaps I could cobble a few together from a number of sources looking to unload what they might need to replace. It would take some time and unbelievable luck to land even a few of these, but I was determined not to come up empty-handed. After all, I took dubious pride in the idea that I was something of a "pro" on the phones.

As fate would have it, after only a few hours of calling I had a decent lead on a summer camp in the East Bay that might be in the market to replace some of their mattresses. After some further back-and-forth phoning, I reached the proprietor of the summer camp, who said he was in fact about to replace the mattresses in his cabins. He even said we could have them for free if we were willing to cart them away. I asked him what kind and how many he had. He didn't have an exact count at the moment, but he was pretty sure there were seventy-six twin-size mattresses available. Whoaaaa, that was a direct hit, with a couple extra to spare.

When I gave Nadeau Sensei the news before the next class, he assigned some of the guys to do a test run that Saturday of a fall, roll, and *koshi-nage* with an old mattress he had dragged in for the occasion. They got the keys to the restaurant space downstairs, and upstairs the test began. They had some sound guy there who measured something or other, but it was all to no avail. Mattress or no mattress, downstairs it sounded like the sky was falling. The plan was abandoned. We all shifted our focus to moving the dojo.

While Nadeau Sensei took the whole thing in stride as just another day in the neighborhood, I must say it had rattled my world. What stood out for me about all this is that it did not require belief because I did not believe. It did not require faith because I had none. And in a way, it did not require trust because I did not trust it would all work out. Looking at this from the perspective of Nadeau Sensei's teaching, clearly just below the surface, beyond all my certainty and doubt, was another dimension. It was a realm with different possibilities and "supporting forces," as Nadeau Sensei often referenced, and it was not very far away.

As Nadeau Sensei might point out about this, my "small-I" was not big enough for the task at hand. A dimensional shift revealed by a kind of surrender or letting-go allowed me to be fully present and open to whatever presented itself as I made those phone calls. I had no attachment to, or expectation of, a successful result. All I did was simply respond from that open space and let it work itself out. This was not a consciously preplanned process that I did back then. It's just how it played out. And upon reflection, it was very indicative of the way Nadeau Sensei taught us Aikido: as a process, with the hidden nature of the Universe giving us glimpses of its underlying harmony and support as we settled and opened.

## Travel Vehicles

Nadeau Sensei recounts watching Morihei Ueshiba transform nearly instantaneously from an elderly man with all the natural frailties of his age into a powerful presence radiating invisible but palpable energy. Osensei described this as a shift from "this old man" to "Ueshiba of Aikido." Because he witnessed this transformation firsthand and directly experienced the energies emanating from Osensei, he knew them to be true phenomena he could trust. On the mat, in dialogues and lectures, or just being in the room, Osensei seemed to glow with an inner force, living in the Manifest Dimension but somehow channeling extraordinary energies from unseen sources.

Inspired by Osensei's transformation, Nadeau Sensei has developed practices that he calls Travel Vehicles to help us move from who we are now to an improved version of ourselves. He uses the word Character in these practices to help distinguish between the levels of energetic support at each stage. Travel vehicles are designed to help us practice shifting from a closed, tight, constricted identity to a more open, relaxed, and expanded character. Travel Vehicles are inherently sequential, helping us practice shifting incrementally from one energy level to the next.

Diagram 9 illustrates a very basic Travel Vehicle that Sensei calls "1x1, 2x2, 3x3." Begin this practice by describing your experience of being in a 1x1 space that allows only one step forward and one step back. Anyone in such a small space might feel constrained and confined. In the next phase, feel and describe a slightly larger 2x2 space with room for two steps in each direction. Does that feel better? Continue by feeling and describing the transition from 2x2 to a larger 3x3 space. The energies associated with each 1x1, 2x2, or 3x3 space, when fully allowed, become easily recognizable. Through this process, we can learn to quickly sense the size of an energetic space and shift or remix our Character appropriately.

Another Travel Vehicle is what Sensei calls "10-pounder, 20-pounder, 30-pounder," using weight as a metaphor for the functional capability to handle a given situation. For example, a Character who is a 10-pounder is comfortable handling a 10-pound situation but cannot deal with 20 or 30 pounds. They would have to grow, evolve, and become a stronger version of themselves. This requires a Remixing of the Character to function with new potential. The goal of this practice is to enable one to shift from a 10-pounder "you" to a more capable 20- or 30-pounder "you" as needed for a given situation.

Sensei's Travel Vehicles use examples from the manifest world to describe a process that works on our inner sense of Dimensionality. The transformational sequences are representations analogous to the energy

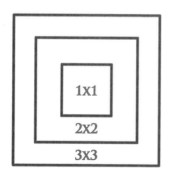

Diagram 9. 1x1, 2x2, 3x3 . . .

levels we can all move through to Remix, shifting internally from our smaller character with its coarser energies and lesser capabilities to our fuller character embodying finer energies and greater capacities.

Perhaps the most personal way Sensei expresses the step-by-step nature of Travel Vehicles is with the sequence "Bobby, Robert, Nadeau, Sensei, Shihan," where he speaks about himself as different Characters, each with better energetic qualities.

He starts this sequence with small, weird Bobby, a 1x1 kind of guy, an unhealthy, tightly wound Character. But Bobby can Remix into his next level as Robert, a more normal 2x2 person. Next, Robert can shift into Nadeau, a fuller and more complete 3x3 being with finer energies he trusts and allows to Remix into a more highly evolved 4x4 Sensei Character with qualities of competence and leadership. Finally, he can shift himself into a 5x5 Character with finer energy and deeper wisdom named Shihan.

In many ways, this is similar to the 1x1, 2x2, 3x3 practice, the 10-pounder, 20-pounder, 30-pounder practice, or another sequence of circumstances and attitudes that Sensei calls "bad day, fair day, good day." All these practices are designed to help students sense the levels of energy and the dimensions of Situations in which they may find themselves, and to recognize their potential to internally Remix into a Character that can "rise to the occasion" as needed.

The lesson underlying all of the Travel Vehicle practices is that we can each express various Characters, in the here and now, that can range from weird to wise. Initially, Remixing to allow different Characters to emerge will be a gradual process of small incremental steps. But once Travel Vehicle patterns become familiar, letting your Character shift to fit the Situation can become nearly instantaneous. This is essentially what Nadeau witnessed with Osensei. And this is how it is possible for Robert, the normal everyday guy who commutes to the dojo, to quickly Remix upon arriving at the dojo into his more refined Characters of Sensei or Shihan who are energetically more capable of leading an Aikido class with wit and *elan*.

For a person with a family, this might involve Remixing into a better parent. For someone in a company, it might mean Remixing into a better manager.

## ◬ *From* Martial *Art to* Marital *Art* ◬

DIANA (WEINBERG) DAFFNER
Aikido 1st Dan
Aikido of San Francisco, Aikido of Mountain View
Founder, Intimacy Retreats
Author: *Tantric Sex for Busy Couples*

In 1970, I was on the massage staff at Esalen Institute. Most of the workshops being offered, in my (somewhat arrogant, twenty-four-year-old) opinion, were geared toward the "straighter" attendees who arrived in their leisure suits, hoping to make a significant change in their lives, rather than those of us considered "local hippies." I was already familiar with lots of what was taught. Heck, I thought I could teach some of the workshops myself! After all, I had a B.A. in psychology, and heightened insights galore to go with my Big Sur lifestyle. Unfortunately, I wasn't very impressed by most of the seminar leaders. (They wanted to hang out with us!)

One workshop that *did* catch my attention was titled "Energy Awareness for Spiritual Development." When the leader, Robert Nadeau, was pointed out to me, I saw a fellow wearing tight jeans tucked into black leather motorcycle boots and a white T-shirt whose rolled-up sleeve held a pack of cigarettes. Really? I thought. Didn't look very "spiritual" to me.

Even though, as staff, I only had to pay a small portion of the workshop fee, I sauntered over to where he sat and brazenly asked if I could attend the first night before deciding whether to sign up. He looked at me and then turned to the young woman with him, Betsy Hill, and said, "She wants to see if we're too tough for her."

"Too tough" for me? Hey, I lived in an old truck with my dog and played flute with the local conga drummers (women weren't even allowed to drum in Big Sur in those days). I had meditated with Indian gurus and hiked alone in the hills. Journeyed with LSD. Too tough for me? Who was he kidding?

I had to ask again since he hadn't answered me, and he finally nodded. *If you know Bob, you know that Nadeau nod!* I walked away, totally unconvinced that this was a good idea.

The workshop blew me away. I thought I knew a lot about energy and states of consciousness. Somehow this totally wrong-looking dude knew more than I did! I was very intrigued.

I loved living in Big Sur and couldn't imagine what would ever take me away. Fortunately for me, a couple of friends were also drawn to Bob's teaching, and they insisted I go with them to visit him in Mountain View. So, we all ended up moving there.

It wasn't Aikido that I was drawn to. I moved to Mountain View to meditate and to learn about energy. Doing Aikido was just part of the program. If Bob had been a basketball coach or a basket weaver, that would have been what I did. What I learned in the dozen years that I actively studied with Bob would fill this whole book, and probably be redundant to what others have said.

What I did with it is another story. My path, my main interest, has always been about "intimacy," deep spiritual connection, eyes open, with a meditation partner. Or energy connection while blending with an Aikido *uke* (attacking/receiving partner). Or connecting through touch as I massaged clients. Or all of these with a lover. Although I didn't know the Japanese word until recently, it was always *musubi* (connection) that I was drawn to. For all his sometimes-seeming-aloofness, Bob Nadeau taught me how to build a foundation for manifesting intimacy, *musubi*, in all aspects of my life.

Together with my husband, Richard, who is neither an

Aikidoist nor a meditator, for the last several decades I have used those teachings to provide effective training for couples wanting more closeness in their relationships. In the process, I moved from practicing a *martial* art to developing and teaching a *marital* art!

For intimacy to take place, a *shift* has to happen. There's a movement, an opening, from "me" to "we." Or really, to something larger, a Presence that is way more than both of us.

Shifting is what Nadeau is so extraordinary at. And he's fast. I learned to recognize "Oh, fuck / Oh, base" moments by training with him.

The "Oh, fuck" is when our attention is grabbed by something outside of ourselves—an *uke* holding my wrist like a vise. A lost earring. Butting heads with my husband. Oh, fuck. The solution, a return to peace, cannot happen if I narrow my focus to that place of conflict.

The "Oh, base" is the reminder to shift from out there, where the trouble is, to in here, under my feet, into the center of my being. Bob taught me to embody the "Be Here Now" that I believe is necessary for spiritual growth.

Establishing intimacy follows the same pattern of shifting. Moving my attention from *out there*—even when it may be pleasant—to fully being *in here* opens me up to the potential of connection. In that "base" place inside myself is the door to a shared experience of who we are. Connecting with myself, I can connect with my partner, we can connect with our finer *selves*, and, in the best of moments, with "It," a term Bob used for that which flowed in, out, and through us on the mat.

I still get caught in the "Oh, fuck" place. But because of my training with this amazing teacher, I (eventually) remember to shift to "Oh, base."

The Zoom classes that came into being due to the COVID-19

restrictions have allowed me to hang out once again and learn from Nadeau. His understandings, experiences, and explanations about the nature of human being continue to evolve, and his ability to translate them into practices have shown him to be so much more than a martial arts teacher.

## ◬ *The Best "Me" I Can Be* ◬

LYN MEACHEN
Dojo-cho, Riai Aikido
Belmont, Lower Hutt, New Zealand

My first experience of Nadeau Sensei was at an Aikido seminar in Rotorua, New Zealand, approximately twenty-five years ago. I had been training for maybe a year or so. My first thoughts were, "Wow, this guy is amazing." He was so powerful and centered, and I believed for the first time I was starting to see what this "Aikido thing" could indeed be.

Nadeau Sensei continued to come to New Zealand over the years, and I attended every seminar, even if injured. It took many years before I understood his messages around energy, and I'm still working on it. An ongoing journey.

For me, a memorable experience occurred during a night

session Nadeau Sensei led at the Aiki Summer Retreat in San Rafael one year when a group of us Kiwis traveled to California. On this particular night, he was working on progressing from 1x1 to 2x2, etc. We had reached 4x4, and I was training with Danny McIntyre Sensei. I was in such a different place, such a different zone, and so into the training that Danny said to me at one point to ease up as I was nearly throwing him through the gym wall. After class, we went out for sushi and beer with Nadeau Sensei and friends, and I remember feeling like I was floating.

Centering, grounding, breathing, feeling, spirituality, dimensionality, connection, and love are vital when applying Nadeau Sensei's teachings in daily-life situations.

For example, my mum was in her nineties, and we walked down the hallway at her rest home. I had linked into her arm to guide her as she was partially sighted. Suddenly her left leg collapsed, and I knew she had a stroke. I centered and took on most of her body weight because dropping her was not an option. I managed to get her back to her room and seated when help arrived. Then, it was about staying calm for her, reassuring, connecting, letting her know I was there because she was very frightened. She pretty much recovered from the stroke.

In a second example, I flew off my mountain bike riding at around thirty kilometers per hour into a large pole and walked away with just severe bruising. Based on years of Aikido *ukemi* (art of attacking/falling/rolling) I curled up to take the fall as I was coming off the bike. After impacting the pole with my cheek and then my back, I ended up about ten feet away. My first thoughts were to stay still, breathe and relax, and check out my body. In doing so, I knew I hadn't broken anything, and I knew I could get up, but first I went through the process.

Trying to grow and develop every time I'm on the mat is a

benefit of trying to follow Nadeau Sensei's teachings. I want to be the best Lyn-character I can be. I feel amazing joy whenever I train, which wasn't always the case. My focus as a sensei myself is to see my students grow both on and off the mat, and I feel immense joy when I see this. I mention Nadeau's lessons in every class I teach, and I believe this is very beneficial for our students.

The longer I do Aikido, and the more I listen to Nadeau Sensei, the more I understand how much of a self-development art Aikido is. Off the mat, my focus is on staying grounded and connected. I'm trying to be the best "me" I can be, a better partner, a better sister, a better friend, a better workmate. I know I have a long way to go, but I am trying.

Training with Nadeau Sensei has made me feel like I know Osensei better. I have some insight into what he (the Old Man, as Nadeau calls him) was all about. That is the gift that Nadeau Sensei has given us all, and it's invaluable. He talks about Osensei in such a loving way and always emphasizes that Osensei was doing more than just physical techniques. It's the "so much more" that Nadeau Sensei has shared that I believe has so deepened my experience of Aikido.

# Trading-in, Clearing, and Stepping into Qualities

Sensei offers various practices to help students let go of their old Characters in order to allow them to energetically remix better, finer versions of themselves. Some of these practices include what he calls Trading-in, Clearing, and Stepping into Qualities.

Trading-in involves completely—physically, mentally, and emotionally—letting our current Character drop away so that a new character can take its place. Giving up our current character is a necessary step to embodying a better character, much like a person must trade in their old car to make space in their garage before they get a new car. For example, in the linear progression described earlier, "Bobby" must trade in his character to become "Robert," and "Robert" must, in turn, trade in his character to allow "Nadeau" to emerge. With practice, trading-in can become relatively fast and effective without conscious thought.

Clearing is another way of relaxing our intentions and expectations and giving up the certainty of what we know about ourselves in order to experience what is yet unknown.

Clearing, like Easy the I and Open and Settle, begins by being Present, here and now. First, Sensei encourages students to look and listen quietly to the physical space around them. Then he asks students to open to the energies of the space, patiently allowing enough time for their internal clearing to progress far enough for them to begin feeling a subtle sense of inner expansion or unfolding.

He encourages us to practice this internal energetic orientation. Feeling more deeply in this way, we can begin to let go of our preconditioned thoughts and habits to allow the emergence of inner spaciousness needed for new growth—spiritually, mentally, emotionally, and energetically.

Sensei will sometimes pause when demonstrating a particular Aikido *waza* (technique) to clear himself, so he can better sense the energies of that moment—his own, his partner's, and the situation—before physically engaging with his partner. Likewise, he will sometimes instruct students to clear before each repetition of a *waza*, so they can better feel the underlying Energy of the encounter with their *uke* more fully and distinctly without falling into habitual patterns.

He consistently teaches that these principles are broadly applicable in many walks of life. For example, a physical therapist or mental health counselor treating successive patients may find it helpful to clear with a moment of quiet breathing, handwashing, or stepping outside between clients.

Another practice for realizing new perspectives is what Nadeau Sensei calls Stepping into Qualities. Students are asked to perform an Aikido technique that begins with an internal process of clearing before stepping into an energetic quality, for example a metaphorical "pool of calm." They are then instructed to stay in the moment long enough to soak in the calm, to "be the calmer one" who can experience subtle shifts of Dimensionality. Sensei cautions against trying to consciously become calm because this creates a kind of entangled mental ownership that only leads to more stress. He points out that this same approach can also be used to sense other energy qualities like "stepping into joy" or "stepping into stability." This is not a mental exercise. It involves sensing and experiencing little improvements along the way. Osensei once told him: "I am not pure. But I can stand in purity." Calmness, joy, stability, or even purity are not the ultimate goals of these practices. They are meant to be utilized as gateways to the next level of dimensional energy, the next level of your Character.

## ◬ *Mapping Levels of Enlightenment* ◬

MARK FITZWATER
Aikido 4th Dan
Aikido Oamaru, New Zealand

I'd been training a few years in Aikido when Robert Nadeau Sensei came to New Zealand for a weekend seminar. It was the first time I had seen him. Up until that point in time, I hadn't had any particularly memorable Aikido experiences other than practicing physical techniques. I was attracted to the art for more than its physical techniques, but looking back, I didn't know why. I enjoyed it, yet sensed there was more to the art.

That first weekend with Nadeau Sensei turned out to be pretty special for me.

I was *uke* (attacking/receiving partner) for my *sempai* (senior partner) when Nadeau came over to show him something. To do that, he reached toward me as his *uke*. From the moment I grabbed him, I was almost in shock. Just grabbing his wrist from behind, I felt my entire body being moved. There was just an amazing sense of energy flowing off him, around him, and moving me. A thought crossed my mind: "I'm in so much trouble here." It was kind of terrifying. He had taken my balance and moved me from behind him to the front of him with a turn of his wrist. All logic had gone out the window. Something else was going on here, and I wanted to know more.

Maybe a year later, he came back to New Zealand. I was again *uke* for someone much higher ranked than myself. I may have been a 3rd *kyu* (third class white belt) at the time, and we were doing *ikkyo-ura* (first-teaching technique done to the backside). I was not resisting, but it might have looked like that from the outside because I stopped not far from the ground. I felt like I wasn't being taken all the way to the ground by my partner, and I don't believe in just falling over for people.

Nadeau had seen this and came over. He did the technique on me. One moment I was up, the next flat on the ground with him pinning me and chuckling at the same time. I had no idea what had happened. How did someone put me on the ground without me knowing what had happened? I learned that day that I have so much more to learn.

Nadeau can see so much. Once I was visiting San Francisco, staying and training in City Aikido. During one class, I felt particularly ungrounded and was doing my best to re-ground. Right at that moment, Nadeau Sensei's voice came booming across the dojo. "Where is your grounding, Mark?" He wasn't even near me, but he saw!

If you listen to Nadeau's teachings, the message is short and almost always the same. Aikido is about personal inner development. It sounds simple, but what does that mean? Well, until you experience even a little of what he teaches, the phrase "personal inner development" is just words.

Lately, the frequency with which I practice has increased dramatically. It is no longer just something I do on an Aikido mat; Nadeau's teachings are never far from my mind. If I settle, center, ground, or sense the space I occupy, I find that whatever I am doing tends to improve. I live in the countryside and look after bees. There is always something to do. So, whether I am rounding up sheep, cutting firewood, or trying to find a queen bee in a beehive, taking a moment to settle beforehand tends to improve the outcome. Having improved outcomes gives me an incentive to practice more. When you have an experience, good; however, there is always more.

The most valuable thing Nadeau has given me is "belief." The belief is that if I can get good enough, and develop well enough, other possibilities will open up. There could be improved outcomes with tasks as well as with family and friends, a healthier body, a better mind, and better overall well-being.

That you, the reader, are reading these words isn't enough. These are still external. The true rewards are within. Everything else is a side effect that we shouldn't get caught up in.

I believe Nadeau Sensei has laid out a map to finer levels of enlightenment—an ongoing journey for anyone interested.

## Taking the Hit. Receiving the Gift

PETER WRIGHT
Aikido 2nd Dan
City Aikido of San Francisco
Founder, Embodying Possible
Mentor, Identity Dynamics

Aikido folks delight in telling stories about Osensei. My favorite is how a janitor hid in a closet, witnessing Osensei responding to a sumo wrestler's challenge; how he saw Osensei spin this very large wrestler around and throw him into the ceiling! We also tell stories about our own sensei. When I visited other dojos or attended an Aikido camp, I would overhear people sharing a particular story about my Sensei, Robert Nadeau Shihan.

"Vintage Nadeau," the storytelling usually begins. The setting is the Aiki Summer Retreat at Dominican College in San Rafael. It's a full evening class, with crowded mats and around two hundred people. Drummers are gathered in a far corner, filling the old wooden gymnasium that serves as our training hall with an intense, primal rhythm.

Nadeau is transformed, prowling as if some great leopard

on the hunt. He calls a male student up to deliver front kicks. Nadeau sidesteps the kick, scooping the leg with one hand and with the other thrusting at the student's neck, driving him to the floor. Nadeau calls for this attack again and again— prowling, dancing, driving. It's brutal, so the story goes. Only, it doesn't seem that way to me. And I would know – *I was that student.*

When I engage the memory, it's like it was yesterday. I'm a brown belt, with all of those typical brown belt qualities surging through me—I'm young, strong, eager. I feel the sweat of the hot summer night, the intoxication of the percussion, the sea of bodies surging, cresting, crashing in rolls in all directions. I am so immersed in the power of the night that when Nadeau points to me to attack, it is not until I've taken my third or fourth step toward him that I realize I am moving into a very different, unfamiliar world.

I am enveloped in an energetic storm: it is magnetic, drawing me into this primal reality he has opened, inviting me to join him.

Music, movement, energy all pulsing together—beyond thought. Kick—feel the ground. Again, the ground. It was not brutality, though I can understand how one could see that from the outside, watching the intensity of our exchanges. Nadeau was not using me, hurting me, or pounding something into me.

Much more than a demonstration, or a lesson, it was intensely personal, a calling forth. As I consider it now, I am tearful in my gratitude. His force in that powerful rhythmic transformation sensed the potential in me and called it forth. "Come, come play with me."

I would not say that I was ready for that moment. Instead, he helped me become ready as I responded to his invitation, moving toward a more direct world of experience. The echoes of that night are still with me: the taste of the untamed, a power of surging aliveness that deeply informs how I work, how I move.

It has been years since I've been in his dojo, and still I can hear Sensei repeating the words in class, time after time: "Take the hit." And his unspoken message: "Receive the gift, while I am here, while you can."

## Downtime and Underworld

When COVID-19 first hit in the spring of 2020, people worldwide were forced to suddenly stop normal activities and shelter at home for months. Nadeau Sensei responded by encouraging everyone to accept the extraordinary situation as Downtime and, therefore, an invaluable opportunity to experience aspects of ourselves that we don't typically take the time to explore. Over the following months of online classes in a virtual dojo, he reintroduced students to many of the Travel Vehicles described earlier because of their suitability for solo practice during the enforced Downtime of the pandemic.

He urged everyone to accept Downtime as a naturally occurring phase in the energy cycles of life and not something to be resisted or wasted. He described Downtime as any interval in life's hectic scramble when we pause what we're doing to clear our heads, reflect on our practice, take stock of our lives, and listen quietly to our inner voice. Sensei recognizes that Downtime may initially feel a bit scary to navigate without all of the familiar "I do" activities that typically occupy our attention and keep us busy. His advice in such cases is, as always, to Open and Settle more to experience the Energy dynamics of the new situation.

To help students accept the naturalness of Downtime, he points to the rhythms of sleep in the life of all mammals. These rhythms involve the temporary cessation of regular activities, a substantial period of inactivity and internal processing that helps us recover from our day-time exertions, rebalance mind and body, and awaken with fresh energy each morning. People may have different sleep patterns, but everyone needs sleep for a healthy, balanced life. The same goes for Downtime, according to Sensei.

Downtime, he says, can be an opportunity to more deeply explore the lesser-known aspects of creation that he calls the Underworld. In diagram 10, the upper half of the circle represents Awareness, the world of conscious activity where people typically spend most of their waking hours, while the lower half of the diagram represents the Energy and

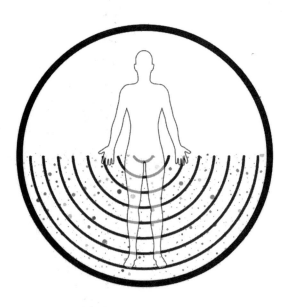

Diagram 10. Exploring the Underworld.

intelligence of the Underworld that is always present and available to everyone through direct Experience.

The Energies of the Underworld will present themselves in various ways depending on the individual. What we Experience and how we react will be uniquely personal for each of us. But, typically, we're just too busy with life's daily activities to take the time needed to delve into the Underworld. He advises students who find themselves in Downtime to recognize it as a precious opportunity to explore their personal Underworld and, in the process, begin accessing previously hidden Energy to realize their fuller potential.

Nadeau Sensei often recounts his own early exploration of the Underworld to make this point. Once, as he sat meditating, he felt like he was surrounded by snakes that were hissing, biting, and looking at him menacingly. He admits to being quite upset at first because he really dislikes snakes. But he kept meditating, Opening and Settling, welcoming the Energy he felt rising within himself rather than giving in to fear. After a short while, the snakes seemed to be smiling at him. He continued to Open and Settle more, and then they presented themselves not as snakes but as Energies spiraling up toward him from a beautiful, life-giving source in a finer dimension. He felt touched by the Experience of that beauty and the truer nature of those Energies.

He realized from this and other personal experiences that while the Underworld is commonly misunderstood to be a region inhabited by hostile, dark, and destructive forces, often portrayed as a place to be feared and avoided, really the Underworld has no "bad" Energies, even if they appear negative at first. Someone's first forays into the Underworld may be scary or uncomfortable because the Energies of the Underworld are heavy and unfamiliar. They may initially present as monsters, as they did for him in his early approaches to the Underworld. But it is important to recognize that these are just first impressions and habitual responses. He assures students that their Underworld "monsters" are really "allies" that, in time, can energetically empower them in unexpected ways.

# ◬ *Opening to the Tiger Within* ◬

### DENNIS BUTLER
Aikido 1st Dan
City Aikido of San Francisco

I can never forget the first time I saw Nadeau Sensei. It was at the Mountain View dojo in 1990 or 1991. I had never imagined that anyone could move with such panther-like power and grace. In those days, new students stayed at one end of the mat learning *ukemi* (the art of attacking/falling/rolling) until we demonstrated some basic level of competence and could join the main class. I remember sneaking peeks out of the corner of my eye just to watch Sensei move. His presence was palpable; he owned the mat.

Have I ever used Aikido? Every day, but not, of course, in a self-defense mode. Learning to settle and open to new spaces has eased my passage through difficult times in my life. Learning to recognize that the process for becoming at ease in a new, unfamiliar, and sometimes threatening space is always the same: settle and open. The idea that the "monsters" we run across in life are simply allies we haven't met before is enormously influential.

I experienced some powerful and maybe even dangerous aspects of myself a couple of times. I had a clear image of a dangerous tiger. Sensei led me through the process of settling, opening, and becoming acquainted with this "monster" until it became clear that the tiger wasn't part of me ready to lash out and destroy, but was instead a mother tiger protecting me and emerging when I was threatened. Since then, when I feel the tiger stirring, I can settle and open, and smile a bit at my protector.

One time, I was riding my motorcycle home from training, crossing the San Francisco–Oakland Bay Bridge. I had crossed this bridge hundreds of times before and was completely relaxed, on that sort of high I often got after training. Then, out of the blue, I felt a very strong and very obvious shove on my left cheek, so strong it forced me to change lanes to the right involuntarily. At that instant, the car to my left made an abrupt lane change, right into the space I had just vacated. Aikido? I think so.

Relax and open.

##  *A Deeper Place to Grieve*

PATRICK FITZSIMMONS
Aikido 1st Dan
Aikido of Mountain View

Nadeau Shihan is the best teacher I've ever had—in anything. And what he has taught me has had a markedly positive influence on how I have lived my life. Shihan's teachings about Aikido, derived from Osensei's teachings, have made me aware that there are better levels of myself that are accessible, if only I engage in a process to discover them.

His practices such as opening and settling, grounding, centering, aligning, connecting, and harmonizing have been helpful on and off the mat. Embodying and enacting these concepts has certainly enriched my life in the realm of personal and professional relationships.

About ten years ago, my wife passed away, causing me to feel a sense of profound loss. As I sought to cope with the loss, my grief was like a tsunami coming toward shore and headed for me. It seemed like I had a choice either to be drowned and swept away by the incoming wave, or to seek a different outcome. My Aikido training with Nadeau Shihan helped me realize that as threatening as the wave appeared, I could still harmonize with it. As I reflected on the meaning of the image of the approaching tsunami, it occurred to me that geologically a tsunami is often generated by movements in the ocean floor deep below the surface. Maybe the psychological tsunami I was experiencing was coming from a place deep in my psyche. My training then helped me realize that I could go to a deeper place within myself to grieve and cope. And when I did, it helped. This was an especially important moment in my life when I was grateful for my Aikido training and Nadeau Shihan's teachings.

## ⬛ *The Monster Theory* ⬛

JACK WADA
Aikido 7th Dan
Chief Instructor, Aikido of San Jose
Student of the Universe

I began Aikido in the fall of 1969, during my senior year at the University of California, Santa Cruz (UCSC). Robert Frager Sensei, a psychology professor at UCSC, started an Aikido club. He was my first home dojo instructor, and we keep in warm contact to this day.

Back then, Frager Sensei worked closely with Robert Nadeau Sensei. Both had been direct students of Morihei Ueshiba Osensei, and both were interested in the vast dimensions that the art could open in the realms of human potential. They would co-teach weekend workshops together where Aikido training was coupled with other things that they had been exposed to by Osensei. Chanting, meditation, and centering were just a few of the topics explored at these weekend-long sessions. I consider them both my first teachers.

After graduating from UCSC, I did a two-year graduate program at UC Davis. Something inside told me to go to Japan, train, and find Osensei, even though he had physically passed away in 1969. So, in 1973, I crossed the Pacific Ocean and began training at the Kumano Juku Dojo in Shingu, Japan. It was intense: a traditional approach to Aikido as a martial art with deep exposure to Osensei's teachings based on the Founder's way of practice and his metaphorical vehicle of *misogi* (inner purification) from the Shinto religion.

By 1975 I was back in Santa Cruz. Robert Frager was leaving to open his own graduate school, and I took over as the chief instructor of the Santa Cruz Aikido Club. Then, in 1976, I heard that a new Aikido dojo was opening in San Jose and was invited to be a part of it. I agreed, and began to also teach Friday evenings and Saturday mornings there, which made it convenient for me to attend Nadeau Sensei's Monday night classes in Mountain View. I was amazed and surprised to find that he went directly to the energy, removing a lot of the Shinto wrappings I had been exposed to in Japan. To quote Bruce Lee, his approach was "simple, direct, non-classical." I found it refreshing. I still, even to this day, value the teaching of my teachers in Japan and their very traditional approach. But Nadeau Sensei helped me to tie together my super intense experience in Japan with what I was trying to achieve here in America.

Once, in the fall of 1974, I was in Japan, practicing at the Shingu dojo when Robert Frager Sensei brought a group of Santa Cruz students to train there. Hikitsuchi Sensei was feeling very energetic and went all out for Frager Sensei and his visiting students, teaching intense classes in staff, sword, and a special class in *kototama* (word spirit).

One evening I decided to try some *kototama* on the roof of the building where we were all staying. I had heard Hikitsuchi Sensei do the "O" chant. I tried the sound as an up-down spiral. The up went fine. But the downward spiral seemed to pull something down with it. I felt great emotion, mainly irrational fear, compressed into that single instant. It was, and still is, the only time in my life that I have ever uncontrollably run away from anything. I felt the urgent need to be surrounded by people. There was a dining area where the other Santa Cruz people hung out after evening class. I figured this was just a figment of my imagination and human contact would probably solve the issue.

To my surprise, the moment I entered the room, the response was, "What have you done?" Whatever it was that I had called up with my *kototama* up/down spirals had freaked the whole group out. Everyone felt "something weird." Group sentiment was "Fix it!" So we all gathered together and I chanted the Amatsu Norito (chanted Shinto prayers) three times. That seemed to quiet things down for the moment. I went to sleep, hoping everything was now okay. But I got up several times during the night and saw rotting corpses floating by my window. Unsettling. By morning, with the sun out, all seemed to be back to normal.

Hikitsuchi Sensei had gotten wind of all this somehow. He admonished me for bringing in *jaki* (dark forces / evil spirits) with my chant, and warned me against practicing such chanting unless I was safely in the dojo or at a shrine, which put a certain amount of fear into me.

Later, back in California, I had a related experience. I was teaching in Santa Cruz at the time. The situation was not good. My mom was very ill with cancer and would soon pass. I was aware the brakes on the car I was driving were not good, but I was too preoccupied to deal with it. One day, I had to drive from Santa Cruz to San Jose to pick up Mary Heiny Sensei at the airport. Normally it's not a very long drive, but it is up and over the mountains. En route on Highway 17, there was some heavy construction going on. Traffic was stalled on a down-sloping curve with cars bumper to bumper. I felt the brakes in my car fading and pulled off to the side, intending to stop the car. But the brakes were totally gone, and my car didn't stop. It rolled off the side, over the edge of the road, and plunged down an extreme slope. Suddenly, trees blocked out the summer sun. Everything turned dark, and the car gathered speed incredibly quickly.

But unlike the incident on the rooftop in Japan, I was calm.

It was like an intense *ukemi* (art of attacking/falling/rolling) where you just open and trust. I was moving so fast there was no time to think.

But my radar picked up something immense in that darkness and speed, and what the energies told me was HIT IT. And so, I did. Head-on. Then I blacked out.

When I came to, I was holding the top half of the steering wheel in my hands. The impact had been so great the steering wheel had been sheared in two. I looked out through the windshield. What was left of the hood was crumpled up just a foot away. And right beyond that was the trunk of an immense tree. That's what I had hit head-on. Looking around, I could see that if I had missed this particular tree, the car would have kept going, gathered more speed, spun further out of control, and eventually hit something else with even greater force. I would have died, for sure. As it was, I had to be pulled from the wreckage, but was largely OK and needed only a few stitches.

After I started teaching in San Jose in 1976, I told Nadeau Sensei about my rooftop *kototama* chanting a few years prior, and how I had pulled down "dark energies" and become fearful. His response was very clear. "Don't buy this 'dark forces' thing. All energies at their source are pure. Don't be afraid of your own power."

This is one of the most important things I have learned from Nadeau Sensei, and he calls it the "monster theory." As we process and go back to the source, forces and energies can become more intense, and sometimes they can appear as monsters. It is up to those of us who journey back to see that the Self individuates into its more original state, where those forces and energies can be experienced as allies instead.

When I did the *kototama* chant on that rooftop in Japan, I called up energies that, at the time, I was not prepared to deal with. I felt fear, but the energies themselves were not necessarily "dark."

During my car crash, the sudden shift into the dark and the unspoken guidance to hit the tree were those same forces "protecting" me.

What I got from Nadeau Sensei has greatly influenced my Aikido journey. Don't settle for ritual and form. Trust yourself.

## ⬠ *Intelligence of the Body* ⬠

RICHARD ESMONDE
Aikido 3rd Dan
City Aikido of San Francisco
Designer

"Intelligence of the body" is a mantra Nadeau Sensei often uttered as he led us through numerous process journeys exploring what it meant to be our physically individual selves. "The body talks," he'd say. I thought he was off his rocker when I first heard this. "I'm the one thinking and controlling this body," I thought. It would take some time for Nadeau's teaching to sink in.

Gradually, it dawned on me that I needed to get out of my own way to realize that, yes, I was trying to control my body when it was quite well equipped to look after itself. I realized the body is trying to tell us this every day.

I was diagnosed with cancer about twenty-one years into Aikido. I couldn't fathom it. I'd lived healthfully up to that point. Long story short, I had a tumor removed. Then the doctors said they needed to do more to be safe. What they had in mind would mean irreversible changes in my life.

A completely different life.

After very serious consideration, with equal parts rage, disbelief, and profound sadness, accompanied by all kinds of very real, very horrid psychological crises, I sank into a deep, lonely, and dark place. Through this maelstrom, the doctors continued to recommend cutting out part of my body and subjecting me to all kinds of radiation and chemotherapy. I'm quite analytical. I did my own research and got at least three external independent opinions. All agreed that "cut and burn" was a reasonable course of action. All except me, that is.

Something simply did not feel right about this. I questioned myself: "Am I in denial?" I knew I was. I questioned my sanity on numerous occasions. Weeks were ticking by. Time is never on your side with cancer. So, I asked myself, "How do you feel? What is the body saying?" Finally, something inside me was talking. It said, "We've taken a few hits, we're down, but we're not out. This might be a big, long scrap, but we're up for it."

Against the opinions of all the doctors and caregivers I spoke with, and despite the concern of many who were rooting for me, I chose a different path, declining the recommended surgery and therapies. This is a path not many live to talk about. But happily, I am still clear of all cancer three years later.

If I hadn't sat with this specter and myself, questioning my intent and this new reality, I'd most likely have followed the logic of Western medicine. Things would have been very different.

I did a lot of work to get here, but I doubt I'd have chosen this particular path toward health without Sensei's guidance about the intelligence of the body over the years. Don't get me wrong. If I had felt like my body was saying things were bad, I'd have listened and taken a different tack. My point is, listen to your unique body. It talks. It's talking all the time.

Thanks, Nadeau Shihan.

## Being Squared Away

In diagram 11, Nadeau Sensei integrates multiple themes, showing a Centered person standing in the "here and now," sensitive to the universal Energies that encircle their Center, harmoniously balanced between Awareness above and Experience below. Such a person can do extraordinary things they might not think they are capable of until their Experience gives them confidence. He calls this being Squared Away.

In a true story of small miracles, one of Nadeau Sensei's student's students was a single mother raising an autistic child. One day, she was having trouble calming her child who was having a meltdown. She tried doing some of the crisis-management techniques recommended by her son's physician, but they were not helping. At a loss on how to help her child who was in such distress, she tried using her Aikido training to Open and Settle herself. Her body began to relax. Her breath slowed and she felt the ground beneath her. Next she did

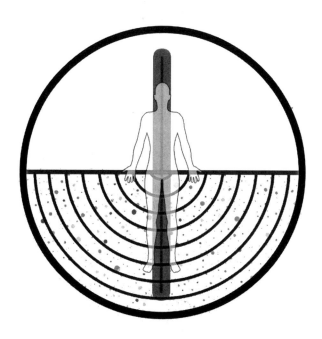

Diagram 11. Being Squared Away.

some Center Circle practice and began to sense a calmer, more peaceful space around her. She allowed this feeling to deepen and felt herself soaking in the experience of the encircling space. Her screaming child quieted himself and began to visibly calm down in front of her eyes. She stayed Present with her son and the storm passed.

Nadeau Sensei likes this story as an example of living and breathing Aikido in the moment, following an inner process to Remix one's Character with finer Energies when faced with a genuinely challenging personal Situation in real life. For him, this is the epitome of being truly Squared Away.

## ◎△ A Map for Understanding △◎

DENISE BARRY
Aikido 6th Dan
Founder, Director, Dimensional Guide
Aiki Consciousness Institute

Nadeau Sensei has a deep interest in psychology and how it influences our ability to live harmoniously with universal energies. He has always been adamant that the practice of Aikido is meant for personal development. This emphasis allows us to better examine ourselves and learn how to function under the pressures of daily life. Sensei has developed a profoundly influential dimensional process for working with universal energies. He is not teaching us how to be better martial artists so much as he is teaching us how to be the kind of people who can help fulfill Osensei's vision of making the world a beautiful and peaceful place.

I first met Nadeau Sensei when I was a junior in high school during a workshop on Aikido principles led by a couple of his students. I became Nadeau's student that day, although I would not meet him in person for another year. The main emphasis of the workshop was connection. We began by being guided into a simple yet profound level of embodiment. Next, we practiced aligning with ourselves and the Universe. I felt whole by the end of the day and immediately knew that pursuing mastery on this Aiki path would be my life's work.

In addition to dimensional practices, I met my *hara* (lower abdomen source of *ki*/heart/mind) for the first time. I could see it through my mind's eye, perceive its location in my body, and feel its empowering qualities of peace, calm, and clarity. We began exploring partner practices from a place of embodiment and centering. Staying centered while exchanging energy with others is one of our ultimate challenges. This is where we learn about blending and harmonizing with energies outside of ourselves while staying connected to the energies moving within. As a sixteen-year-old, I was struggling with many things. The experience I had that day was life changing. It was an immense relief to feel myself in such a complete way. The tangible connection I felt to the world was an experience I will never forget. Inner/outer alignment continues to be the lifeblood of my daily practice.

I have had the opportunity to study with many different Aikido teachers. Several of these teachers studied directly under Osensei and each had come away with a particular perspective on his teachings. While everything I learned from these instructors helped to weave the fibers of my Aiki tapestry, it was Nadeau Sensei's teachings that were the blueprint for my life and my practice.

Nadeau Sensei would spend long periods exploring different qualities and principles and the process for accessing and embodying them. He gave us time to explore the process ourselves in solo practices and then, of course, with the mirroring we received from our training partners. He always included some psychological references in these lessons.

Because there was an ongoing emphasis on using our practice to navigate the pressures of daily life, Sensei would often speak about the impact of being overwhelmed by too much energy hitting our systems. This is where he would help us explore how a psychological misunderstanding might need to be addressed before we could effectively harmonize with the energies that Sensei calls "allies."

The first major teaching I can remember from Nadeau Sensei was about the dimensional aspects of "ground." He taught us a process to use grounding as a tool for transcending fear. We learned to direct our attention downward to our feet and notice how they felt on the mat. Feet in relationship to the earth is a first basic. Sensei guided us well beyond that basic connection to discover what happens internally as we descend into the different layers of the earth. I learned that I could get underneath my fear. Somehow, my fear disappeared when I allowed my consciousness to go deep enough into the earth.

I have come to love being grounded! It is my go-to place. Nothing happens without first establishing some ground. The higher the stakes, the deeper the grounding. The greater the fear, the deeper the grounding. A difficult situation or training partner, the deeper the grounding. This gives me additional options in response to pressure, not by pushing back but by going deeper into the dimensional world of ground. An energetic intelligence emerges far greater than my own in this deeper place.

Another lesson that affected me profoundly was that of "sizing." Nadeau Sensei used many examples to illustrate what happens when too much energy tries to move through too small a space. He emphasized that we cannot control how much energy the Universe gives us. The only thing we can manage is our sizing.

We learned how to recognize our sizing in a variety of ways. One way was through a practice Nadeau called "bad day, fair day, good day, great day." Who we are on a bad day can be very different from who we are on a great day. This practice is so immediate and decisive that I began to offer it to my beginning students. I was stunned to see students with just three months of training go from confusion and disorientation to impeccable technique when they did it from their "great day" place. I have always enjoyed training with Nadeau Sensei's newer students as they first learn that feeling and allowing the wisdom of the system to prevail is more important than getting the technique right.

Another way to practice sizing is through "naming." Sensei is famous for his descriptions of himself as "Little Bobby." He always said that trying to teach Little Bobby anything was useless because Little Bobby would never improve. So, rather than trying to improve our smallest self, we should go dimensionally to our better self and see how we can function at a finer level.

Nadeau Sensei tied this naming practice to Osensei's habit of referring to himself by different names in different situations. Sometimes he was "this old man," "Mr. Ueshiba," "Osensei," or "Ueshiba of the Universe." As Nadeau Sensei pointed out, these names implied dimensional locations. The capabilities of "this old man" were different from those of "Ueshiba of the Universe." "This old man" did not experience himself as embodying the Universe, but "Ueshiba of the Universe" did. According to Nadeau Sensei, this is partly why Osensei took so much time with his personal inner process. He went through a process to be in his chosen dimensional locations. He didn't just magically become one with the Universe. Instead, he prepared himself methodically to have stability while navigating the dimensional realms.

Being "squared away" is also something Nadeau Sensei has emphasized. Of all of his teachings, this one has become particularly useful for me. Because Sensei teaches everything as a process, being "squared away" is a dynamic hybrid of assessing and adjusting. We need to sense the quality of our stability at any given level and make appropriate adjustments. When one enters a new level of development, shakiness and uncertainty can appear. Rather than fighting or resisting this feeling, Sensei encourages us to "allow" the system's intelligence to make adjustments along the way, which provides us the space, the ground, and the presence we need to embody our power with balance and dignity.

I feel Nadeau Sensei has given us a beautifully clear map for understanding and working with the human and universal intelligences that exist in all of us. When these deeply intelligent systems function harmoniously, peace within us and a peaceful world around us are manifested. My gratitude for Nadeau Sensei's abundant generosity and patience as a teacher and friend knows no bounds.

# Potted Plant Theory

To describe the growth and development of character, Nadeau Sensei sometimes refers to his Potted Plant Theory, where an individual, specifically the individual's character, is analogous to a living plant. Plants

Nadeau explaining his Potted Plant Theory in the virtual dojo, 2021.

are relatively simple systems with three essential components: leaves, stems, and roots. The roots may be unseen, but they anchor the plant as they draw power from the soil below. Roots are also essential for absorbing nutrients from the Earth—minerals and water—that the plant needs for healthy growth. In gardens, as in life, pots (Situations) can come in all shapes and sizes. Wide varieties of plants (Characters) can grow and thrive in pots as long as they can fully draw nutrients (Energies) from the soil (Underworld) they are rooted in.

He uses the Potted Plant Theory to help students acknowledge the parts of their Characters that are, by nature, rooted in the hidden Underworld but still integral to who they are. Whatever Character they embody to fit a given Situation, that Character will naturally function more fully if it is well rooted and able to draw Energizing Experience from the Situation.

Sensei will often encourage students in an Aikido class to be more rooted and grounded in order to establish a better base for enhancing their *waza* (techniques). Similarly, he would say, a golfer needs a stable, well-rooted stance from which to generate a smooth stroke of just the right power to navigate to the next hole.

As every gardener knows, sometimes a plant's roots outgrow its pot. The plant needs to be shifted to a bigger pot or put in the earth so its growth is not stunted. Similarly, a person might come to feel they have outgrown their current Situation and need a change in circumstances and more space to allow their true nature to express itself more fully. When this happens, Sensei urges students to trust their instincts and trade in their old Situation (the too-small pot) for something that will support and nurture their continued development in a healthy way.

One of Nadeau Sensei's students tells the story of how he was once living in a small town in western New York, with a good job at a major company. His family was well settled because his wife's relatives also lived in the area. Then he got an attractive job offer that would require moving to Northern California. He was very interested in going to California but was having a difficult time making the decision to stay or move. He talked with Sensei on the phone, who suggested he visualize himself as two potted plants: one plant staying put in New York and the other moving to California. The visualization practice revealed to the student that moving was an important opportunity for further growth, so he took the new job. Shortly after moving to California, the corporate office in New York where he had been working was closed and his wife's relatives all moved to Florida. So he was very glad to have transplanted his family when he did, on all levels!

## Original Self, Space, and the Design of Creation

All of the developmental processes described in these pages can help bring us closer to experiencing our true nature, who we really are. Reflecting Osensei's teachings, Nadeau Sensei calls this our Original Self, who we were before we were born. Some call this our soul. He declines to define it, explaining there is no way to adequately describe Original Self with words. Language cannot fully convey, and the mind cannot fully understand, the essence of Original Self. By nature, it remains hidden to these normal tools of human intelligence. It only reveals itself through direct Experience. We can sense it, feel it, Experience its Energies. But we can't think our way to it.

Sensei teaches that Original Self is the less obvious supporting partner underlying Character. They each have their distinct natures, coexisting within us all. In practice, Character and Original Self both energetically influence developments in the Manifest, Hidden, and Divine Dimensions.

Character is the one who functions in Situations. Original Self enlivens the Character with a vibrant glow that emanates from within.

"I" can express various Characters depending on the Situation. Original Self is constant.

One role of the Original Self is to give vitality, support, and direction to the Character of the moment. One role of the Character is to allow the fullest possible expression of the Original Self.

Practices like Easy the I, Open and Settle, and Clearing are designed to engender in each of us an expanded sense of inner Space, a bit more inner room that allows the distinct Energy fields of Character and Original Self to reveal themselves more fully. Conversely, when there is more Space, practicing Easy the I, Open and Settle, and Clearing is going to be easier.

For Sensei, Space is not a matter of bigger physical dimensions but of a finer Energetic Dimensionality. It is not empty, vacant of qualities. Space itself has its own distinct Energies, alive with the dynamics of a given Situation. Sensei stresses the importance of patiently allowing Space to reveal itself because it has qualities that are subtle and take some time to fully emerge.

According to Sensei, Space is like a stadium, architecture that provides a capacious enough environment for a sports match to occur but doesn't predetermine which of many possible sports are to be played on a given day, or the outcome of a particular match.

Generally speaking, he says, more Energies can show more easily in more Space. For example, a particular expression of the Two Beats of Creation might become more apparent. Or an archetypal figure might reveal itself. Or a 1x1 Character might transition to a 2x2 and then a 3x3

Spiral Galaxy.

version of itself. Space has innate intelligence that will unfold in its own time if "I" can rest easy and not interfere by thinking too hard about Space as a concept. Space is an inviting presence that can only be directly Experienced. Its nature is not something that can be cognitively understood. It is enough to be Present in Space, fully allowing whatever you Experience, without preconception or expectation.

Sensei uses the term Design of Creation to describe the organic structure of the Universe, the self-organizing shapes and intrinsic relationships, the underlying forces and principles that operate according to what he calls "the universal laws of nature."

The Design of Creation functions naturally, inevitably, everywhere, all the time. Practicing in harmony with these principles guides us on the path of authentic spiritual growth.

For Sensei, the Design of Creation is expressed in constructs like the Two Beats of Creation, or Center Circle, described earlier in these pages. He also points to the Vortex of Creation spiraling ever inward from the ethereal Energies of the Divine and Hidden Dimensions to create the denser physicality of Manifest reality, and spiraling ever outward toward the Original Source of Creation. He recalls Osensei describing how the inwardly and outwardly spiraling forces of Creation echo each other.

## △ *Deep Dive into Universal Consciousness* △

VINCE SALVATORE
Aikido 6th Dan
Chief Instructor, Aikido of Reno
Author: Fight Flight Flow

Doing Aikido with Nadeau Sensei always feels like you are doing a deep dive into universal consciousness. His work always deals with the alchemical Way of Aikido and how it applies to the larger realms of life outside of the dojo.

I've had many discussions, practices, and trainings with Nadeau Sensei, and he never fails to open me up to new ways of being, so that my Aikido is ever moving forward, going in the direction of expansion. His focus transcends the basic idea of physical training and goes into territories of spiritual growth well beyond Aikido rank and basic practices.

## ⬡ *Best Decision I Ever Made* ⬡

### AIMEE BERNSTEIN
Executive Life Coach, Organizational Consultant, Trainer
Author: *Stress Less Achieve More*

When I was twenty-three, I lived on Formentera, a small Spanish island in the Mediterranean. There I met an astrologer and psychic who told me that when I was twenty-eight, I would begin studying with a master teacher who would change my life. I thanked him for his prediction and immediately stowed it away in the shadows of my mind, where his message was forgotten.

Five years later, I was at a martial arts festival in San Francisco. It was the end of the day, and participants stood in a circle holding hands and *om*-ing. Then, a door opened across the room, and in walked Robert Nadeau, who joined the circle next to me and held my left hand.

I had been introduced to Nadeau a couple of years earlier by friends who were training with him. As a consultant to Marin County Juvenile Probation Services I had hired him to make a presentation to probation officers, but never chose to train Aikido with him myself. The idea of having my body thrown across a mat didn't appeal to me.

I had a B.A. in music and had sung semi-professionally, so my attention was immediately captured when Nadeau began to chant *om*. To my surprise, it seemed as if the sound was coming from below the ground. The next thing I knew, I was standing under the ground, not physically, of course, but energetically. When the sound stopped, I told myself that I had imagined it. Then Nadeau began to sound again, and once more, I sensed myself under the ground. This time I became annoyed. "I'm from the Bronx," I told myself. "I don't buy this stuff." But when it occurred a third time, I admitted to myself that I had experienced something I couldn't explain. "This man knows something important that I don't," I realized. And that's when I made the decision to train with him and find out what that was.

My first life lesson happened the night I was being taught to do a forward roll. I was instructed by an advanced student to practice rolling on the empty mat, which was closest to the office window at the Turk Street dojo. I felt awkward and self-conscious in my attempt to manifest a smooth, effortless roll. And then, with my arm on the mat and my butt in the air, I spotted Bob at the office window smoking a cigarette and looking amused as he watched my disjointed efforts. At first, I was appalled and ashamed. Then I realized that, of course, I didn't know how to roll. I was a beginner! At the moment I let go of my self-consciousness, Bob snubbed out his cigarette and moments later returned to the practice hall. I learned that night that if I was serious about learning, I needed to leave my ego at the door.

Nadeau's prowess as an Aikido master proved to be extraordinary. But what surprised me even more was his exceptional ability as a teacher. His use of simple metaphors, such as *water hose* as we practiced *ki* (vital energy) extension, generated a heightened level of experience. And his use of settle to shift from the thinking mind to a grounded presence has been a lifeline for many of us in challenging times.

As an extraordinary teacher, Nadeau doesn't have a one-style-fits-all teaching approach. Instead, he senses how each student needs to be taught and skillfully blends with it. For example, one night he called Bob Noha, one of his longest-practicing students, to the center of the mat. Noha was told to raise his fists and no matter what, freeze. Then Nadeau proceeded to throw punches at him. As Nadeau expected, Noha unfroze and lifted his arms to protect himself. Then Nadeau called me up to demonstrate and gave me the same instructions—raise your fists and freeze. With heart pounding,

I waited for the punches. Instead, Nadeau walked around me and began nibbling on my ear. Immediately I unfroze and turned my head toward him. Bob knew that whereas Noha, the skilled martial artist, would respond to punches, aggression would close me down. However, if he were gentle and caring toward me, I would be open to receiving his teaching. And for over forty years now, he has remained so.

As a lifelong helper and fixer, my energetic habit has been to focus my attention on what other people think, feel, need, and want. Nadeau's practices taught me to bring my attention back inside me and allow my energy to center/ground. With training, I learned to extend my *ki*, dialogue with energy, and blend with its flow. And thus, an upgraded version of me emerged that ran deeper and was more effortlessly powerful. By the time I was forty, I could skillfully apply these principles to my coaching, consulting, and training work with executives. I credit Bob for much of my corporate success.

However, the greatest gift I received in training with Bob was experiencing that I am not only a physical being. I am an energy being living in an energy world. While the Aikido and energy practices developed this knowledge, it was Bob's ability to shift into a finer dimension and take his student with him that deeply confirmed it for me.

For example, one evening, Bob called me up to *uke* for him and he threw me in a *sutemi-waza* (sacrifice technique). As I flew through the air, time slowed, and I sensed a circular energy field around me. As I landed, the energy ball hit the ground first, then came up and escorted my body gently down to the mat. When I stood up, Bob looked deeply into my eyes, and I sensed that he knew I had experienced a dimensional shift.

Over the years, Bob has provided guidance in meditating, pointed out my misunderstandings, provided encouragement, and urged me, even when I experienced a WOW, to be easy with it and go deeper into my inquiry. After forty years, I thought I had received all the gifts he had to give me. How wrong I was.

When the COVID-19 pandemic hit, and dojos closed, Bob began teaching online. Now his focus is on the Self, which is our essence. Unlike most spiritual teachers who teach spiritual truths that their students can discuss but often are not ready to experience, Bob teaches us to experience the emergence of a finer Self by going "inch by inch." Now, as my focus turns toward my essence, the Self, my identity begins to shift. In my dreams, meditations, and waking state, I receive downloads from my Self that are supported by my experience. I sense I am functioning more often from a finer version of me. And in my initial foray into the domain of the Self, I experience its largeness and brilliant, beautiful colors. I recognize that who I am is so much greater than who I have known myself to be.

Compelled by this internal shift, I have begun to offer a virtual training series to help others evolve. The training blends my self-awareness work with Bob's experiential teachings. Participants find great value in the series, and Bob is supportive of it. I am over-the-moon happy teaching this work as I sense it is a greater manifestation of my Soul's purpose in this life and that, in a small way, I am contributing to making the world a better place.

Then yesterday, Bob called and reminded me that my number one purpose in this life is for my *Self*, which exists on numerous dimensions, to return to its origin—the *Original Self*. He told me that because I came in with love, much of my life has been dedicated to caring for others and helping them grow. He told me that the aim of learning in this life is to experience a deeper power. Once again, he awakens me and guides me along my inner journey.

When the call ended, I was left with deep heartfelt gratitude to my Sensei and friend. I don't know who I am becoming. But I know that choosing to train with Bob was the best decision I ever made.

## Four Major Expressions of Universal Creativity

According to Nadeau Sensei, Character, Original Self, Space, and the Design of Creation are four major expressions coming forth from the Original Source of Creation that vitalizes and connects all living beings, underpinned by what Osensei called Universal *Ki*.

These four aspects have distinct energy patterns but are profoundly and harmoniously interwoven.

Character has its own energy field. Original Self has its own energy field. When Character and Original Self align, their respective energy fields blend, merge, and unify into a "oneness," expanding the sense of inner Space within which the Design of Creation can show.

More Space allows Character and Original Self to align themselves, as long as "I" doesn't interfere by insisting that it knows better, needs to control, or wants to stubbornly hold on to its current Character, oriented as it has always been.

Aligning with the Design of Creation allows Character, Original Self, and Space to be more fully experienced. As this journey progresses, the fuller dimensions of these four major expressions reveal themselves more and more.

Many of the training practices described here are intended to refine our Character's adaptability beyond the habitual limitations of our tight, controlling "I" so that we can more fully sense the Energy in every Situation without losing our Center, cultivate a healthy balance between Awareness and Experience, and in the process discover our own ways to harmonize the Two Beats of Creation within us all. In the process, our Character can begin to sense the next Dimensions of Energy, leading to further opening of inner Space within which Character and Original Self can come into better alignment. They "want" to align and will do so naturally if freely allowed to express themselves. Easy the I practice can help!

When this happens, Sensei encourages students to enjoy their newfound sense of balance and the feelings of harmony and calm that may accompany it. He tells them to play with it, appreciate it, and reflect on it. But don't stop here, he urges. There is more!

He teaches that these are just stepping stones along the path of personal development. They help us allow more inner Space to emerge, opening a subtle energetic portal within us, a gateway to the next dimensional Space. He encourages students to metaphorically step through the portal courageously and without hesitation. And he tells them to not be surprised if they notice a sensation of additional Energy previously hidden and inaccessible. They should welcome these fresh Energy. They should do their best to sense the fullness and depth of their Experience of this Energy. It is vital in such moments to keep breathing. Continue to Open and Settle. Allow what Nadeau Sensei calls "the more of Creation" to unfold.

## △ *Compelling Movement* △

ELAINE YODER
Aikido 6th Dan
City Aikido of San Francisco, Two Rock Aikido
Feldenkrais Practitioner, Feldenkrais Assistant Trainer
California Aikido Association President, 2023–2026

When I was about five years old, my parents piled us into our old Chevy wagon to see an art show at the de Young Museum in San Francisco. I remember entering a room that was busy with people moving along a series of artworks on the walls, hovering in front of each for a while and then moving on to the next one. No one seemed to be aware of me, a child, likely too small and too young to "see" what was hanging on the walls.

As I approached, I found the artworks to be long paper hangings rather than rectangular paintings. The perception of height and depth in the strokes of ink swept me away into a world of high cliffs and waterfalls. There was usually a tiny man somewhere on a precipice, often with a little shrine nearby, their smallness enhancing the vast space of the painting. And always there was the pull of movement upward toward the clouds and emptiness above. I was so small that no one cared if I stood right in front of each scroll. My short stature was perfect for viewing the images from below, looking upward.

I felt like I woke up, even lit up, while looking at these inviting and gorgeous scrolls. Each one seemed to hold a mysterious and compelling world. I could have stayed in that room forever, rooted in place and swept away at the same time, gleefully following the flow of ink toward the point of interest in each painting: a man, a tree, a shrine. The switch from large focus to tiny, from detail and then back to spaciousness, left me feeling porous and light. I didn't want to leave, ever.

Need you wonder why some of us so avidly continue to train in Aikido?

I found the art in 1977 at a conference of New Age sports that included Inner Tennis, t'ai chi, and many other forms. Aikido seemed particularly interesting. I liked the partner practice right away, and the feeling of the movement. Richard Strozzi-Heckler, Wendy Palmer, and George Leonard were the three Aikido presenters at the conference. They were also the dojo-cho (dojo heads) at Aikido of Tamalpais, which was close to my home. I joined. The people were welcoming, even playful, and seemed accepting of my initial disorientation. I came to Aikido from a background of dance, running, and scuba diving, and I was used to picking up on movement patterns fairly easily. This time, though, I felt like I was learning a completely new language. Gradually, the careful and creative teaching of grounding, centering, and sensing a flow of *ki* began to make sense internally. I couldn't get enough and trained almost every day.

Nadeau Sensei was invited to teach at the Tamalpais dojo fairly regularly. I felt his teaching included something of what I had first experienced while looking at those art scrolls as a five-year-old. There seemed to be movement that traveled around and through all of him. The room felt animated, both by his teaching presence and by the participation of the rest of us on the mat.

I grew up without the expectation that anyone would be able to explain, or guide me back to, my elusive young experience at the museum. There was no place for those feelings in my life, except for a few experiences while running or swimming when I felt porous and joyful once again. Eventually, I joined a group of students from the Mill Valley dojo who drove to San Francisco to train with Nadeau Sensei, which was the beginning of my long study with him. And thanks to his training, Aikido has become my base for the formation of a landscape of transitions toward experiencing the vastness of the universe and its grounding in each of us.

Nadeau Sensei has spent most of his life working to make the experience of "more" available to each of us. Rather than being told to take it down a notch, when I train with Nadeau I am finally in an environment where "More, please" is said every day. His processes, maps, diagrams, and insistence that we clarify, witness, and name these levels of experience have made Osensei's Aikido more real, for me and for many others.

Many people have written about what it was like to take *ukemi* during a class with Nadeau Sensei. A few of us were fortunate to become his preferred attackers because we were willing enough and brave enough to inhabit that role. We got to enjoy the freedom, the air, and the unknown, beckoning again and again. I initially found taking *ukemi* to be a more accessible doorway than being *nage* (throwing partner). *Ukemi* compelled me to move, to learn how to step up, to stay present, and to develop a relationship with myself as a grounded listening presence.

Aikido became my home base, the first place I found where a teacher was generous enough to guide us students to experience our potential. Nadeau Sensei has continued to refine and clarify his teachings, and continues to ask for the same rigorous study from each of us. My life is vastly richer because of his teaching.

# Do the Aikido that Cannot Be Seen with the Human Eye

When Osensei spoke about Aikido as an art of transformation, he naturally used Japanese vocabulary with richly nuanced meanings in the traditional arts of Japan, like *kokoro* (heart/mind), *shugyo* (personal development), and *misogi* (inner purification). His explanations were often very esoteric, his themes universal. He described Aikido as an expression of the workings of Shinto *kami* (deities) and mystical *kototama* (word spirit) vibrations. Other times, he explained Aikido as *takemusu aiki*, the spontaneous actualization of the harmony of the universe, a kind of transformational alchemy. He drew on his own training in multiple Japanese martial arts, as well as Shinto (especially Omoto-kyo), Buddhism (especially Shingon), the syncretic Shugendo religion, and other shamanistic traditions of Japan.

He memorialized many of his key concepts in calligraphies of various sizes. As the noted author and translator John Stevens wrote in *The Essence of Aikido*:

> In East Asia, the calligraphy of a master teacher is always revered, for it is felt that the brushstrokes are a direct expression of the master's spirit. Long after a master such as Morihei is gone his calligraphy is thought to retain his physical presence, and his brushwork continues to inspire each new generation of Aikido students. The content of the calligraphy is also important, since the master reveals what he deems most essential by the themes he selects.[1]

Nadeau has always prominently displayed, in his dojo and in his home, a large calligraphy that he received from Osensei. It reads "*katsuhayabi*" and is composed of three Japanese characters: *katsu* (victory), *haya* (fast/quick), and *bi* (sun/day).

The meaning of *katsuhayabi* is obscure, deeply rooted in Osensei's vision of human nature, personal development, and the workings of the

Universe. It has been translated as "day of swift victory." It has alternately been described by senior Japanese teachers who studied directly under Osensei as "the speed that transcends time and space" (*jikan kukan koeru hayasa*). Others have stated *katsuhayabi* is "the eternal victory which goes beyond time and space."

These same three characters are the concluding triplet of one of Osensei's most famous Aikido mottos: *masakatsu agatsu katsuhayabi* (literally, "true victory / self victory / victory swift day"). The full motto, which Osensei reproduced with brush and ink on many occasions, is itself a reference to a Shinto deity named *Masakatsu agatsu katsuhayabi ame no oshihomi no kami*, who appears in the eighth-century Japanese *Kojiki* (Record of Ancient Matters), which Osensei was known to study. He once described its esoteric meaning this way, as translated in *The Essence of Aikido*:

> *Masakatsu* represents the masculine fire element of the left; *Agatsu* stands for the feminine element of the right; *Katsuhayabi* is the perfect combination of both that empowers the techniques. If the techniques are true like this, victory will be directly at hand.[2]

Katsuhayabi, written left to right, signed and sealed as Aiki Morihei.

When Nadeau received this personal calligraphy from Osensei's hands, he asked the meaning of the characters and why he was being given this particular gift. Osensei did not lecture him about the phrase's Shinto antecedents. He did not attempt to translate *katsuhayabi*. He simply told the young Nadeau that it was meant to exhort him to "do the Aikido that cannot be seen with the human eye." In many ways, this became Nadeau's bestowed mission, an aspirational goal for his own personal practice, which continues to this day, and a defining theme that motivates and underlies all that he teaches.

##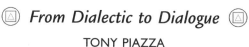

TONY PIAZZA

Mediator

Grateful Student of Robert Nadeau

Training with Nadeau Sensei provided the foundation for my Mediated Negotiations practice, and this, in turn, has enabled the resolution of thousands of complex civil disputes without large-scale, disruptive, and expensive courtroom battles.

In the words of a Sufi poet:

> *Awakening from this dream of separation*
> *I find I have misplaced my most precious fears.*
> *Reaching for them, I touch your smile in my heart*
> *   instead.*
> *Some boundary has been passed, and it is no longer*
> *   spacious enough to collide.*

Bob Nadeau taught me that in the absence of reactivity, the operative force is cohesion.

Criticism of Aikido in the past has been the lack of practical demonstration through the traditional martial arts metric of competition and contests (such as mixed martial arts matches).

That perspective, of course, misses the point: as soon as one agrees to participate in a fight—even a ritualized fight like a contest—an art like Aikido, predicated on *ai* (harmony), is severed from its base.

How else, then, can it be demonstrated that Aikido is not only real, but an accurate reflection of fundamental physics?

The gold standard for empirical evaluation of the validity of a theory—or the efficacy of a medication—is replicable testing over an extended duration, preferably with a large subject base.

We now have empirical data that Aikido works. I can point to a forty-three-year study with more than four thousand tests (and upward of forty thousand participants). And the results are conclusive.

When you structure a process so as to redirect energy from a dialectical relationship (opposing parties with conflicting positions) to a dialogue (where each of the opposing parties and a third-party come from a place of *ai*), the outcome dramatically changes toward resolution—exactly as Osensei perceived.

In my life, eight or nine times out of ten, year after year, courtroom battles that had been raging for as long as a decade, in which investments in each fight ranged up to more than $100 million per dispute, have been resolved peacefully (if not always entirely amicably) through this process of applying Aikido off the mat in real-world conflicts.

## 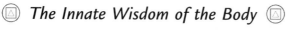 *The Innate Wisdom of the Body*

**WAYNE ROTH**
Aikido 3rd Dan
Longtime Student of Nadeau Sensei

Osensei gave Nadeau Sensei a scroll that roughly translates: "Do the Aikido that cannot be seen with the human eye." What does that mean? How do you teach that? Nadeau Sensei has focused on such questions for more than half a century.

I will try to describe my experience in one of Nadeau Sensei's classes, circa 2002.

After leading the group bow-in to the *shomen* (ceremonial front of a dojo) and turning to bow to the class, Sensei does not immediately start a series of exercises or techniques. He stays seated in *seiza* (formal seated posture on the floor) for some moments. We sit waiting, wondering. He slowly rises to a high kneel and begins the class with a practice of settling from high kneel back into *seiza*. Sensei talks about how sitting practice, because of its quietness, is an excellent way to explore subtle currents in the body. The body has its own feelings, its own understanding and experience. It often doesn't get a chance to feel itself during activity; it's too busy. We break after a moment, and then practice the same approach a number of times. Each time my body feels different: a little deeper, a little straighter, calmer, oddly bigger.

We stand in *hanmi* (triangular stance) and practice a simple arm extension. "Let the arm feel itself," Sensei says. He wants us to let ourselves discover our other half—"the body," "the system," or "the unit" as he calls it—so we will begin to let go of the sense of ownership and control of our bodies. He wants to free us from translating every "body" experience into an "I" understanding. "Let this system find its own way to do this stance. Let the body feel itself," he continues.

His way of presenting this simple exercise seems almost bizarre. It is so different from how classes are usually taught—from how we think our world works—that students are initially confused, lost. "Let the body feel itself?" What the hell does that mean? Don't we practice so "I" can perfect "my" body, so it will be a great tool for me?

Nadeau Sensei feels the "I's" ownership of the "body" is a critical misunderstanding that limits our perception. Yes, that's the obvious reality, but Sensei is interested in the not-so-obvious. "Do the Aikido that cannot be seen with the human eye," Osensei's scroll said. Maybe if we can find a way outside the obvious, we will discover something extraordinary, another dimension. Sensei trusts in an innate intelligence of the body system, an intelligence that is seldom given a chance to express itself. Sensei's "job," our "job," is to let go of our control so the body/system can feel and learn about itself. But if "I" let go of control, how am "I" going to learn anything?

Aikido class is turning into a moving Zen *koan*. This is frustrating for students who came to learn a martial art. Is all this philosophical-sounding bullshit worth it? But once you watch Nadeau Sensei move, you see that he walks his talk. His Aikido is mesmerizing. As his *uke* attacks, Sensei moves like wind and water, yet still grounded like a boulder. There is no effort, no work, no struggle, no separation, no conflict. And when his *uke* flies away or crashes to the mat, they come up glowing, smiling, as if they had just received a wonderful gift. "Wow! I want to learn to do that," I mutter to myself, not recognizing I've translated what Sensei is teaching back to "I" learning it. Our language traps us, keeps us away from what he wants us to learn.

While teaching, Sensei quietly talks to himself. It's an odd conversation. It goes something like, "Ah, this system likes to settle deeper. It likes to be supported. Oh, there's a flow of energy out of my fingers. What's the 'more' of that? Ah, the arm feels surrounded by a glowing, humming tube of energy. Hmmmmm . . . energy is coming from deep under the feet and enlivens this whole system. There's a glow and swivel to its hips. This unit has a straighter back. Oh, it has a front AND a back. Front back, back front, out in. There's a two-beat going through this system. Easy the I." And usually after saying each phrase, Sensei's body system moves on its own again, reaffirming what it has just discovered and feeling even more of that quality.

Deeply wrapped in his own experience, Sensei notices that most of his students are just casually standing and watching him. He is mildly annoyed and wryly says, "Come on people. I'm not a television set. Move. Feel the body. Let the body system feel itself." Like a group of kids on their first field trip to the ocean, we look inwardly over the huge, obvious, and unknown shimmering sea that is ourselves, and tentatively stick a toe in the water.

As the class progresses, Sensei continually asks us about our body experiences. We are hesitant to respond—these waters are so unfamiliar—but with his encouragement, we start to speak up. "I feel like I don't have to work at timing. I just know it," someone says. Sensei could simply respond from his past experiences, his knowledge, but instead his body moves, feels itself and seems to play with this notion, and then he responds, as the body's spokesperson, "Yes, this system, at this level, is so open to *uke* that it just knows right timing. Easy with the 'I' statement. Are you just aware of the body, or was that really the body feeling itself?"

Nadeau Sensei knows what he wants to share is difficult to communicate. He is patient, encouraging, offering guidance, pointing the way. "The system itself is feeling itself, discovering itself." These words are very tricky, precise and vague at the same time because Nadeau is inventing a new language.

We practice a simple *tenkan* (turning blend) movement with a two-hand grab by *uke*. Keeping the hand low with the palm up leads into an open spiraling *kokyu-nage* (breath throw). Sensei continues to ask students what they are discovering as their bodies become more settled, more open. He demonstrates, not the techniques per se, but the two beats that our body systems are exploring, a full flow in one direction followed by an equally full flow in the opposite direction. He talks about the fullness within your own body system, how this unit seems to be fed from under the ground, and the sense/experience that *nage* and *uke* are connected even before *uke* begins to move on the attack.

Suddenly, like an old pinball machine when the ball connects with the bumper and all the bells sound off and all of the lights start flashing, my body has its own knowing, its own connection to *uke*, to flow, to a two-beat, to a solid yet fluid base. The system senses its own power and fullness, its own beauty, caring, and connectedness. I don't have to work it; I just have to be present, open.

A wave surges from deep underground and infuses and lights up every cell in my body. The body system feels like a huge and glowing ball of energy that flows in playful, powerful, circular patterns that effortlessly sweep up my *uke* and deposit her on the mat. This feeling is so strange and satisfying that both of us—my partner has felt it too—smile and giggle.

Laughter is a clear sign we are on the right track. Laughter is the hallmark of surprise, not ownership. Shared laughter is unexpected agreement, not forcing someone to do your bidding. True Aikido is a harmonious blend, so subtle, so powerful that when it happens, both *nage* and *uke* often don't know what happened, or why it worked so effortlessly.

Tonight has been a good night. It's after class, and the magic is slipping away. Still, an inner glow remains. It's a body feeling, a playful hum, not just a thought in my head. "I" am learning how to let go, to allow "the system," to trust it. Functioning from a body system level, unexpected energy doesn't fluster me. I go with the flow rather than push to be first or try to get my way. Being open is a wonderful tool to have.

Studying with Nadeau Sensei is a deep challenge. His process, the way he explores getting inside Aikido, is not a familiar path. He guides us away from our self-imposed limits. He offers a doorway to unforeseen new dimensions, vast and unlimited. This is why Aikido is a lifetime practice, maybe many lifetimes.

## ◬ *Lifelong Dimensionality* ◬

DIANNE HAYNES
Aikido 6th Dan
Rotorua Aikido
**Head Instructor, Tatsu Gi Kai, New Zealand**

I first met Nadeau Shihan at a Riai Aikido *gasshuku* (training retreat) in 1987–88 at Kiwi Ranch in Rotorua, New Zealand. Our local Aikido club lent our mats for the camp. Richard Moon Sensei came with Nadeau Shihan that year. I remember Nadeau Shihan talking about Osensei and thinking, "Wow, he trained under Osensei." His Aikido movement was very energetic, very powerful at that time, and he taught lots of techniques.

I remember him focusing one *gasshuku* on the Māori saying of "*kia kaha*" (used by the people of New Zealand as an affirmation, meaning "stay strong"). Nadeau Shihan searched with us for the true meaning of this saying over the entire three-day retreat. It meant a great deal to me then to be able to explore the depth of *kia kaha* through Aikido since the saying had originally been popularized during World War II by the 28th Māori Battalion from New Zealand as a way to focus the men in battle.

As I have gotten older, I have found Shihan's style of training very helpful to continuing Aikido. He was a role model on the mat for his attention to the details of Aikido beyond mere technique. He has inspired me as a longtime student of Aikido. His training has helped me to continue in this art I love and am so passionate about.

I used to go to *gasshuku* as a younger student, in many ways, to throw and be thrown. But in the end, I was searching for another path, one that would challenge me to dig deeper into Aikido and change my training to better reflect Osensei's teachings of inner power, resoluteness, and inner growth. Essentially to be a "better me." Nadeau Shihan gave me this self-imposed challenge.

It is a work in progress. I think I'm making inroads into these teachings. I am more grounded and settled on the mat and can convey to students the importance of growth in Aikido for each of them. And that it's their journey, not mine.

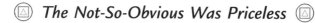

## *The Not-So-Obvious Was Priceless*

CHARLOTTE HATCH
Aikido 5th Dan
Creating Harmony Wherever I Can, Enthusiastically

I can remember my experience with Nadeau Sensei during the first year of my Aikido training. I had studied judo for a few years, so I already knew how to fall and roll a bit. I felt comfortable because I could tell that Sensei cared deeply about his students, both about their progress on the mat and in their lives off the mat. He clearly had a deep commitment to Aikido, and showed it every day in every class.

My judo teachers hadn't talked at all during class. Instead, they showed what to do and let you work it out yourself. When I came into Nadeau's classes, I was struck immediately by how much he talked. Sometimes I felt my head would explode. Were the talks helpful? On a deep level, yes, very. On a more superficial level, they were mystifying. After class, I remember telling people, "He talks, and he's talking English, but I don't understand a word!"

Using Aikido as a metaphor, Nadeau Sensei helped us look beneath the surface of our day-to-day personalities we showed the world. As my partner was coming to attack me, I remember Nadeau saying, "Everyone has depth; everyone has a past, a present, and a future path." I thought he was suggesting that the blend entailed a deep understanding of my path and my partner's. If I had that depth, the resulting throw would be the art of Aikido. I worked on it.

In actuality, I was in way over my head in that class. Sensei would often come around to give me some instruction. Sometimes he would suddenly appear by my side, see what I was doing, and laugh. This laughter was disarming, but I felt a little worried about it at first. After all, I was trying as hard as I could! Obviously, my attempts were ridiculous. Then I realized that Sensei laughing was much better than Sensei crying when he saw my techniques, and I felt better. He seemed like a kindly shepherd, and I was a sheep. At least, that's what I thought, and I realized this was OK.

I appreciate how Nadeau Sensei introduced me to Aikido, showing me the obvious and the not-so-obvious. All of it was a gift, but the not-so-obvious was priceless. Thank you Sensei, for speaking what can't be spoken. I don't know how you learned to do that, but you're a master at it, and I'm so grateful!

## ▲ *Speaking My Language* ▲

PEGGY BERGER
Aikido 5th Dan
Shidoin, Aikido of Columbus
Columbus Center for Movement Studies
Dance/Movement Therapist, Teacher of Authentic Movement
Feldenkrais Practitioner

My history with Bob Nadeau was brief, but his teachings have been long lasting. I trained with Bob in San Francisco from 1977–79, attended a few retreats, and sponsored a few seminars in the 1980s. In my twenties and not at all athletic or embodied, I truly had beginner's mind. What compelled me to train was that

I could see the energy that Bob embodied, and the processes or experiments he created on the mat opened a door inside of me to something that somehow felt familiar, and I wanted more. What I saw and longed to experience (though I had no words for it at the time) was that form arises from formlessness, and that by dropping into myself in a different way, I could do things I didn't know I could do; I could be "more" than my usual ego-experience of myself.

My ex-husband, Paul Linden, introduced me to his teacher, Nadeau Sensei, early in 1977. After the first class, he asked me if I could see what Nadeau Sensei was talking about. I said, "Of course!" I was so excited to see a teacher who spoke my "language," although I didn't know I could speak that language! Paul was amazed because, at that time, Bob's language didn't translate for him, and he spent the next fifty years developing his own method that, he later admitted, must have been what Bob was talking about all along. "Equal and even," "4x4," and all those other evocative phrases wouldn't have made any sense to me if they hadn't been accompanied by the most beautiful movement, the huge shifts in energy. For me, it was like coming home.

After moving to Ohio, I continued to train and teach Aikido for thirty-two years. But, again, I was a stranger in a strange land. Most of my East Coast and Midwest Aikido experience consisted of mimicking external techniques. I was lost and disappointed. I didn't recognize it as the Aikido I'd been introduced to and fallen in love with. But I persisted because I knew that the internal and external would somehow come together. Admittedly, I wasn't very patient. And I was more than a little judgmental!

As I taught, I always returned to my initial experiences of my two years with Nadeau Sensei. As I bowed in and led the class in warm-ups, I would return to the practices I learned from Bob for dropping into that state within myself from which Aikido techniques would arise. Because there were conflicting approaches in our dojo, which gave rise to emotional turmoil and self-doubt in me, I had to teach from this more expanded state. And, of course, some of the students could sense and see my process and begin to do it themselves.

Now, more than forty-five years after first training with Bob, and without the "form" of Aikido in my life currently, I continue to drop into that place of "knowing." I carry Bob's gift inside me when I'm hiking, engaged in a discussion, trying to determine the next step in my life, or cooking. I've used his embodied teachings and my own movement "medicine bag" to heal my relationships with many people, to journey through my own medical issues, to accompany my mother as she died, and to support dear ones when they have life challenges. It is the place from which wisdom, compassion, and peace flow.

What Bob embodied and taught me to embody was, perhaps, the most significant "tool" I've ever received—a process to intentionally shift myself to an inner place of Love, Joy, and Wisdom. For this gift, Bob, I will always be grateful.

## Pivotal Moments in Training

RENÉE GREGORIO
Aikido 3rd Dan
Poet and Writer
Author: *Abyss & Bridge,*
*The Writer Who Inhabits Your Body*

The resonance and reverberations of Nadeau's teaching have been with me since I first set eyes on him in the San Francisco dojo in 1990. At the time, I'd never seen an Aikido class and was immediately struck by the spirit I found there.

I began training in earnest with my first teacher in Taos, then my second in Santa Fe, and loved what I felt and learned on the mat. But something unspoken kept nudging me. I was slowly learning the pins and throws that make up Aikido, but something much more subterranean was always at work in me. Why at times did I feel cracked open like an egg about to be scrambled? Why at other times did I sense myself so full of possibility I could barely recognize myself? I wanted to understand, and no one I trained with seemed to be addressing this unseen, unspoken territory. What was it I was so drawn to if it didn't have a name?

When I eventually attended a summer Aikido retreat in San Rafael, I began to understand. I attended Nadeau's energy sessions most mornings and recall how he asked us to encounter our bodies and the space around them in ways that were totally unfamiliar to me. I remember at first not having the words to describe such an encounter. But the fact that Nadeau asked, and how he asked, let me know that I could settle into myself and explore—and something would arrive. And it did—a kind of knowing that exists within and around each of us, that only needs to be coaxed a bit to come forth. Our bodies hold so much knowing and so much yearning to be more. Nadeau always led me toward that "more."

Another incident at the retreat occurred when I had a hard time executing a throw that involved a sweep of the leg to unbalance my *uke*, something I'd never done before. Someone (certainly not me!) called Nadeau over to help me. The next thing I knew, I was lying flat on the mat, having been shown exactly how to do such a sweep! I'll never forget the feeling of that throw—the clean energy of it—and how I flew up, then down quite quickly, completely unharmed and energized in a way I didn't know possible.

Nadeau made a few trips to teach in Albuquerque in the ensuing years and, when I could, I attended his seminars. Two distinct learnings from those times on the mat with Nadeau have stayed with me for decades. The first was when I could feel him watching me as I attempted to throw my partner. I recall the technique was not complicated, but I had no results. He approached us and let me know that he'd been watching and saw me attempt the throw three times, and each time he was waiting for me to make a shift, but after the third time, he knew it was a "pattern." He asked me to show him again, and when I did, he whacked my bicep, saying at the same time, "You don't need this! I watched you over and over. You must think that you have to work very hard to get anything done in your life!"

At another juncture, he asked me to come up and demonstrate *shiho-nage* (four direction throw). Although pretty scared in those moments, I ended up feeling really good about my openness and energy as I did the technique in front of everyone. Then he broke down my technique and what he'd seen. He spoke of how I began so open and full. I smiled. But then he added that as the technique progressed, I finished it in a way that showed I just wanted to be done with it and that I somehow "threw it all away" at the end. Then Nadeau did the technique, demonstrating an openness throughout the entire technique. Even after its completion, his body was a conduit for the energy it received and then emanated out into the universe. I truly felt his movement and energy within myself, felt the beginning and ending as one, and I was enthralled. Then, as if this weren't enough, Nadeau did *shiho-nage* again. What he said as he attempted to "be me" was: "I am trying to be her, but it is making me very tired."

Something happened deep inside me in those moments as I got to witness my habit of effort in both instances. I felt something collapsing from within. Honestly, at the time, it frightened me. Nadeau walked by and acknowledged that my technique was looking better. But I was just feeling the effects of my internal collapse, coupled with a sense that I was shape-shifting into another self, and I didn't know who she was.

Yet when the seminar ended, I felt much lighter. I knew I couldn't get away with using my biceps anymore without noticing my "effort" pattern. I now knew *in my body* what the habit felt like, and how much energy I'd exerted over and over, no matter the task, by "effort-ing" rather than allowing. I also came away with a deeper curiosity to understand my relationship to completing things. I caught myself using effort in the oddest of places—the one I remember most is cleaning basil to make pesto and noting the strain I was giving the task as I released the leaves from their stems. And thus noticing, I could let go. And what replaced the habit of effort was a new energy, maybe even joy—certainly presence.

The lesson about my relationship to completing things that began on the mat with Nadeau all those years ago is still with me, too. The quality of *zanshin* (sustained energetic connection) that he exhibited that day, even though I couldn't name it then, has entered my blood and bones, seeping in slowly over all these years, taking up residence. Rather than throwing-away, I can stay-with. Rather than giving up, or giving in to my resignation, I can choose to keep extending and directing my energy into relationships or projects.

I might even venture that such giving of energy makes a difference in this world of ours.

Since meeting Nadeau, I've found many ways to continue what began on the mat with him—through further study in somatic work, coaching, teaching, and blending body-centered learning with my love of writing. I owe a lot to those pivotal moments when I learned a new direction from Nadeau Shihan. I am ever grateful.

## ◬ *Getting Closer to the Truth* ◬

DENNIS KYRIAKOS
Aikido 3rd Dan
City Aikido of San Francisco
Professional Magician

About four years into my Aikido training in Nassau County, New York, our dojo hosted a weekend seminar with Nadeau Sensei.

It was perhaps the second time I'd ever participated in a seminar, and Nadeau Sensei's appearance was hyped for weeks. My biggest challenge that weekend was deciphering what he was saying, and trying to keep up. He may as well have been speaking Greek because I couldn't understand him. And I speak Greek!

There was no technical discussion. There was no "put your foot here" or "lift your hand like this." Instead, the movements were vehicles to study energy and how you function in a relationship. That first encounter was like drinking from a fire hose.

In the final few moments of the last class that weekend, we sat as Sensei lectured and attempted to recap his thoughts. I was sitting at the end of the first row of students when he began looking for someone to demonstrate a technique. I perked up, and he invited me up to take *ukemi*.

Sometimes you don't know you're ready for a change until it happens. Then things become clear.

He invited me to grab his shoulders, and just as he was in striking distance, he vanished. It was the most incredible magic trick I had ever experienced. Suddenly he was standing behind me, and I turned to face him again. Then the ground swelled up from behind, and I was swept away.

It was as if someone had turned off gravity for the briefest moment, and I found myself floating in space. Then it felt like someone dropped a house on my chest. I must have blinked because I don't recall hitting the floor.

When I got up to one knee, Sensei stood about ten feet away, and the entire dojo giggled. *What happened? Why are they laughing?*

Then I became aware of the look on my face. *What the fuck was that?*

I was very confused, but he motioned to come again. This time I would pay attention.

*Keep your eyes open. Where does he put his left hand? Where was his right hand? How did he slam you down?*

I moved in and found myself on the ground again. He never put his hands on me.

*W.T.F.*

He thanked us all for joining him and for our attention. Then, almost as an afterthought, he mentioned hosting a yearly summer retreat in San Rafael. I thanked all my partners for the training and sprinted into the office after him. *Uh, how do I sign up for this camp?*

Over the next few years, I would make the trip out west for summer retreats, to spend a week training with Sensei and other teachers I had never known existed.

Eventually, I met the woman who would be my wife while training at New York Aikikai. She was born and raised in Berkeley, and on our visits to see her parents, I'd always sneak away for an evening of training with Nadeau Sensei, followed by after-practice conversation and fine dining (?!) at Max's Opera Café not far from the dojo. In 2012, we moved to the Bay Area and continue to get closer to the truth.

## ⬡ *Taking the Highest of High Falls* ⬡

XAVIER FAYANT
Aikido 3rd Dan
City Aikido of San Francisco
Massage Therapist, Bodyworker

Twenty-eight years ago, I had a motorcycle accident. I was a blue belt at the time. I broke my knee and fractured my thumb. I flew thirty feet in the air over a car and landed in the middle of the road on my back. The knee broke from hitting the roof of the car as I was passing over it! Thanks to my Aikido practice, I landed on the pavement safely, avoiding more serious injury. Clearly, my newly acquired *ukemi* skills kicked in.

I had a brace and crutches for a few weeks. I could not practice Aikido, but I would watch Nadeau Sensei's classes anyway. As soon as I got rid of the crutches, I started training slowly, avoiding rolls and high falls.

One day, I was sitting on the side of the mat, watching Sensei demonstrating high falls. He called me up, and I thought, "You've got to be kidding, I am not ready to take high falls yet!" I kept the thoughts to myself and prayed to the gods he was not going to throw me. He surely knew I was still weak and fragile from the accident, and that in no circumstances was I ready to take a high fall!

Sure enough, there I was standing next to him, surrendering my body and soul to the universe, and BAM, he went for it. For a split second, I was one with the universe; it felt like I must have crossed dimensions or something because I sensed an internal explosion deep inside my guts. Then I was lying on the mat, a big smile on my face, with a feeling of being reborn. Nadeau looked at me, and asked, "You OK?" I felt fine, more than fine. It's as if the throw healed me in an instant. I was no longer afraid. Guess I was ready to resume practice, after all!

## Direct Transmission

Robert Nadeau has invented his own distinctive approach for conveying the Way of Aikido to his students, a direct transmission from his seminal teacher Morihei Ueshiba, inevitably interpreted through the uniqueness of his own being.

The circle in diagram 12 contains some of the main themes and principles of Nadeau Sensei's transformational practices. They are purposefully not laid out in a specific order inside the circle because they are all part of a holistic teaching approach. Many of the themes are interrelated in multiple ways. Sometimes just one or two aspects are presented, sometimes more. Physical training, guided energy processes, dramatic demonstrations, and quiet instruction are all part of the mix.

In any Nadeau class, there is always a rich potential for personal development through better integration of Experience and understand-

Diagram 12. Themes and Principles.

ing. Concepts may be connected to stimulate development. Lessons may be overlaid to provoke embodied insight into the underlying principles of the Universe. There is no fixed sequence, with no beginning—other than to be present—and no end point because, as he says, there is always more to explore in the Universe within.

His message for an Aikido student training diligently in the dojo, or a schoolteacher facing a classroom of eager first-graders, or someone playing a round of golf, is that this is the time to be all you can be, Present in the Situation, Experiencing the here and now as fully as possible. It is not the time for conceptual thought or self-judgment. Afterward, at the proverbial coffee shop, in conversation among friends or in dialogue with your teacher, there will be plenty of time for reflection and assessment.

Nadeau Sensei sometimes describes himself as a maker of maps, a cartographer of inner space, energy flows, and human nature. For over sixty years, he has pointed the way forward for students on a path to fuller vitality as balanced individuals—Open and Settled, Centered, Grounded, and Squared Away, able to live harmoniously and realize their full human potential.

He consistently teaches that words, ideas, and Awareness are good and useful, up to a point, but they are not sufficient for true personal transformation, true Aikido. Words describe concepts, and the concepts can be assembled into a valuable map for the journey of personal development. But ultimately, it is a journey we must each travel in person and Experience firsthand to be truly meaningful.

Nadeau would likely tell anyone reading these paragraphs to take a moment now to be with yourself, to absorb the implications that can carry us beyond words into the knowing that is available only through subjective experience. This "writing about" is unavoidably presented linearly using written language, but the path itself can lead to non-linear transmissions of potentially life-changing Experiences and profound insights about who we are and how the world works. This is a Way of inquiry, practice, and transformation open to all.

## △ *The Universe Is My Teacher* △

JOEL RIGGS
Aikido 3rd Dan
Founder, Aikido Decatur

In 1993, on the first night I met Nadeau Sensei, I sat on the side of the ballroom of the Oak Street YMCA building in San Francisco and watched the class. Midway through class, Sensei came over to say hello and see if I had any questions. I asked, "Osensei died twenty-four years ago; who has been your teacher since then?? He smiled, stepped back, opened his arms wide, and said, "The Universe!"

In 2019, at the yearly Osensei Revisited workshop in Occidental, I asked Nadeau Sensei, "What would you say Osensei's teaching is at its most fundamental level?" He replied, "Body."

It has taken quite a few years for me to really get what he meant.

## △ *Teacher of Direct Experience* △

TOM LEWIS
City Aikido of San Francisco
Founder, Tom Lewis Restoration and Consulting, Inc.

Once or twice in a century, there comes from a deep manifest experience a rare individual whose teaching and practice transform the world. It takes decades to forge, tool, and refine the essence of these rare gifts. The sheer individual will, wisdom, love, compassion, and strength it takes to accept one's calling and share it with the world is one of the greatest tests of valor and sacrifice we know. Their stories and legends inspire us. They give us direction, resolve, and nourish our beings. They help us understand where we truly come from and where we are going. We find purpose and see a path to our full human potential.

One such truly remarkable man was Morihei Ueshiba Osensei, the Founder of Aikido, who forged a new way, a path for us to follow if we so choose.

Generations and decades later, through the careful teachings of those who trained with Osensei himself, we have perspectives into Morihei Ueshiba's creative process. Robert Nadeau is one of Morihei Ueshiba's personal students who breathed the "rare air" and experienced the "spark of creation" directly from Osensei, and in the process himself became an extraordinary Aikido teacher, passing on Osensei's gifts and their potential to change our world.

Language can be the source of illusion, but through careful guidance and nurturing, Nadeau Sensei guides us through the challenges of interpreting that which at times cannot be named in any language. By demonstrating his practice, with clarity and vision, Nadeau guides us to the source of Osensei's teachings. He offers us a window into that "rare air" where we feel our own "spark." He inspires us with his passion and love for Osensei's teachings.

"Experiencing awareness, awareness of experience."

What we think we see can also be the source of illusion. I recall Nadeau's story about Osensei instructing him to "teach the Aikido that is not seen." In my personal experience, this has been the aspect of greatest value, offering the greatest opportunity to improve my practice on the path toward my full potential.

"Easy the I. Easy the I."

I initially decided to do Aikido to fulfill my longtime interest in energy work, connecting with the "other," that could be combined with a physical practice. I decided to go for it at age sixty-two, after my knee replacement. (My only regret is that I didn't start forty years earlier.) Bob Noha Sensei in Petaluma took care to ease me into the practice gently. After a few months, I wanted to practice more frequently, and was told there was a dojo south of Market Street in San Francisco. It was just blocks away from my office, and I could practice there during weekdays. I was also told that it was run by a tough instructor named Nadeau Sensei, and I better be prepared to train hard and get my arse kicked.

I was a bit nervous when I first showed up, but what I found was a teacher who is passionate about what he teaches, cares deeply for his students, and can uncannily recognize what each person has been through that day without asking. It was as if you were getting your own personal lesson while in a group class. I saw a dojo where real friendship, sharing, and learning were happening regardless of rank. I joined a real community and felt a part of something larger.

Aikido has connected me with a global community. Although I traveled the entire globe in my youth searching for truth, I've found that everything I'm looking for is right here in the "immediate adjacent." Everything in the Universe is within reach of the Self within. We can be the Universe because we are in it, and it is in us.

Thank you, Nadeau Sensei!

 *Soul Connection*

SHAWN McCRACKEN
Aikido 4th Dan
Visual Artist, Yogi, Teacher

My time with Robert Nadeau Sensei began when I moved to California in 1995. At the time, I was convinced that something quite magical was at play when he threw me, beyond the obvious technique demonstrated. I figured the mats must be pressure sensitive since I'm not myself capable of leaping ten, fifteen, twenty feet, even with a running start. Yet that's what was happening when Nadeau Sensei turned and touched me with no overt force. Time and again, I'd be astounded at the "airtime" suspended between heaven and earth, so to speak.

Due to COVID-19, on-the-mat practice with Nadeau Sensei was impossible for most of 2020 and 2021. But he continued his efforts to clarify and articulate Osensei's inner Aikido by adapting to the situation and teaching weekly virtual dojo classes via Zoom. When we finally returned to the mat in mid-2021, I could feel in myself how the process of referencing our internal landscape, as opposed to an external achievement-oriented technique or form, had somehow become much clearer after fifteen months of pandemic downtime.

Over the years, Nadeau Sensei has been severe and stern in his instructions to me, on and off the mat. Perhaps it has to do with our history, which seems to transcend this current time and place; call it a soul connection. My appreciation for my teacher runs deep. His generosity of heart never ceases to amaze me. He never gives up on anyone, not even on me. His perseverance and willingness to engage with me personally in my Aikido evolution are truly endearing. His remarks are timely, precisely cutting to the heart of the matter. His suggested adjustments reverberate, which usually result in my acknowledging a deeper sense of

"Core." His encouragement to step up and check out "Next," to play with an entirely different sensibility, has struck a chord and resonates.

I believe the energetic exchange between teacher and student is vastly more subtle and significant if both are open to it. I will always be humbly grateful to Nadeau Sensei for the opportunity to share time and space with him. Namaste!

## ⊿ *Lineage of the Ancient Sword* ⊿

CATHERINE TORNBOM
Aikido 3rd Dan
Founder, Interfuse Associates
Organization Development Consultant and Mediator
Adjunct Professor, University of Arizona,
School of Government and Public Policy

How curious it is for me that a martial art that emerged from feudal Japan into the modern world, for which the sword was considered the ultimate transformational tool, would become my transformational tool.

The will of the gods
permeating body and soul
is *aiki*—polish that sword
and make its brilliance
known throughout this world. (Osensei)

I am enduringly grateful that Nadeau Sensei has made it his life's work to facilitate the manifestation of *aiki* (spiritual harmony), as Osensei brilliantly taught, into our lives as a community, and into every aspect of my life.

Here's my summary of his teachings: there is an inexhaustible source of energy; I am the co-creator with this energy; and the energy expresses through me in an exquisite balance of cognitive awareness, the sense-feel of embodiment, and profound love.

Nadeau Sensei does his part—he offers a myriad of approaches, methods, and techniques. He offers coaching to be sure we don't get carried away with conceptualizing and therefore miss the entire experience. But, as he continues to admonish, I must do my part. Whether I am doing a seated meditation, engaged in mundane everyday tasks, or mediating high stakes conflicts, it is my responsibility to become more and more skillful in my own inimitable way at manifesting ever finer levels of energy so that my contribution is brilliant. Thank you, Nadeau Sensei. After more than four decades of practice with you as my primary teacher, I am still filled with curiosity and wonder, more engaged than ever.

#  *A One-Handed Ukemi Conversation*

## ALEJANDRO ANASTASIO
### Aikido 4th Dan
### Dojo-cho, Three Shapes Aikido

Let me begin by saying I was born without my left hand. I started doing Aikido when I was twenty-six to proactively support my body alignment. I knew that over time my spine would start to feel the effects of my one-handedness, and I wanted to take preventative action sooner rather than later. Additionally, I was drawn to the harmonious movements, the resolution of aggression, and the internal aspects of Aikido, and I thought Aikido was such a cool martial art.

As my understanding of Aikido deepened, I began to realize I had some very one-handed quirks in my training. Since I do not have two hands, I take *ukemi* (art of attacking/falling/rolling) differently on each side. I fall and take rolls one way on my longer, handed arm, and take different types of falls and rolls on my shorter, non-handed left arm. As I started to take more and more advanced *ukemi*, I began to notice something unique. The people throwing me would often throw me on my left side as if I had two hands. If you throw me on my left side as if you are throwing someone with two hands, neither the throw nor the fall will fit my body. If someone deeply throws me as if I have two hands, it is difficult to take that fall safely because I do not have two hands. Over the years of consistently almost getting hurt, constantly being thrown like I have two hands, and continually having apprehension about taking specific kinds of advanced falls on my "short side," I developed a problem taking falls on that side of my body.

One day while walking on the path of Aikido, I had the great fortune of meeting Teja Bell Sensei. Since Teja was a long-term student of Nadeau Sensei, I spent more time with Nadeau on and off the mat. Often I would go to California to train with Teja Bell Sensei, and we would train at Nadeau Sensei's dojo or at the bi-yearly California Aikido Association's Aiki Summer Retreat "Friendship Seminars." As time went on, I made it a point to attend more and more seminars with Nadeau Sensei, especially when he taught anywhere near Boise, Idaho, the location of my dojo. Around that time, I received a flier at my dojo advertising a seminar with Nadeau Sensei in Reno, Nevada. Little did I know that the short forty-minute flight from Boise to Reno would have the longest-lasting and most profound impact on my one-handed Aikido.

When the seminar began on Friday evening, it was clear to everyone training that Nadeau Sensei was choosing me to take a lot of *ukemi* for him. Once, when he was throwing another student, I believed that he was not just looking for a good *uke*. I sensed he was also looking for someone to communicate with, an *uke* who was open and could listen and be receptive. Perhaps he was looking for a student who wanted to communicate and grow at a deeper level through the practice of Aikido. I had heard stories about this quality of Nadeau Sensei. I could see my opportunity unfolding right before me on the mat. Initially I was scared, as I had seen Nadeau Sensei throw people very hard in the past. However, I was inspired by the advice Teja Bell had given about taking *ukemi* for Nadeau Sensei: "Trust and allow, and sincerely give yourself to the moment." As I closed out the first night of training by taking falls, I energetically engaged in the dialogue that Nadeau Sensei was asking.

The Saturday training day had two two-hour training sessions. I took 90 percent of the *ukemi* for Nadeau Sensei that day. As he was throwing me I could feel him communicating while throwing me from many different techniques. It was almost as if he was asking me, "What do you really need to work on in your body, your person, and your Aikido?" I would respond by opening myself to what he was energetically asking and taking those falls. As the physical part of our Aikido dialogue became more intense, the deeper energy levels of our communication started to evolve.

Two qualities began to arise. First, on a more physical level, Nadeau Sensei isolated one technique for the remainder of the second training session and had me take falls from that one throw with more and more intensity. Secondly, within the boundaries of that one technique, I began to realize Nadeau Sensei was asking me something. I became aware that he was communicating with me about how I fall differently on each side of my one-handed body, on both a physical and energetic level. It was at that point that I truly opened up. Nadeau Sensei had discovered the most challenging fall for me to take on my non-handed left side. He isolated my most significant obstacle to growing in Aikido through taking *ukemi*. This fall was also a huge source of fear for me as an *uke*. Nadeau Sensei only threw me in that one technique for the rest of that training day.

In the evening, we all celebrated, ate dinner, and enjoyed our time together as students of Aikido. Throughout the night, people told me how much they enjoyed watching me take *ukemi* for Nadeau Sensei. I was complimented on the grace of my falls and for the amount of *ukemi* I took. Some people even commented on how the level of intensity grew toward the end of class and how I met that challenge. These were all very kind and appreciated compliments. However, my thoughts were focused more on the dialogue in which Nadeau Sensei and I engaged on the mat. I was contemplating where it would lead and what the result would be. All I could hope for was that he and I would finish the conversation during the last Sunday class.

The following day, after Nadeau Sensei bowed us in, he said, "We will just pick up where we left off yesterday." He called me up, and I started taking that one fall from that one technique. At first his pace was soft and relaxed, as it was a morning class.

But soon enough, the "warm-up" time ended, and the pace and intensity began to build. The next thing I knew Nadeau Sensei and I were right back in that one-handed *ukemi* conversation. As I took falls on each side of my body, I could feel him "inquiring" as he threw me. The intensity quickly rose as he began to throw me faster and harder. Finally, I found myself at the edge of my capacity to take that fall on my non-handed side. As I was taking what I can only call "very deep *ukemi*," I felt Nadeau Sensei "asking" me to go past the edge of my one-handed *ukemi* capacity. In a very real way, he was asking me to trust him. At that moment time dilated and everything started moving in slow motion. I knew I had to make a choice.

I had heard of this kind of thing happening while training with Nadeau Sensei. Now the opportunity was right before me. I chose to give myself to the moment and to Nadeau Sensei. I simply trusted it and allowed it. He had just finished throwing me on my right side. As I got up, I knew I would be grabbing his wrist with my right hand and taking a fall on my left, non-handed side. Just before I grabbed him, something happened that I cannot really explain. Everything just went black. It felt like I fell into something that was unexplainable. I do not even remember grabbing his wrist. There was no time, no movement, no nothing, just blackness. The next thing I was aware of was hitting the ground with more force and speed than I ever thought possible on that side. It was the greatest *ukemi* I had ever taken in my entire life. Far beyond anything I ever thought I could do. In that one moment of impact, all my fears, obstacles, and quirks about taking advanced *ukemi* were destroyed.

After the seminar, a small group went out to eat lunch with Nadeau Sensei. At one point, before the meal was served, I started to lean over to Nadeau Sensei, implying I wanted to say something heartfelt. He responded by leaning toward me with a similar receptive energy. I said, "Hey Sensei, thanks for everything." He replied, "Don't mention it, kid." Everyone at the table could sense I was thanking him for giving me something very profound. And I could tell they did not know what that was.

My Aikido grew more in that one moment and in that one fall than at any other time in all the years I have done Aikido.

# FOUR

# Recollections and Reverberations

##  *Lucky to Have a Teacher at My Age*

LAURIN HERR

Aikido 6th Dan

Aikido of Mountain View, City Aikido of San Francisco

President, Pacific Interface Inc.

Translator: *Heart of Aikido* video, with Michio Hikitsuchi Sensei,
10th Dan (1990)

Director/Translator: *The Essential Teachings of Aikido* video, with Michio
Hikitsuchi Sensei, 10th Dan (2000)

In 1999, Danielle Smith Sensei invited me to participate in a one-day workshop to be taught by Robert Nadeau Sensei at Aikido of Monterey. I had seen Nadeau's name in books and knew he had been a direct student of Osensei back in the '60s, but we had never met. I decided to attend.

My first impression of Nadeau Sensei was the beautiful fluidity of his Aikido *waza* (techniques), which to my eye had no obvious *suki* (vulnerable gaps) despite how open he appeared. I noticed how smoothly he moved his feet and how he kept his hips low to support himself with a broad stable base. There was a clear center and circle when he worked with his *uke*. Great connection. His posture was straight, balanced, expansive, and more than a little "springy," with lots of up-and-down dynamics. He was full of *ki*, though he didn't use the word as he talked about the energy processes involved in what he was demonstrating. He referred to Osensei a lot, which I liked. But Nadeau Sensei was describing Aikido concepts using a strange idiosyncratic vocabulary I couldn't follow. Then he completely surprised me. He asked us what we were feeling. I was stunned! I was a forty-nine-year-old 4th Dan (4th degree black belt) and had practiced in Japan and America for decades. Until I met Nadeau Sensei, none of my teachers had ever asked for student feedback during a class.

At the workshop dinner that evening, I sat across from Nadeau Sensei and tried to strike up a conversation with him. I was very pleased to have a chance to talk with him for the first time. I thanked him for class and introduced myself. Nadeau Sensei listened but didn't really engage with me. He seemed more interested in ordering his dinner. But I was bubbling over with questions. I asked him about Osensei, what it was like when he was in Japan back in the day, and so on. He seemed to take this as his cue to step outside for a smoke. He returned to the table, ordered another drink, and the conversation moved on. We didn't interact again until dinner was winding down and everyone started saying their goodbyes, at which point he looked over at me and said, "Come practice sometime."

Soon after meeting Nadeau Sensei in Monterey, my Silicon Valley company was acquired, and my new company's headquarters was just a few minutes from his dojo in Mountain View. I was up to my elbows developing new business deals with two major Japanese manufacturers, while simultaneously trying to figure out how my new company's organization really worked, who was who, and where I fit within the management team. I was succeeding and liked my job, but I felt under a lot of pressure and busier than I had ever been in my life. Much too busy, I told myself, to commit to any regular Aikido practice or join a dojo. I had put work and career ahead of Aikido for some years, to the point where I only went to a few seminars a year. But I was deeply intrigued by my first class with Nadeau Sensei, attracted to his Aikido, and more than a little curious about him and how he taught. So, after work one evening, I drove over and sat on the sidelines watching a class. Nadeau came over to chat.

He asked, "What do you think?"

I told him that I liked what I saw.

He asked, "Did you bring your *keiko gi* (practice uniform)?"

I had just come from work, so no, I had not.

I explained I couldn't really commit to regular practice because of my job.

He said, "OK."

I explained that I traveled a lot for business and might be absent for weeks at a time.

He replied, "No problem."

I explained that I might be tardy for class because I sometimes worked late talking to colleagues overseas.

He said, "Don't worry about it. Come when you can."

We stood together in silence for a moment, then he turned back to lead the class and I drifted out the door.

But Nadeau Sensei had been so unexpectedly accommodating, absorbing all my self-imposed objections without any pushback, that I did, in fact, return the next week with my *keiko gi*. And just like that, he drew me back onto the mat after my long hiatus.

In those first years with Nadeau Sensei, training in Mountain

View, he offered what I needed most at that stage of my life: space and time and structure to rediscover myself as an older *Aikidoka* (Aikido practitioner). He didn't so much "teach" me as "allow" me to open and settle back into the energetic rhythms of full-bodied Aikido. Training with Nadeau Sensei left me sweaty and tired, refreshed and energized.

It seems obvious in hindsight, but adding steady Aikido practice into my busy routine was exactly what I needed to help me find balance living life in the fast lane. I was better able to navigate corporate politics. I was able to accept additional responsibilities without overloading my circuits. I even found the resolve within myself to finally complete a personal project on which I had long procrastinated. I didn't initially make the connection between these developments and my practice with Nadeau Sensei, but I kept going to his classes and giving it my all. In the process, we developed a loose, informal relationship we were both comfortable with.

When I left my Silicon Valley job and began working instead from my home in Oakland, Nadeau Sensei invited me to continue practicing with him in San Francisco at City Aikido, which I did. I attended as many of his classes as I could, and we started having lunch together after his weekly midday class. He soon invited me to become one of the dojo's regular teachers, which I was pleased to do.

Whereupon, he immediately started giving me a harder time on the mat. One day, as we practiced a technique utilizing *tegatana* (hand sword), he brought me up short, standing right in my face, with the comment, "They taught you very well in Japan how to put a sharp edge on your sword. Now how are you going to use it?" I didn't have a response. Another time he yelled at me across a crowded mat to "stop doing what I remembered" about a particular technique, one that I had practiced for many years, but which just would not work for me that day. What exactly was

I supposed to "stop doing" or "stop remembering?" In another class he criticized how consistently I was doing a particular *waza*, and when I protested that I was doing the technique exactly the way he had taught it a few weeks prior, he grumbled that I was "too much into learning."

Once, I described some of these upsetting interactions to Motomichi Anno, 8th Dan, one of my oldest sensei who has known me since I was a gangly twenty-three-year-old white belt practicing at the Kumano Juku Dojo in Shingu, Japan in the 1970s. He listened attentively and then told me with a smile, "Laurin, you are very lucky to still have a teacher at your age."

These words, and the smile they came with, gave me new perspective on my relationship with Nadeau Sensei. Did I truly trust him as my teacher to guide me correctly, or not? If he didn't care, he wouldn't comment. If he didn't think I was capable of more, he wouldn't waste his time on me. I realized Nadeau Sensei's approach wasn't a bug, it was a feature! Yes, he might still confound me on the mat. But I could accept what he does, and the way he does it, as part of my *shugyo*, my personal spiritual training on my chosen path with my chosen teacher.

To be clear, Nadeau Sensei doesn't always confront and challenge. I clearly remember a class when he had us responding to a one-handed grab from behind by "stepping back into calm." Sensei must have sensed something as he watched me practice from across the mat, because he quietly slid in behind me without my noticing and whispered in my ear, "Inner . . . inner . . . more inner." I was completely surprised by the sound of his voice up close. Maybe this is what allowed his quiet words to penetrate me so deeply, resonating within me like a bell vibrating harmonically after being cleanly struck, just so.

The global pandemic that began in 2020 opened a new chapter in my practice with Nadeau Sensei. More than three years of telephone conversations about the themes he wants to articulate each week and devising appropriately pithy titles for his Friday-night Zoom classes in the "virtual dojo" have helped me reach a more fully nuanced understanding of what he's been trying to tell us all these years.

Now that we're back on the mat, post-pandemic, Nadeau Sensei still admonishes me to "open and settle—more," to "activate my lower half—more." I have come to welcome his instruction, difficult as it might be to follow at times. The pandemic has given me a deeper appreciation of how precious such moments can be. Under his watchful guidance, I can sense my Aikido maturing, becoming even more grounded, more spontaneous, more flowing, more connected, fuller, finer. My life outside the dojo also seems more balanced, more "squared away," as he would say.

I don't know if I would have kept practicing Aikido through my fifties, sixties, and into my seventies without Nadeau Sensei in my life. From our very first encounter, he has always emphasized the inner process of personal development at the heart of Osensei's Aikido. As I reflect on my evolution as his student, these have been the most valuable lessons in Robert Nadeau's *jikiden* (direct transmission) of Aikido: passing along, in his own inimitable style, the essential teachings of his teacher, Morihei Ueshiba, for the next generation to absorb and actualize, as best we can.

For that, and so much more, I am lucky to still have him as my teacher.

# *Finding Your Genuine Self*

PATRICK CASSIDY
Aikido 6th Dan
Chief Instructor, Aikido Montreux
Founder, Evolutionary Aikido Community

It isn't easy to describe the impact that someone like Robert Nadeau has on one's life. So I have written a list of snapshots that I hope give my appreciation for his work and presence.

- Bob is a skilled facilitator who can use metaphor to spontaneously communicate experience.

- He is like a force of nature. In that way, I did not take him personally. If he was in a foul mood, I took it like I would take foul weather. It is a part of life, and the time to use an umbrella.

- He got the coding of what Osensei was teaching and was able to embody and transmit it to his students. But his process work demanded complete involvement. Anyone sitting back in concept-land would get burned.

- His take on accessing energies, like communicating with allies, is genius.

- His take on speaking with energies, allowing energies, is groundbreaking.

- His approach to "body allowed" opened a door for me personally that showed Aikido could be a healing art. I had always intuited that, but until Robert introduced that "doorway," it was only a concept. He showed me how it could be accessed.

- Bob introduced me to the idea of alchemy. Combining two energies—frame/flow, he/she—was an important theme. Bringing these energies together created a new thing, a new experience.

- His focus is on using Aikido to become better versions of ourselves. Rather than focusing on what we want to do, he helps his students give attention to who we are, and how we can transform into who we need to be.

- Bob's teachings are so simple and yet profound. The doorways he opens are always fresh, and we always need to approach them as if it were the first time. This is why Aikido with Nadeau can be very frustrating for so many. Developing any skill in his approach required a naked vulnerability and willingness "not to know."

- You have to start from square one every time.
- Bob was a catalyst within the Human Potential Movement, with students such as Michael Murphy, Dan Millman, Richard Strozzi-Heckler, George Leonard, and so on. He was a creative participant in a movement that changed the world.
- He has also been a great inspiration to serious martial artists, which says a lot about his approach.
- Bob opens a dimension of Aikido that enables students to evolve independently. He strives to give the keys to the kingdom and allow each student to access that kingdom directly.
- Bob is his own man. He does not live by anyone's standards but his own. In that way, he is like the teachers of old. If you want to train with him, you need to accept him as he is.
- Bob has a deep loyalty to Osensei and a deep reverence for his work. I feel this more in him than in any other student of Osensei that I have trained with. I feel a living connection to Osensei's presence and perspective through Bob.
- Like a channel, Bob transmits energy and perspective that is tangible. It opens pathways in the student. I always feel that I am walking on the path that Osensei walked.
- Bob is passionate about what he teaches, inspired, and in love with the art. And he gives each person in his class the same space to access the art with the same passion.
- Bob is a genius and, in that way, a little mad. Genius does not conform to social niceties and can be challenging to accept. I appreciate Bob for that, but you need to develop your center to receive his perspective.
- Bob's work is always new. He made a joke that writing a book

would be too complicated because by the time he finished, he would want to change the whole thing. His understanding is constantly developing. His work is in a state of perpetual evolution.

## ◬ *Oil and Water* ◬

### BOB LEICHNER
Aikido 6th Dan
Aikido West, Aikido of Mountain View
Electrical Engineer, Medical Devices (ret.)

My earliest memories of Nadeau Sensei are from decades back, when I was a new student in the Bay Area. At that time, my exposure to Sensei was sporadic—classes at summer camp or when he was a visiting instructor at one or another dojo. Pretty much without fail, I would find myself furious at some point in his classes.

It felt like oil and water. I thought we just did not mix. I did not know how to be with, let alone "welcome," Nadeau's energy in those classes.

A couple of decades passed, and I began to encounter training partners with a quality of movement and presence on the mat that I was able to recognize as something special. These partners brought something to their practice that was intriguing, something I wanted to explore. Very often, I discovered they were students of Nadeau Sensei. As a result, I found myself drawn to more regular training with him.

It might have been that my experience of Sensei had somehow morphed over the years into something more comfortable for me. But that was not the case.

Nadeau Sensei remains one of the most challenging instructors I have encountered in my lifetime. Training with him often takes me well outside my comfort zone into regions where I encounter uncomfortable energies. A significant part of my practice is learning to welcome the energies "pushing me" and using Osensei's process to settle, ground, and open to a finer and more appropriate self.

Sensei is also one of the very few teachers who has changed my life. Nadeau's transmission of Osensei's process is with me whenever I encounter situations that ask more of me than I might otherwise have available. People do not come at me with *shomen-uchi* (frontal strike to the forehead) on a typical day. Life regularly comes at me with far more significant challenges. Thanks in no small part to my time with Nadeau Sensei, I have learned to "work the process" in order to rise to the occasion.

I do not think I am ever going to be completely comfortable when training with Nadeau Sensei, and I do not want to! I am grateful for the challenges Sensei has presented me with, and the personal growth that has (sometimes) resulted. I am especially grateful to Sensei for his patience as I stumble along the path!

##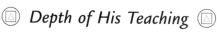

SETH PARIS
Aikido 2nd Dan
**Feldenkrais Practitioner, Occupational Therapist**

I had been training with Richard Moon Sensei for some months at Aikido of Marin before I first met Nadeau Sensei. I was enamored with Richard and his style of teaching *jiyu-waza* (freestyle techniques), which was his unique approach to teaching the art of creatively responding to incoming attacks without planning or forethought. I had already fallen deeply in love with the art of Aikido and had been hearing stories of Richard's own sensei, Bob.

Many of these "Bob stories" had an implicit air that something was intimidating and amazing that needed to be experienced. So I was a bit nervous when I decided to go to Richard's semiannual Point Reyes weekend Aikido retreat for the first time, where Nadeau would teach on Sunday. Indeed, upon his entry Sunday the feel of the whole dojo changed. Just his presence seemed to raise the intensity level several notches. I remember feeling worried that perhaps I would have to take his *ukemi*.

Watching Nadeau's Aikido that first time was fantastically inspiring as a relatively new student. It seemed almost otherworldly how he moved so powerfully and effortlessly. The black belt students would just seem to fly across the room when attacking him.

Over the next couple of years, I continued to go to these retreats twice per year, and Bob would occasionally come to

Aikido of Marin to teach. Once I earned my blue belt, I was finally able to take some *ukemi* for him, and it was exhilarating.

As I fell more and more in love with Aikido, something called me to Nadeau. I think it was the depth of his teaching. I wanted to be around him and soak it up. It was unlike anything else I had experienced. There was a different quality with Nadeau. He was not just grounded or centered; he would embody these concepts to a unique degree. His teaching offered a window into his "process" that allowed us as students to glimpse what these ephemeral concepts actually feel like when we can get out of our own way and experience them directly.

I began attending weekly classes with Nadeau Sensei, as well as his annual summer retreats. As I was young and flexible, and as he liked the young ones for their bounce, I increasingly got opportunities to take his *ukemi*, which had become not so much intimidating as intensely thrilling. What was once such a scary thought—to be chosen to take *ukemi* from Nadeau Sensei— became pure joy. To feel the ground disappear in the blink of an eye, to feel like I was being sucked into a vortex or whirlpool or black hole of some kind, became one of my favorite experiences in Aikido. To be sure, one always had to be keenly attentive to what Sensei was asking for nonverbally, in terms of direction, force, energy, and quality of attack. Still, I found myself eager to try again and again; to take flight and experience the intense swirling of energy around him was quite the experience!

While I have not trained for many years, I still have frequent visitations in my dreams from both Nadeau Sensei and Moon Sensei. Their teaching continues.

## The Thrill of Ukemi

ALAN VANN GARDNER
Aikido 6th Dan
Senior Instructor, Two Rock Aikido
Mindfulness Meditation Teacher
Coach for Leaders in Schools and Other Settings

I can recall many evening treks from Marin each week to train with Nadeau Sensei.

Turk Street dojo. Early 1980s.

What a thrill to take *ukemi*. How exciting. Some degree of trepidation. Be sure to give a wholehearted, sincere attack. Stay awake! Pray that I return upright, centered, and all in one piece.

Have to come back for more. Have to understand and unravel the mystery and magic about how to source such power.

Reflecting back decades later, so much appreciation and gratitude to you, Bob Sensei, for leaving a legacy—for pioneering the way, inviting us all into a more personal, how-to-relate-Aikido-to-life mystical exploration of this great art.

## ⊠ *Seeking Beginner's Mind* ⊠

### PETER RALSTON
#### Founder, Cheng Hsin Center
#### Teacher/Facilitator

First, some context: I am not an *Aikidoka* (Aikido practitioner). I am the first non-Asian to win the Full-Contact World Tournament in Asia. I have studied pretty much every martial art there is, and have worked to develop my skills and understanding beyond all traditions. But I did study Aikido and become friends with Robert Nadeau.

I first encountered Robert around 1980 or so when I was part of a one-day seminar composed of about a half-dozen teachers taking turns demonstrating their respective arts. I wasn't very impressed with most of the others, but Robert caught my attention. He talked of principles and experience, not just techniques and beliefs.

At the time, it was becoming difficult for me to relate effectively to beginners. So, I decided to create some "beginner's mind" for myself to relate more effectively to the challenges of a beginner. I decided to take up a new art. Previously, I hadn't been very interested in Aikido as demonstrated by other teachers, but after meeting Robert I decided to study with him.

It proved an interesting and fruitful study. I enjoyed his no-nonsense approach, as well as his delving into principles that apply to a greater context than merely doing Aikido techniques— such as centering, joining, and being whole and total. These principles aligned with my own work and contributed significantly to deepening my abilities and powers. Plus, I got to rejuvenate my beginner's mind.

I attended some of the crowded Aikido camps at the Dominican College. I wore a white belt and didn't want anyone to know who I was, but of course, after a few days, the word got out.

One time, a *shodan* (first degree black belt) was applying a *nikkyo* (second-teaching technique) that went way too far and would have damaged my wrist, so I dropped quickly to the floor and used my foot to slap his hands off my wrist. He was shocked, of course.

Robert later told me he saw this guy being abusive and started to head our way, but then saw what I did and decided I could take care of myself. After people found out who I was, the black belts would come up to me during breaks and ask if Aikido was really effective. I had to communicate that you can't learn to fight without fighting, but it was still a useful practice and a beautiful art. I also appreciated that Robert distinguished between strictly fighting arts and Aikido, emphasizing that Aikido offered life-lessons training.

He has shared many stories of his experience and life with Osensei, some of which I use in my own classes or books to make a point. Robert and I became friends over time, and even after I stopped training Aikido, we would meet for lunch from time to time—but it has been way too long, since I live in Texas now. We are both old guys now, and I, at least, am winding down a bit. I wish him all the best and congratulations on his 8th Dan and a life well lived!

##  *Inner and Outer Harmony*

PHIL BOOTH
Aikido 5th Dan
Dojo-cho, Aikido Aotearoa, New Zealand

My first impression of Nadeau Shihan was in the mid-1980s when I heard that there was a very high-ranking Aikido practitioner teaching at a five-day *gasshuku* (training retreat) at Lake Taupo on the North Island of New Zealand. I paid for one day of training, starting the first class in the morning. At this point, Nadeau Shihan had been teaching for two days. The class began with some extension exercises, and Shihan then asked, "How do you feel?" There was a deathly silence, and I stood there rather dumbfounded. Asking a young New Zealand male to express his feelings back in the 1980s was like trying to squeeze blood out of a stone. I finished the day thinking Shihan was a tree-hugging, hippie space cadet, so I was not all that impressed.

After the training was over, I stayed for the group meal. Well, this was a surprise, as it was vegetarian, which just made my day! But, again, in 1980s New Zealand, getting a rugby-playing male in touch with his feelings and eating vegetarian just wasn't how we rolled. Anyway, I loaded up my dinner plate, then turned to find a seat at a table. All the tables were pretty much packed with people I didn't know, but Bob was sitting at a table all on his own, so I sat down next to him. He was sitting there looking at his plate of food, so I turned to him and asked if they were serving any meat. He said no, we hadn't had any meat for two days. I suggested going to town for some steak and pizza and a few drinks. He readily agreed. Within a few minutes, we were off to town with three Americans in my car and another five cars following. I spent approximately three hours talking to Bob over steak, chips, and beer, and saw him in a different light, as a man who sees more in life and the universe.

Since that day, he has taken me on a lifelong journey of more deeply looking at myself. I am now able to achieve some amount of harmony in my existence on this planet. Nadeau Shihan's contributions go beyond just Aikido. The message that he offers is more critical in these times than ever before, and I hope people out there can still listen.

## Don't Stand There, Move!

ANDREW WATSON
Senior Instructor, Riai Aikido, Belmont, New Zealand

In the early 2000s, Nadeau Shihan ran a class at the Wellington Dojo in New Zealand ahead of a larger camp. It was a fantastic opportunity to attend a Nadeau class just with our club members present. During the session, I remember *Aikidoka* forming a circle, with Shihan moving around the circle being everyone's *uke*. We were to perform the technique he had just shown. I was a *kyu* grade (white belt), and when it came to my turn, Shihan grabbed my arm, and I froze. A glancing strike followed with a message from Shihan I remember today and tell all my students: "Don't stand there, move!"

This is an excellent self-defense reflex to have.

At a post-camp class back at the Wellington Dojo, we had the largest class ever with Shihan—around fifty *Aikidoka* were present. During the class, Shihan stopped and declared that some *nage* were dramatically waving their hands at the end of techniques, akin to Osensei. Shihan then stated he had news for us—we were not Osensei!

In the same class, Shihan stopped the class and, rather frustrated, stated he was giving us "Gold"—but we did not get it. It is only recently, after listening to Shihan on Zoom sessions during 2021–22, that I believe I understand what the "Gold" was. Thank you, Nadeau Shihan.

## ⬙ *The Beat of a Different Drummer* ⬙

### GINA MEARS

One of my favorite Nadeau stories . . .

Nadeau was in my living room, which at the time was full of musical instruments, as I often had band practice there.

I began to hear conga drums being played perfectly, with an amazing beat, from the back of the house.

I thought my drummer had come by, but as I entered the living room, there was only Nadeau standing in front of the congas. So, I said, "Robert, I didn't know you played drums."

He gave me his mischievous look and said, "I don't. . . ."

## ⬙ *Unconventional Methods Appreciated* ⬙

### MICHAEL FRIEDL
Aikido 7th Dan Shihan
Chief Instructor, Aikido of Ashland
California Aikido Association, Division 2 Head

I moved to the West Coast in the late '70s and was not familiar with Aikido teachers in California. On a whim, I decided to register for the Aiki Summer Retreat in San Rafael, and that was my first experience with Nadeau Sensei. He seemed bigger than life in some respects. He carried himself with confidence and a flair for the dramatic, and I don't mean that negatively. He verbally shared with his students a process for personal discovery that was very unfamiliar to me. I was used to very physical training, and few words were exchanged during training unless the teacher explained a technique. In contrast, Nadeau Sensei talked about dimensions, colors, feeling, emotion, various realms of consciousness, and energetic states of being.

I must confess that I was often puzzled and could not comprehend what he shared with us. Yet his Aikido had such depth, power, expansiveness, and mystery that is still evident many decades later. I continue to enjoy his classes and witness his students' love for and devotion to him as a teacher and mentor.

Nadeau Sensei's experiences with Osensei in Japan were profound. I love the stories he tells with such reverence about Osensei and the benefits of Aikido for personal growth and self-discovery. You see this in Nadeau's passion for Aikido and his takeaways from Osensei each time he bows to the *shomen* (ceremonial front of dojo), begins class, and taps into the knowledge and experience from his decades of training.

Nadeau Sensei employs unconventional methods to challenge his students, and I appreciate that very much. For example, I recall a class at the Aiki Summer Retreat over thirty years ago at Dominican College where he had drummers present in his class. I think Nadeau Sensei was exploring primal energies and wanted to set the stage for training without thinking, emphasizing instead feeling the energy and allowing it to mature and evolve as the class progressed.

It was a memorable experience. The rhythms, the cadence, and the deep resonance of the drums created an energy that at times seemed frenetic and out of control. Those of us who attended his class that evening had never practiced Aikido that way before. Even Nadeau Sensei appeared to take on the raw and powerful energy, perhaps untamed and unpredictable. For the rest of the event, people continued to share their personal experiences from this class.

Nadeau Sensei has been such an influential figure in the spread of Aikido, both in the United States and abroad. He loves teaching and will try to convey his thoughts and ideas in various ways. Since the pandemic and the popularity of Zoom, Nadeau Sensei has embraced this new media platform to share his Aikido and continue Osensei's dream of providing Aikido to everyone to help us become true, sincere, and authentic human beings. I look forward to more classes where I can experience his teaching firsthand, in person, and glimpse what Osensei shared with Nadeau Sensei so many years ago.

## ◬ *Weird and Wise* ◬

### KAYLA FEDER
### Aikido 7th Dan Shihan
### Chief Instructor, Aikido of Berkeley

I met Nadeau Shihan at age twelve in 1976, and I vividly remember my first few meetings with him. I remember being struck by how unusual he seemed. At that age, the only word I could come up with was "weird." At the same time, I was inspired and grateful to have been introduced to the notion that there was so much more to Aikido than technical prowess.

Since then, I've been deeply grateful to him for introducing me to aspects of the art that I may not have otherwise discovered until I was a bit older. I continue to note him in my thoughts quite often, especially when I'm spending time off the mat studying Aikido. I also refer to him sometimes while teaching and then feel gratitude again for his having opened me to the great depth of Aikido at a young age.

Also, I remember choosing to go to the Aiki Summer Retreat in San Rafael, in large part to challenge myself by practicing with this "weird," wise, super interesting, esoteric teacher. My daily instructor at the time focused on very different aspects of the art, so I enjoyed Nadeau's musings and the challenge of training with him immensely!

## △ *Let's See What They Can Do* △

### DANIELLE SMITH
Aikido 7th Dan Shihan
Founding Member, Aikido of Monterey
Dojo-cho, Aikido of Monterey (1983–2019)

In June of 1976, I took my *shodan* (1st degree black belt) test before the testing committee of the Aikido Association of Northern California (AANC). The next day, my teacher, Stan Pranin Sensei, shocked all of us at Aikido of Monterey (AOM) by announcing that he was leaving the Monterey area. I had expected to be sempai (senior student) in the dojo. Instead, I suddenly was AOM's only black belt teacher.

I was told that AANC leadership considered inviting a Japanese teacher to come over to run the AOM dojo. Then Bob Nadeau Sensei suggested: "Let's see what they can do." His suggestion created a path that led to my becoming a teacher and a leader, continuing my training while developing Aikido of Monterey.

The support of the AANC was absolutely essential to our fledgling dojo in Monterey. In those early days, Jack Wada Sensei and Linda Holiday Sensei came down to help out once a week, teaching and instilling their energy and expertise into the development of AOM as a dojo. Then, and in the years that followed, I often received supportive calls and visits from Nadeau Sensei, Doran Sensei, Mary Heiny Sensei, and others.

We pulled through that first year, and by 1977 the dojo had three students with *shodan* ranks. We continued to train, teach, and grow. Because of Nadeau Sensei's suggestion to "see what they can do," AOM survived, grew, and operated continuously for forty-three years, producing more than sixty *yudansha* (black belt holders), many of whom have reached high levels, including two 6th Dan (sixth degree black belts) and three 7th Dan (7th degree black belts). Several have gone on to lead successful Aikido dojo.

One of the most significant gifts I received back when I lost my first teacher and felt in over my head was understanding that we are all connected, and how precious the whole Aikido community is for all of us. I have friendships and mentors that go back more than four decades. I am deeply grateful to Nadeau Sensei for his willingness and foresight that allowed AOM to flourish and contribute to the growth of Aikido.

## ◻ *Beyond My Limitations* ◻

DAVID FLOETER
Aikido 3rd Dan
Aikido San Miguel, Mexico
Songwriter, Musician, Performer,
Award-Winning Documentary Videographer

My introduction to Aikido was mostly in Iwama style because that was the style of the dojo closest to my home in the East Bay. However, I sometimes practiced at the Turk Street dojo in San Francisco, which was led by Nadeau Sensei, Doran Sensei, and Witt Sensei. Practicing at Turk Street offered a wonderful plethora of perspectives on Aikido, which I appreciated a great deal. Every time I attended any event with Nadeau Sensei, what he taught intrigued and excited me.

I left the San Francisco Bay Area for many years, but when I returned, I began training consistently with Nadeau Sensei. This was a challenge for me initially because I had to face the part of myself that I had been "taught" to avoid while growing up in Texas. For example, I had been brainwashed to be "the perfect little boy," and it was that thought (among others) that was always in my way. Whether I was taking a test in Aikido, performing onstage as a musician, or doing whatever, mistakes mattered a lot to me then.

My experience with Nadeau Sensei has proven to be fruitful. He helped me grow beyond my self-set limitations and be more "present" as a human. Thanks in no small part to Nadeau Sensei, I am now becoming the artist that I came here to be: a songwriter, musician, and performer.

Thank you, Sensei, for all the trials and tribulations you have presented. I wish I had made it easier!

## Ⓐ *Guiding Principles* Ⓐ

### KEN KRON
Co-Instigator of the Moonsensei YouTube Channel and Website
Exploring Ways to Enhance Resilience, Safety,
and Creativity for Young Human Beings.

When I was growing up, I could tell that people were doing things to make themselves unhappy, yet they kept doing actions that an outside observer could tell would contribute to unhappiness. I remember frequently wondering if that was the way the world was supposed to be.

Then I saw the television series *Kung Fu*, which felt right and motivated me to look into martial arts. I read George Leonard's book *The Ultimate Athlete* and was captivated by his description of Aikido and the whole idea of noncompetitive athletics and movement. I searched for Aikido and martial arts instruction in my small town of Ponchatoula, Louisiana.

There were no martial arts schools anywhere near where I grew up, but I did run into a couple of Green Beret alumni who showed me a few things. My first teacher fired me because I was chronically late. I found another teacher in the country of Colombia, in South America, but he was less into formal classes and more into hanging out. When I returned to the United States I found some black belts who would work out together, but it never really jelled into serious training, so I focused on running and working out at the gym until I met Robert Nadeau Sensei— I've always called him just "Bob"—and started Aikido training with him.

For many years my guiding principle has been to face my fear and move toward it like a Buddhist novice, not away from it. This has been my North Star because my most embarrassing life events have happened to me when I was afraid.

I have faced life-and-death moments on a few occasions. Once, when I was attacking Bob, I thought he would kill me. Another time, I was on a sailboat and got tangled up in the line. I imagined myself dragged over the side and drowned in San Francisco Bay. Then I realized that there was nothing I could do about it, and I relaxed completely, without pretense.

Since that moment, I've discovered how arrogant I really am. I've talked for several years about how our cognitive biases lead us to see only what supports our beliefs and to discount other views, to avoid what doesn't support our preconceptions. The big breakthrough for me came when I was on a conference call, and someone said something I disagreed with. I heard an inner voice say, "Oh, they're just wrong," and instantly my attention left the present moment, imagining instead an alternate reality where I would deliver a barrage of facts to prove they were wrong.

In no small thanks to my Aikido training with Nadeau Sensei, a part of my self was aware of my experience at this moment. Reflecting, I've come to understand that no one is either entirely right or entirely wrong. Instead of playing the game of trying to win every argument, I'm trying to be skeptical of all my beliefs. It probably doesn't sound like great progress, but it is for me!

I once heard Nadeau Sensei, quoting Osensei, say, "Aikido is not a religion. Aikido completes religion."

Aikido has become my philosophy of life. I don't mean to say that I've mastered Aikido or live a life that anyone should admire, be jealous of, or strive to reproduce. I only mean to say that when I think about my life and how I make important decisions, my guiding principles have been the lessons of Aikido, lessons I've learned from Bob.

##  *Improvement Depends on Inner Work*

### KEN LAWS
Aikido 1st Dan
Aikido of Mountain View
Computer Scientist (ret.)

Robert Nadeau Shihan is one of those rare people who is really worth writing about, like Johnny Appleseed or Jaime Escalante. I can't write that story, but I do know that he played a large role in bringing Aikido to the United States. He and the teachers he trained have taught Aikido to thousands of students at hundreds of dojo in America and other countries.

I started Aikido training in 1982, taught by students from Aikido West. I encountered the group by accident and was intrigued. The training was fun, but difficult for me. I was physically awkward, poor at learning sequences, and had an extreme lack of confidence. My usual refuge in intellectual skills was not applicable. ADHD and ASD (autism spectrum disorder) traits—then undiagnosed—and related emotional limitations were embarrassingly evident. For eight years, I worked on physical Aikido technique, but made very little progress, physically or spiritually. My greatest progress was simply joining and becoming comfortable in a *gi*.

When I moved to Washington, D.C., I tried a little Tang Soo Do. Not my thing. It made me aggressive and unhappy rather than calm. After returning to the Bay Area, I joined a *kata*-based (form-based) Karatedo Doshinkan group for a few years, but learned nothing of practical use.

I missed Aikido.

After a thirteen-year gap, I returned to Aikido in 2003 when I discovered Nadeau Shihan's Mountain View dojo. Good teachers, plenty of classes and students. I was so ashamed of my lack of skill I avoided Shihan's classes for a year. Even after joining his sessions, I still felt self-conscious and timid. I hadn't come close to "mastering" anything despite all my training. I was still "up in my head" and trying to control every part of every move.

Since then, I've attended about fifteen hundred classes under Mountain View instructors, more than half of which were taught by Nadeau Shihan himself. I am much, much improved, though it still takes some time for me to translate an intellectual understanding into non-thinking physical movements. (Not the recommended approach, but it serves me for now.)

I have found Nadeau Shihan to be a sensitive observer who reacts more to how students move than to where they place their hands. His patience with our incompetence has been impressive. When correction is necessary, Shihan often says, "I'll exaggerate" before demonstrating our mistakes. A small matter, but one that avoids any sense of harsh parody or bullying. This may be one of the reasons why I have stayed with Aikido instead of switching to yoga or t'ai chi.

For me, an advantage of the Mountain View dojo has been the consistency of instruction, even though teachers each have their own styles. Nadeau Shihan himself invariably focuses on posture, presence, grounding, centering, awareness, openness, allowing, blending, and leading, in some combination. He uses Aikido training as a vehicle to cultivate these qualities, not just to make the techniques work better but to make *us* better people. That's a big difference, and in line with Osensei's hopes for Aikido as I understand them.

Over time, I've learned what I'm good at and what just isn't my style. As my confidence has grown, my techniques have improved. Training sessions have become more fun, and I'm addicted to them. I have faced and overcome real limitations, some of them congenital mental and emotional problems, some from social rejections, some from decades of bad posture and lack of exercise. I still haven't mastered anything, but I've become a better person. Nadeau Shihan helped save me from my limitations, and I love him for that.

### ⊿ *Using Our Own Words* ⊿

LINDA ESKIN
Aikido 3rd Dan
Aikido of San Diego
Author of Articles and Books about Fitness and Aikido

A writer and horseman, Mark Rashid, initially suggested I try Aikido, and his excellent *Horsemanship through Life* was the first book I read about the art and what training might look like.

Intrigued, I started thinking about training, and wanted to learn a bit about the art. So I read about Aikido. It happened that the books that affected me most were written by Nadeau's early students: Wendy Palmer, Richard Strozzi-Heckler, and George Leonard. Each of them, in their own way, painted a much bigger picture of Aikido than just what's practiced on the mat. This appealed to me.

I first encountered Nadeau Shihan in George Leonard's book *The Way of Aikido*, where he wrote about his experiences of being a new student with Nadeau as his teacher. Leonard Sensei wrote about how Nadeau owned his perspective on Aikido and encouraged others to own theirs as well, and how he focused his teaching on personal growth rather than martial application. For example: "He insisted. . . that everything he taught us could be applied to every aspect of our lives. 'What you do with Aikido off the mat,' he said one day, 'is really more important than what you do with it on the mat.'"[1]

Everything I read about Aikido by these authors encouraged me. After all, my original reason for considering Aikido was to become a more centered, grounded leader—calmly taking effective action under pressure. The context I had in mind was horsemanship—being a solid, calming presence for my young horse when things "got a little Western," which they did with some regularity.

I next encountered Nadeau via the excellent Aikido podcast *The Way of Harmony* by Jeff Davidson and Bob King. Their hour-long interview with Nadeau was a series of "Aha!" moments for me.

In the interview, Nadeau shared a story about grasping ideas conceptually versus learning through embodied experience. As an example, he said that in his mind, he could be in his favorite restaurant in Hawaii in seconds, but that the body has its way of getting there, and that takes a little longer. Understanding this distinction helped me be patient with myself when I eventually started training.

During the podcast, he also discussed how *who we are* affects our ability to *do* things. Nadeau told a story about fishing. If you have a rod, reel, and line designed for 5-pound fish, that's what you'll catch. Someone with 5-pound tackle would be in trouble if they were to catch a 20-pound fish! If you want to catch 20-pound fish you need sturdier equipment, a heavier line, and a bigger hook.

Likewise, being a 5-pound version of ourselves and trying to do 20-pound things doesn't go well. We often struggle to take on big tasks or achieve grand goals from our smaller 5-pound state of being. Instead, if we can learn to inhabit a better level of ourselves, *doing* at a better level will come naturally—just as someone fishing with 20-pound tackle will naturally catch larger fish. This lesson shaped how I approach my Aikido training—and everything else.

"Don't ask how to do this.

Ask who you need to be that this is possible."

ROBERT NADEAU SHIHAN

Researching about Aikido before actually training, I knew I should check out a few dojo to find the best fit. But when I visited the first one and saw a poster for their upcoming annual seminar with Robert Nadeau (whoa!) I knew I'd found someplace special. I stopped my search right there, at Aikido of San Diego, and have been training under Dave Goldberg Sensei ever since.

When I've had the rare and precious opportunity to work directly with Nadeau Shihan—whether in a brief private interaction on the mat or taking *ukemi* for him during public seminars—he's often pushed me right to my edge. High falls, once. An hour of *nikkyo* (second-teaching techniques) another time. Then there was the time at a retreat when he scooped me up by my chin and planted me flat on the mat. My attention had wandered off into the gym rafters someplace. You can bet it didn't wander after that!

He has never given me more than I can handle—but he has gone right up to that edge and trusted me to deal with it, whether physically, emotionally, or cognitively. I take that as a sign of respect.

As a woman starting out in Aikido in my mid-forties, it would have been easy to write me off. Too old. Too fragile. Not worth investing the time. But he has never babied me, never excused me from high expectations, never looked past me hoping to find someone more promising to work with. And I've seen him demonstrate this same level of commitment to all his students at every level.

I am deeply grateful for being taken seriously as a student. It has helped me take *myself* seriously, expect more of myself, and not write myself off. I hope I show that level of trust and respect to everyone I have the honor of sharing the mat with.

Nadeau doesn't stop at helping us find the more of *ourselves*. In his annual Osensei Revisited retreat, he regularly gives tips—to everyone, not privately to his senior instructors—on how to teach this work, to new students, to children, and even in non-Aikido contexts. He wants it shared freely and widely, not held close for a select few. I appreciate his inclusion, as if everyone is a potential teacher, showing us that it's not only important that the work *is* shared, but that *we* can be the ones sharing it.

Nadeau Shihan doesn't insist the way that works for *him* is the One True Way. Just the opposite. He encourages those of us who train with him to approach the work in our own way and at our own pace. This is such a gift. I have had days (or months!) when I've felt like I'd fallen behind, when I didn't have the energy or focus to train at the level I thought I should. What a relief to hear Sensei assure us that we can work from wherever we are at that moment. Some days that might mean simply standing a little taller and breathing a little more deeply. I can clearly recall Nadeau's words. . . .

"You do it in your way, at your level."

"Feel yourself. Experience yourself."

"Open. Settle. Hush. These are my words. You use whatever words do it for you."

Not only can we use our own words, and develop our own processes for accessing better, finer levels of ourselves, but Nadeau emphasizes the context, or lineage, in which we apply this work doesn't even have to be Aikido. It might be a sport, our job, music, parenting, or the practice of medicine.

I have created my own processes to help me get to where I need to be in order to do good work with less struggle, whether in my Aikido practice, or in my work as a writer and a fitness coach. When I forget to apply these practices and try to dive into a project as a lesser version of myself, my work can be a hard slog. I take on small ideas, procrastinate, find myself distracted, and can't seem to make headway. But when I remember to use my personal processes to get to a better place before I begin, I can find my voice and the courage to take on bigger topics. The words come easily. I can focus, ideas flow, and there's a sense of lightness and joy.

During a seminar at Aikido of San Diego, speaking of our continuing growth as people, Nadeau once said, "You don't know who you are. Not really." This was a tantalizing idea for someone coming off a long string of difficult times and feeling rather defeated. There might yet be *more* ahead of me. New adventures. Bigger possibilities.

Through my Aikido journey, and thanks to Nadeau Shihan's teaching, I've learned I'm capable of much more than I knew—that I *can* be more than I'd ever imagined. Growth can be exciting; it can also take us way out of our comfort zone. As I'd originally hoped when I started on this path, I'm becoming a more centered, grounded leader—able to take effective action under pressure calmly. It's a little scary, and a lot of fun, to keep discovering, new level after new level, who I am, really.

# Glossary

*aiki*: spiritual harmony

Aikido: way of spiritual harmony

*Aikidoka*: Aikido practitioner

*Aikikai*: Aikido Foundation headquarted in Tokyo

*budo*: way of the warrior

*dan*: Nth degree black belt

*deshi*: disciple

dojo: training hall/martial arts school

*dojo-cho*: dojo head

*gasshuku*: training retreat

*gi*: practice uniform

*hakama*: traditional divided skirt

*hanmi*: triangular stance

*hara*: lower abdomen source of *ki*/heart/mind

*Hombu Dojo*: Aikido Headquarters Dojo in Tokyo

*ikkyo*: first-teaching techniques

*ikkyo-nage*: first-teaching throws

*irimi-nage*: entering throws

Izanagi: name of Shinto deity; "male-who-invites"

Izanami: name of Shinto deity; "female-who-invites"

*jaki*: dark forces / evil spirits

*jikiden*: direct transmission of teachings

*jiyu-waza*: freestyle techniques

*kami*: Shinto deities

*kata*: form

*keiko*: practice

*keiko gi*: practice uniform

*ki*: vital energy

*ki musubi*: energy connection

*koan*: Zen question

*kohai*: junior student; the junior in a relationship

*kokoro*: heart/mind

*kokyu-nage*: breath throws

*kote-gaeshi*: wrist-twist techniques

*kototama*: word spirit

*kyu*: Nth class white belt

*misogi*: inner purification

*musubi*: connection

*nage*: throwing partner

*nidan*: second degree black belt

*nikkyo*: second-teachings techniques

*norito*: chanted Shinto prayers

*ofuro*: bath

Osensei: Great Teacher (Morihei Ueshiba)

*seiza*: formal seated posture on the floor

*sempai*: senior student; the senior in a relationship

*sankyo*: third-teaching techniques

sensei: teacher

*seoi-nage*: shoulder throw

*shihan*: master teacher

*shiho-nage*: four-direction throws

*shikko*: knee walking

*shodan*: first degree black belt

*shomen*: ceremonial front of a dojo; front face

*shomen-uchi*: frontal strike to the forehead

*shomen-uchi ikkyo*: first-teaching technique for a frontal strike to the forehead

*shugyo*: personal development

*suki*: vulnerable gaps

*sutemi-waza*: sacrifice techniques

*suwari-waza*: seated techniques done on the knees

*takemusu aiki*: spontaneous actualization of the harmony of the universe

*tegatana*: hand sword

*tenkan*: turning blend

*tsuki*: straight thrusting punch

*uchideshi*: live-in disciple

*uke*: attacking/receiving partner

*ukemi*: art of attacking/rolling/falling

*ushiro katate-dori sankyo*: third-teaching technique from rear one-handed grab

*waza*: techniques

*yudansha*: black belt holders

*zanshin*: sustained energetic connection

# Notes

## Chapter One. The Life of Robert Nadeau

1. Cassidy, "A Life in Aikido."
2. Cassidy, "A Life in Aikido."
3. Cassidy, "A Life in Aikido."
4. Pranin, "Interview," 42–49.
5. Perry, "Interview," 7–11.
6. Perry, "Interview," 7–11.
7. Leonard, *The Ultimate Athlete*, 52.
8. Murphy, *Golf in the Kingdom*, 170.
9. Stone and Meyer, *Aikido in America*, 45–56.
10. Bernstein, *Stress Less Achieve More*, 3–4.

## Chapter 3. Teachings of Robert Nadeau

1. Stevens, *The Essence of Aikido*, 79.
2. Stevens, *The Essence of Aikido*, 29.

## Chapter 4. Recollections and Reverberations

1. Leonard, *The Way of Aikido*, 15.

# Bibliography

Bernstein, Aimee. *Stress Less Achieve More.* New York: American Management Association, 2015.

Cassidy, Patrick. "A Life in Aikido." YouTube. October 28, 2021. Interview, 1:27:34.

Leonard, George. *The Ultimate Athlete: Re-Visioning Sports, Physical Education and the Body.* New York: Viking Press, 1975.

———. *The Way of Aikido: Life Lessons from an American Sensei.* New York: Dutton, 1999.

Murphy, Michael. *Golf in the Kingdom.* New York: Dell Publishing, 1972.

Perry, Susan. "Interview: Robert Nadeau Sensei." *Aikido Today Magazine*, no. 26, Feb/March 1993.

Pranin, Stanley. "Interview with Robert Nadeau." *Aikido Journal* 26, no. 2 (1999): 42–49.

Stevens, John. *The Essence of Aikido: Spiritual Teachings of Morihei Ueshiba.* New York: Kodansha America, 1993.

Stone, John, and Ron Meyer, eds. *Aikido in America.* Berkeley, California: North Atlantic Books, 1995.

# Additional Resources

For anyone interested in learning more about Robert Nadeau's life and teachings, additional resources are available at **NadeauShihan.com**.

For those who would like to watch Nadeau Sensei in action, please visit the Moonsensei Channel on YouTube to access an extensive collection of curated video recordings showing him teaching, lecturing, and demonstrating over many years. The collection includes more than 200 short clips excerpted from live Aikido classes, a variety of medium-length compilations focusing on particular themes, and more than 120 full-length recordings of his weekly online classes in the virtual dojo begun in 2020.

As of the time of this writing, Nadeau Sensei is still actively teaching at his dojo in San Francisco and Mountain View, California. New students are welcome. More details can be found at **cityaikido.com**.

# Authors/Editors and Contributors

### Teja Bell, 6th Dan

Teja began practicing Aikido in 1971 and has been studying with Robert Nadeau Sensei since 1979. He has also practiced with many of Osensei's first-generation teachers, including Francis Takahashi, Morihiro Saito, Akira Tohei, Kazuo Chiba, Hiroshi Ikeda, Terry Dobson, Mitsugi Saotome, and Mitsunari Kanai Sensei. Teja's relationship with Frank McGouirk Sensei of Aikido Ai spans over thirty-five years, integrating Aikido, Zen, Chinese internal arts, and healing arts. An ordained Rinzai-lineage Zen master/priest and lineage dharma teacher, Teja Bell Fudo Myoo Roshi is the 84th ancestor of this Zen tradition.

### Laurin Herr, 6th Dan

Laurin began his Aikido training in 1971 as a student at Cornell University. Inspired by his first experience on the mat, he studied Japanese intensively, moved to Tokyo, and entered Aikido Hombu Dojo as an unranked white belt, earning his *shodan* there in 1976. He subsequently spent formative years affiliated with the Kumano Juku Dojo in Japan, training under Michio Hikitsuchi, Motomichi Anno, Motokazu Yanase, and Yasushi Tojima. Returning from Japan, he continued his practice with Terry Dobson and Ken Nisson at the Bond Street Dojo. After living in New York City, then Tokyo, then New York again, Laurin settled in the San Francisco Bay Area. He met Robert Nadeau in 1999 and has been training with him ever since. Herr was a senior instructor at City Aikido of San Francisco and is currently a senior instructor at Aikido of Mountain View. Off the mat, he is president of Pacific Interface Inc., an international consulting company based in Oakland, California.

### Richard Moon, 6th Dan

Richard began his study of martial arts in 1969, training in Shotokan karate, Kenpo, and kung fu under various teachers. In 1971, he began his practice of Aikido under Robert Nadeau Sensei, a relationship that continues to this day. Richard was also a personal student of Bira Almeida, Mestre Acordeon of Brazilian Capoeira, practiced Cheng Hsin with world champion Peter Ralston, and trained in qigong with B.K. Frantzis. Richard was the founder and chief instructor at Aikido of Marin. He was also a cofounder and senior instructor at City Aikido of San Francisco for many years.

### Bob Noha, 6th Dan

Bob began practicing Aikido in 1966 in Mountain View and shortly thereafter began training with Robert Nadeau Sensei, which started a lifelong friendship. Bob opened the first Aikido school in the Washington, D.C. area in 1970 and taught arrest/restraint tactics to U.S. Military Police at Andrews Air Force Base in 1974. Then, in 1975, he established the first Aikido school in Buffalo, New York. He founded Aikido of Petaluma in 1983 and continues to serve as its chief instructor. Bob traveled to Japan to further deepen his Aikido training in 1998, 1999, and 2006. In addition, he is also a devoted student and teacher of t'ai chi and has a background in several other martial arts.

### *Susan Spence, 3rd Dan*

Susan has studied with Robert Nadeau since 1984 and has been an instructor at his schools in Mountain View and San Francisco. She currently works as a physical therapist and biofeedback specialist treating children and adults.

### *Elaine Yoder, 6th Dan*

Elaine began her Aikido training with Robert Nadeau Sensei in 1977. She has continued training and teaching in the Bay Area ever since. She is currently president of the California Aikido Association (CAA). The focus of her Aikido teaching, as well as her profession as a Feldenkrais Practitioner, is to use movement to help humans live full and healthy lives.

### *Story Contributors*

Jeff Adams

AlejAndro Anastasio

Mike Ashwell

Denise Barry

Teja Bell (Fudo Myoo Bell Rōshi 老師)

Peggy Berger

Aimee Bernstein

Laurence Bianchini

Philip Booth

Dennis Butler

Patrick T. Cassidy

Diana (Weinberg) Daffner

Jade Dardine

Joop F. Delahaye

Linda Eskin

Richard Esmonde

Xavier Fayant

Kayla Feder

Mark Fitzwater

Nicola Fitzwater

Patrick Fitzsimmons

Steve Fleishman

David Lee Floeter

Chip Forman

Michael Friedl

Dave Goldberg

Renée Gregorio

Molly Hale

Jeff Haller, Ph.D.

Charlotte Hatch

Dianne Haynes

Mary Heiny

Patricia Anne Hendricks

Laurin Herr

Linda Holiday

Mark Housley

Roy Johnston

Andrei Karkar

Kenneth Kron

Dennis Kyriakos

Kenneth I. Laws

Robert C. Leichner

Tom Lewis

Hiram David Little

Henry Lynch

Ross Madden

Shawn-Patrick McCracken

Danny McIntyre

Lyn Meachen

Gina Mears

Dan Millman
Richard Moon
Dr. Justin Newman
Bob Noha
John Menard O'Connell Jr.
Olive
Wendy Palmer
Seth Paris
Antonio Piazza
Andreas G. Pefanis
Peter Ralston
Joel Riggs
Wayne Roth
Vincent Salvatore
Stephen Samuels
Carol Sanoff
Amy Shipley
Danielle Smith
Susan Spence
Roland Spitzbarth
Ellen Stapenhorst
Richard Strozzi-Heckler, Ph.D.
Sonja H. Sutherland
Oliver Thorne
Sasun Torikian
Catherine Tornbom
Alan Vann Gardner
Nancy Vayhinger
Jack Wada
Andrew A. Watson
Peter Wright
Elaine Yoder

## *Photography Contributors*

Mark Fitzwater
Laurin Herr
Alexander Kolbasov
Richard Moon
Robert Nadeau
Michael Smith
Tom Tabakin
Jan Watson

Photo courtesy of Mark Fitzwater appears on page 185

Photos courtesy of Laurin Herr appear on pages 54, 56–58, 62, 112, 178, 192, 196 (right), 205, 244, 246–247, 258, 267, 273, 277

Photos courtesy of Alexander Kolbasov appear on pages 49–50, 52–53, 55, 78, 80–81, 83, 89, 91, 94, 96, 103, 108, 111, 118, 121, 124–126, 128, 132, 134, 136, 145, 149, 156, 158, 161–162, 167, 172, 180, 187, 191, 198, 204, 209, 214, 218, 222, 227–228, 232, 236, 238–239, 242, 262, 269–271, 274–275, 279, 282, 286

Photos courtesy of Richard Moon appear on pages 51, 99, 143

Photos courtesy of Robert Nadeau appear on pages 2–3, 7, 9–11, 13–14, 16–24, 26–33, 35, 39–40 (top), 41–43, 46–47, 85, 196 (left), 220

Photo courtesy of Michael Smith appears on page 48

Photos courtesy of Tom Tabakin appear on pages 44–45

Photos courtesy of Jan Watson appear on pages 38, 40 (bottom), 64, 66, 69, 71, 74–75, 77, 138, 141, 165, 230, 252, 261, 264–265

Images in the public domain appear on pages 8, 12, 208

Diagrams created by Teja Bell appear on pages 95, 104, 119, 142, 150–151, 159, 173, 188, 199, 240

# Index

Adams, Jeff, 162–63
"Ahhh" and "Ohhh," 151–52
*ai* (harmony), 222
Aikido
  art of, 122–24, 164
  developmental process, 100
  as lifetime practice, 227
  as process of self-discovery, 107
  religion and, 279
  that cannot be seen, 219–38
Aikido Association of Northern
  California (AANC), 274–75
Aikido Hombu Dojo
  Morihei Ueshiba Osensei at, 24, 27
  Nadeau at, 18, 19, 20
  newsletter, 28
  returns (1966 and 1967), 31
  *shihan* (master teacher)
  appointment, 46
*Aikido in America* (Dobson), 37–39
*Aikidoka* (Aikido practitioners), 99,
  160, 256, 269
*Aikido* newsletter, 28
Aikido of Monterey (AOM), 275–76

Aikido of Northern California
  Yudansha-kai, 37, 39, 78
Aikido of San Francisco, 37, 38, 67,
  81, 296
Aikido teachers, 14, 18, 31, 43
*Aikido Today Magazine*, 29
Aiki Shrine, 28, 29, 50
Aiki Summer Retreats (ASR)
  about, 37, 52
  "Friendship Seminars," 249
  photos, 39, 52, 53
  as a revelation, 65
  student experiences, 271–73, 274
  teachers of, 47
  Terry Dobson as guest instructor,
  37–39
alchemy, 259
"allies," 202
Allowing
  about, 94–95
  Being Squared Away and, 203–4
  effort versus, 235
  practicing, 97
  student experience, 95–97

Amatsu Norito, 194
Anastasio, Alejandro, 248–52
apologizing, not, 91
"art of peace," 163
Ashwell, Mike, 87–90
autism spectrum disorder (ASD), 280
*Autobiography of a Yogi* (Yogananda), 13
awareness
    balance with sense-feel of
        embodiment, 247
    energy, 34, 43, 59, 63
    experiencing, 243
    of ki, 99
    Nadeau use of term, 103–12
    self, developing, 140
    in Underworld diagram, 188
    upper-level, integrating, 94
Awareness and Experience
    about, 103–4
    balance, 105, 118, 199, 215
    diagrams, 104–5
    incompletion without Experience,
        105
    interaction, 104
    opening to new experiences and,
        105
    relationship between, 116
    student experiences, 106–12

"bad day, fair day, good day, great
    day," 202–3
Baptiste, Walt, 13
Barry, Denise, 75–76, 200–204
Bateson, Gregory, 34
beginning basics, 86–92
being Present, 87, 93, 117, 118, 140,
    153, 181, 208

Being Squared Away
    about, 199–200
    assessing and adjusting and, 203–4
    diagram, 199
    student experience, 200–204
belief, 184
Bell, Teja, 163–65, 248–49, 295
Berger, Peggy, 230–32
Bernstein, Aimee, 41–42, 210–14
Bianchini, Laurence, 138–41
Blavatsky, Madame Helena, 12
body, the
    experiences, 119, 225
    feeling of, 226
    flow, 226, 227
    innate wisdom of the, 223–27
    intelligence of, 197–98
    listening with, 89
    ownership misunderstanding, 224
    posture, arrangement of, 136
    Sensei terms for, 223
    structure, aligning, 113
    understanding and, 223
books, about or inspired by Nadeau, 41
Booth, Phil, 268–69
*budo* (way of the warrior), 84
business card (early 70s), 32
Butler, Dennis, 190–91

CAA Doshu Workshop (2019), 55
California Aikido Association
    (CAA), 37, 48, 81
calmness, 36, 93, 182
Cassidy, Patrick, 14, 15, 23, 259–61
Center
    about, 118–19
    energy, expanding, 150

Energy and, 120, 199
in energy practice, 119
enhancing, 150
Experience of, 120–21
exploration of, 119
person, 152–53
standing, 119
Center Circle
about, 54, 149
"Ahhh" and "Ohhh" and, 151–52
Design of Creation and, 209
development, 153
energy flows, 151
harmonization, 153
inner nature, 152
practice, 151
resonances, 149
standing, 150
student experiences, 154–58
Certificate of Recognition, 31, 32
Character. *See also* Situation and
    Character
Energy fields of, 207
next dimensions of Energy and, 215
Original Self and, 207, 214
from Original Source of Creation,
    214
principles, 132–33
Remixing, 200
role of, 207
student experiences, 117, 133–36
Travel Vehicles and, 174
Circle person, 152–53. *See also* Center
    Circle
"Clear I am" mantra, 100
COVID-19, 55, 156, 177–78, 187,
    213, 245

Daffner, Diana, 175–78
Dardine, Jade, 144–45
Delahaye, Joop, 72–74
DeMello, Ed, 8, 9
deshi (disciples), 19, 73
Design of Creation
about, 208
aligning with, 215
constructs, 209
functioning of, 208–9
from Original Source of Creation,
    214
student experiences, 209–14
diagrams
Awareness Experience, 104
Awareness Experience Interact,
    104
Being Squared Away, 197–98
Center Circle Energy Flows, 151
Dimensionality: Manifest, Hidden,
    and Divine, 159
examples of, 173–74
Standing Center, 119
Standing Center Circle, 150
Themes and Principles, 240
Think, Feel, Sense, 95
Travel Vehicle, 173
Two Beats of Creation, 142
Underworld, 188
Dimensionality
about, 159
diagram, 159
fearless, 166–67
lifelong, 227–28
from mattress to, 167–72
in space-time continuum, 160
Stepping into Qualities and, 182

student experiences, 109–10,
160–72
Travel Vehicles and, 173–74
Dimensional Process, 166
dimensional shifting, 123
Dimensional Mapper, The, 162–63
dimensions
coexistence, 160
Divine, 159
Hidden, 159, 160–61
Manifest, 159
mapping, 162–63
moving between, 165
direct transmission, 240–52, 258,
260
Divine Dimension, 159, 209
Dobson, Terry, 37, 71
Dominican College, San Rafael, 39,
65, 67, 185, 266, 272
Doran, Frank, 37, 52, 54, 164, 275,
276
Downtime
about, 116–17
accepting, 187–88
COVID-19 and, 187
in exploring the Underworld,
188–89
student experiences, 190–98

Easy the I
about, 97
as long and challenging path,
99–100
practicing, 97
student experiences, 88–90, 98–103
"Easy the I, Open and Allow," 88, 90
8th Dan promotion, 54

Energy. *See also ki* (vital energy)
about, 247
accessing, 259
allowing, 123, 189
Center and, 120, 199
description of, 120
Divine Dimension, 209
experiencing, 119–20, 129, 215
feeling and sensing, 119
flow, 136
harmonization with, 122
Hidden Dimension, 209
"IT," 121
Open and Settle and, 188
opening to, 123
Situation and, 133
Space and, 207–8
students experiences, 121–32
through Centering, 120
transmission of, 124
Underworld and, 189
"Energy Awareness for Spiritual
Awareness," 175
Energy Awareness Workshops, 51,
143
Esalen Institute, 34, 35, 63, 130
Eskin, Linda, 282–87
Esmonde, Richard, 197–98
*Essence of Aikido, The* (Stevens), 219,
220
Everett, Tom, 72
experiences, memories, and insights
Andrei Karkar, 77–78
Dan Millman, 62–64
Dave Little, 60–62
John Menard O'Connell Jr.,
69–71

Joop Delahaye, 72–74
Linda Holiday, 78–80
Mark Housley, 81–83
Mary Heiny, 75–77
Nancy Vayhinger, 74–75
Patricia Hendricks, 80–81
Richard Strozzi-Heckler, 66–69
Roland Spitzbarth, 64–66

Fayant, Xavier, 238–39
fear, 122, 123, 148, 202, 278
fearless Dimensionality, 166
Feder, Kayla, 273–74
Feldenkrais, Moshe, 34
Feldenkrais Method, 135, 145–46
Fiedler, Margie, 9, 13, 15
Fitzsimmons, Patrick, 191–92
Fitzwater, Mark, 182–85
Fitzwater, Nicola, 93
Fleishman, Steve, 157–58
Floeter, David, 276–77
Flora (mother), 40, 41
flow. *See also* Frame and Flow
    the body, 226, 227
    energy, feeling, 136
    practicing, 140
    under pressure, 137
Forman, Chip, 166–67
Founder's Aikido, 160
Frager, Robert, 32, 79, 192–94
Frame and Flow
    about, 136
    harmonization, 137
    principle of, 136
    student experiences, 137–41
Friedl, Michael, 54, 55, 271–73
"Friendship Seminars," 249

Fudoshin Dojo, 56, 57, 58, 139
Full-Contact World Tournament, 266

Gardner, Alan Vann, 265
*gasshuku* (retreat training), 227–28
*Get Tough* (1942), 8
*gi* (practice uniform), 75, 82
Goldberg, Dave, 160–61, 284
gratitude, 95–97, 103, 158
gravity, aligning with, 92, 97, 119
Gregorio, Renée, 233–36
grounding, 92, 202, 212

Hale, Molly, 95–97
Haller, Jeffrey S., 135–36
*hanmi* (triangular stance), 223
*hara* (lower abdomen source of *ki*/
    heart/mind), 119, 201
harmony, 85, 222, 229–30, 268–69
Hatch, Charlotte, 229–30
Hayes, Dianne, 227–28
Heiny, Mary, 52, 53, 75–77, 275
Hendricks, Patricia, 54, 55, 80–81
Herr, Laurin, 253–58, 295–96
Hidden Dimension, 159, 160–61,
    209
high school years, 8–11
Holiday, Linda, 78–80, 275
honesty of the first-step, 157–58
Housley, Mark, 81–83
Human Potential Movement, 33,
    72–75, 85, 260
Huxley, Aldous, 34
hypnosis, 74

inner development, 154, 228
"intelligence of the body," 197–98

intention, 77
"IT," 121

jaki (dark forces / evil spirits), 194–95
Japan
    first arrival in, 16
    leading group of students to
        (2006), 48
    move to, 15–16
    return in early 60s, 60–61
Japan Karate Association, 16, 17
jikiden (direct transmission), 258
jiyu-waza (freestyle techniques), 263
Johnston, Roy, 167–72
judo
    conclusion of training, 15
    Hawaiian Island Judo
        Championship, 12
    in high school, 8, 9
    training with Watanabe Sensei,
        11–12

Karkar, Andrei, 77–78
katsuhayabi ("speed that transcends
        space and time")
    meaning of, 219–20
    Osensei and, 220, 221
    written, signed, and sealed, 220
ki (vital energy), 71, 81, 98, 254
Kisshomaru Ueshiba Doshu, 43–45,
    48
Kodokan Judo Institute membership
    card (1962), 17
Kodokan member's oath, 17
kohai (the junior in a relationship), 76
Koichi Tohei, 18, 19
Kojiki (Record of Ancient Matters), 220

kokyu-nage (breath throw), 106, 226
Kono, Henry, 76
Kornfield, Jack, 34
koshi-nage (hip throw), 168, 171
kote-gaeshi (wrist-twist technique), 99
kototama (word spirit), 194, 196
Kron, Ken, 277–79
Kumano Juku Dojo, 193, 257
Kyriakos, Dennis, 236–38

Laws, Ken, 280–82
Leichner, Bob, 261–63
Leonard, George, 34–36, 93, 217,
    278, 282–83
Leonard Energy Training (L.E.T.),
    63–64
Lewis, Tom, 242–44
Lilly, John, 34
listening
    with the body, 89
    deeply, 114
    grounded presence, 218
    inner, 67, 68
    without judgment, 87, 89
Little, Dave, 60–62
Lynch, Henry, 125–26

Madden, Ross, 98–100
Manifest Dimension, 159
marriage to Katja Simona, 46
marriage to Margie Fiedler, 13
McCracken, Shawn, 245–46
McIntyre, Danny, 133–34
Meachen, Lyn, 178–80
Mears, Gina, 271
meditation, 12, 13, 18, 176
Millman, Dan, 62–64

Mingo, 10
*misogi* (inner purification), 193
Mitsuteru Ueshiba, 49
"monster theory," 196
Moon, Richard, 122–24, 263, 296
Morihei Ueshiba Osensei
  at Aikido Hombu Dojo (photo),
    24, 27
  Aikido lineage connection, 43
  Aikido written, signed and sealed,
    85
  at Aiki Shrine (photo), 28
  Bob Frager training under, 32–33
  bowing to, 29
  deep connection to, 76
  direct disciple of, 84
  as founder of Aikido, 18, 63, 80, 243
  at home (photo), 33
  interview with Nadeau about, 26–28
  *katsuhayabi* and, 220, 221
  with Nadeau (photo), 3
  Nadeau's time with, 1–4
  photos, 2, 18
  process, transmission of, 262
  respect and love for, 80
  stories about, 185
  with students (photo), 26
  teaching Nadeau, 26
Morihiro Saito, 45, 65
Moriteru Ueshiba Doshu, 43–44,
  48–49
Murphy, Michael, 34, 36

Nadeau, Robert
  adaptive rephrasing of teaching, 3
  birth and childhood, 7–8
  body development, 10

high school years, 8–11
  photo with Morihei Ueshiba, 3
  spiritual journey, 1
  time with Morihei Ueshiba, 1–4
Nadeau Roku, 4–5
*nage* (throwing partner), 86, 106–7
Nakano family, 16–18
naming practice, 203
Newman, Justin, 100–103
New Zealand, 87–88, 93, 125–26,
  178, 268–69
*nidan* (2nd degree black belt), 31
Noha, Bob, 108–11, 211, 244, 296

Oberlin Aikido Club, 64
O'Connell, John Menard Jr., 69–71
"Oh, fuck/ Oh, base" moments, 177
Olive, 137
1x1, 2x2, 3x3 practice, 174–75
Onisaburo Deguchi, 153–54
Open and Settle
  about, 92
  accessibility of, 92
  as basic practice, 123
  into Experience, 119
  to experience Energy dynamics,
    188
  grounding and, 92–93
  practicing, 92–93
organization, this book, 5–6
Original Self
  about, 206–7
  Character and, 207, 214
  as constant, 207
  Energy fields of, 207
  from Original Source of Creation,
    214

role of, 207
student experiences, 209–14
Osensei Revisited (OSR) workshops,
   53–54, 141, 242, 285

Page, Floyd, 10
Palmer, Wendy, 121, 217, 282
Paris, Seth, 263–65
Pefanis, Andreas, 111–12
Perls, Fritz, 34
photos
   at Aikido Hombu Dojo (1964), 19
   at Aikido of San Francisco (1980s),
      38
   at Aiki Summer Retreat (1981), 39
   bowing to Osensei, 29
   CAA Doshu Workshop (2019), 55
   with Eddie Hagihara, 23
   at Energy Awareness Workshop
      (2000s), 51
   at Esalen (1970s), 35
   Francis Takahashi, Frank Doran,
      Moriteru Ueshiba and Nadeau
      (mid-1980s), 43
   Frank Doran (1980s), 38
   with Frank Doran, 8th Dan
      promotions (2017), 54
   with Frank Doran at Aiki Summer
      Retreat (2008), 52
   holding 2nd Dan Certificate
      (1964), 31
   in Iwama Dojo (2006), 50
   with Julian Silverman at Esalen
      (1970s), 35
   with Koichi Tohei (1962–64), 19
   Margie, Verell Sugano, Terry
      Dobson, Eddie Hagihara, 23

   with Margie, Yoshimitsu Yamada,
      Eddie Hagihara, 21
   with Margie and Nakano family
      (1963), 17
   with Margie Fiedler (age 17), 9
   in Marine Reserves (age 18), 11
   with Mary Heiny and Jack Wada at
      Aiki Summer Retreat (2011), 53
   with Michael Friedl and Patricia
      Hendricks (2019), 55
   with Mingo (age 20), 10
   with Mitsuteru Ueshiba, Moriteru
      Ueshiba, Katja Simona (2006),
      49
   Morihei Ueshiba Osensei, 2
   Morihei Ueshiba Osensei at home
      (late 1960s), 33
   with mother Flora (1980s), 40
   Nadeau, Moriteru Ueshiba,
      Kisshomaru Ueshiba (1998), 44
   Nadeau Sensei (1970s), 42
   Osensei at Aikido Hombu Dojo
      (1962–1964), 24, 27
   at Osensei Revisited workshop
      (2014), 53
   Osensei with students (1962–64),
      26
   practices with Katja Simona (early
      2000s), 47
   at public demonstration (1964), 30
   remixing, 143
   Robert Nadeau (age 7), 7
   Robert Nadeau and Morihei
      Ueshiba (1964), 3
   with Roy Suenaka, Morihei
      Ueshiba, Seiichi Sugano, 20
   with Seiichi Sugano, Morihiko

Ichihashi, Shuji Maruyama, 21
with students and Morihiro Saito
(1998), 45
with students at Aiki Shrine
(2006), 50
with students in Tokyo (2006), 49
with Takeo Nakano (1962), 16
at TamaAikikai demonstration
(1964), 30
teaching at Aiki Summer Retreat
(2011), 52
teaching at Fudoshin Dojo (2022),
56, 58
teaching in virtual dojo (2020), 57
Terry Dobson (1980s), 38
throwing high school judo coach
(age 16), 9
wedding, with Margie Fiedler
(1960), 13
wed to Katja Simona (2001), 46
in weight-lifting gym (1990s), 41
with Yoshimitsu Yamada and
Margie, 22
with Yutaka Kurita, Mitsunari
Kanai, Nobuyoshi Tamura, 22
Piazza, Tony, 221–22
Potted Plant Theory, 204–6
practice. See also specific practices
daily, 20, 135, 201
deepening, 105
with forces and pressures, 148, 201
lifetime, Aikido as, 227
nature of, 163
numbers in describing, 123
orientation to, 86–87, 181
process-oriented, 110
repetition, 94, 139

solo, 187
struggles in, 79
sustained, 95, 136
presence, 73, 92, 109, 138–41, 144,
177, 208
Present, being, 87, 93, 117, 118, 140,
153, 181, 208
process circle, 164
Process, The, 162–63
"pump the pump," 118

Ralston, Peter, 266–67
recollections and reverberations
Alan Vann Gardner, 265
Andrew Watson, 269–70
Bob Leichner, 261–63
Danielle Smith, 274–76
David Floeter, 276–77
Gina Mears, 271
Kayla Feder, 273–74
Ken Kron, 277–79
Ken Laws, 280–82
Laurin Herr, 253–58
Linda Eskin, 282–87
Michael Friedl, 271–73
Patrick Cassidy, 259–61
Peter Ralston, 266–67
Phil Booth, 268–69
Seth Paris, 263–65
redirecting energy, 222
Redwood City Police officer, 13, 14,
15
Remixing
about, 143
benefits, 143
Character, 200
photo, 143

student experiences, 144–49
Travel Vehicles and, 174–75
Riggs, Joel, 242
Rolf, Ida, 34
Roth, Wayne, 223–27

Salvatore, Vince, 209
Samuels, Stephen, 128–32
Sanoff, Carol, 90–92
*seiza* (seated posture on floor), 92–93,
148, 223
self-development, 138–41, 163
seminars, 43
shifting, 123, 146, 172–74, 177
*shihan* (master teacher), 46, 269–70,
281, 285
*shiho-nage* (four direction throw),
234–35
*shikko* (knee walking), 89
Shinshin Toitsu Do, 33
Shipley, Amy, 106–8
*shodan* (1st degree black belt), 29, 68,
73, 267
*shomen* (ceremonial front of a dojo),
223
*shomen-uchi ikkyo* (first-teaching
technique for frontal strike to the
forehead), 108
*shugyo* (personal development), 6
Simona, Katja, 45–46, 47, 49
Situation and Character. *See also*
Character
harmonization, 133
principles, 132–33
student experiences, 133–36
sizing, 202–3
Smith, Danielle, 253, 274–76

Space
about, 207
being Present in, 208
Energies and, 207–8
intelligence, 208
from Original Source of Creation,
214
student experiences, 209–14
Spence, Susan, 154–56, 297
Spitzbarth, Roland, 64–66
stability, 182
Standing Center Circle, 150
Standing Practice
about, 112–13
practice, 113
student experience, 113–18
Stepping into Qualities, 182
Stevens, John, 219, 220
Strozzi-Heckler, Richard, 66–69, 217,
282
student practice and experiences. *See
also specific practices*
Aimee Bernstein, 210–14
Alejandro Anastasio, 248–52
Amy Shipley, 106–8
Andreas Pefanis, 111–12
Bob Noha, 108–11
Carol Sanoff, 90–92
Catherine Tornbom, 246–47
Charlotte Hatch, 229–30
Chip Forman, 166–67
Daffner, Diana, 175–78
Danny McIntyre, 133–34
Dave Goldberg, 160–61
Denise Barry, 200–204
Dennis Butler, 190–91
Dennis Kyriakos, 236–38

Dianne Hayes, 227–28
Elaine Yoder, 216–18
Ellen Stapenhorst, 127–28
Henry Lynch, 125–26
Jack Wada, 192–97
Jade Dardine, 144–45
Jeff Adams, 162–63
Jeffery Haller, 135–36
Joel Riggs, 242
Justin Newman, 100–103
Laurence Bianchini, 138–41
Lyn Meachen, 178–80
Mark Fitzwater, 182–85
Mike Ashwell, 87–90
Molly Hale, 95–97
Nicola Fitzwater, 93
Olive, 137
Oliver Thorne, 113–18
Patrick Fitzsimmons, 191–92
Peggy Berger, 230–32
Peter Wright, 185–87
Renée Gregorio, 233–36
Richard Esmonde, 197–98
Richard Moon, 122–24
Ross Madden, 98–100
Roy Johnston, 167–72
Sasun Torikian, 126–27
Shawn McCraken, 245–46
Sonja Sutherland, 145–49
Stephen Samuels, 128–32
Steve Fleishman, 157–58
Susan Spence, 154–56
Teja Bell, 163–65
Tom Lewis, 242–44
Tony Piazza, 221–22
Vince Salvatore, 209
Wayne Roth, 223–27

Wendy Palmer, 121
Xavier Fayant, 238–39
*suki* (vulnerable gaps), 253
surrender, 158
*sutemi-waza* (sacrificing technique), 212
Sutherland, Sonja, 145–49
Su-U-A-O-U-E-Re-E-Gi chant, 51
*suwari-waza* (seated techniques done with the knees), 92
system, the. *See* body, the

Tama Aikikai demonstration, 30
Tann Sensi, 14–15
teacher, influence as, 41
teaching and practices
    adaptive rephrasing of, 3
    Aikido at UC Santa Cruz, 75
    Aikido that cannot be seen, 219–38
    at Aiki Summer Retreat, 52
    Allowing, 94–97
    approach to, 84–85
    attraction to, 23–25
    Awareness and Experience, 103–12
    beginning basics, 86–92
    Being Squared Away, 199–204
    Center, 118–19
    class architecture and, 68
    Clearing, 181–82
    deeper lessons of, 73
    depth of, 263–65
    Design of Creation, 208–14
    diagrams, 85
    Dimensionality, 159–72
    direct students of Osensei, 65
    "doing" versus "allowing" and, 86
    Downtime and Underworld, 187–98

Easy the I, 88, 90, 97–103
Energy, 119–32
expressions of universal creativity, 214–18
first encounter description, 14–15
Frame and Flow, 136–41
at Fudoshin Dojo, 56, 58
Human Potential Movement and, 72–75
idiosyncratic vocabulary, 254
initial attraction description, 15
inner, transmission of, 86
interest in deeper aspects of, 25
introduction to, 13
Japanese characters, 85
language evolution, 86
lectures, 85
lessons of, 86
one-liners, 134
Open and Settle, 92–93
Original Self, 206–7, 209–14
as a path, 64
patois, 85
Potted Plant Theory, 204–6
Remixing, 143–49
in San Francisco, 33–34
schedule, 51
self-defense and, 93
Situation and Character, 132–36
Space, 207–8, 209–14
Standing Practice, 112–18
Stepping into Qualities, 182
themes and principles, 240–41
Trading-in, 181
Travel Vehicles, 172–80
Two Beats of Creation, 142
universal themes, 86

in virtual dojo, 57
as *The Way of Spiritual Harmony*, 85
Tempu-Kai, 33
10-pounder, 20-pounder, 30-pounder practice, 173, 174
*tenkan* (turning blend), 107, 226
Theosophical Society, 12–13
Thorne, Oliver, 113–18
threat, reaction to, 67–68
Torikian, Sasun, 126–27
Tornbom, Catherine, 246–47
Trading-in, 181
Travel Vehicles
  about, 172–73
  diagram, 173
  Dimensionality and, 173–74
  lesson underlying practices, 174
  student experiences, 175–80
trust, 154–56, 159, 166, 195, 227, 249
Two Beats of Creation, 142, 143, 209, 215
Two Beats process, 152

*uchideshi* (live-in disciples), 20, 81
UC Santa Cruz, 75, 78, 192–95
*uke* (attacking/receiving partner)
  aligning as, 156
  energy field as, 144–45
  feeling underlying Energy of, 182
  *nage* and, 86
  in *nikkyo* demonstration, 82
  Osensei, 20
  shifting and, 146, 148
  student experiences, 67, 69, 106, 144–45, 183, 224
  in *sutemi-waza* demonstration, 212

*ukemi* (art of attacking/falling/
   rolling)
   advanced, 248
   learning, 190
   one-handed, 248–52
   for Osensei, 23
   student experiences, 69–71, 89, 91,
      111, 114, 155, 166, 179
   taking with Nadeau Sensei, 218,
      237, 249
   thrill of, 265
Underworld
   diagram, 188
   Downtime and, 188–89
   early exploration of, 189
   energy of, 189
   as misunderstood, 189
   student experiences, 190–98
universal consciousness, 209
*ushiro katate-dori sankyo* (third-
   teaching technique from rear
   one-handed grab), 99

Vayhinger, Nancy, 74–75
virtual dojo, 55–57, 156, 177–78, 187,
   205, 245, 258

visualization practice, 206
Vortex of Creation, 209

Wada, Jack, 52, 53, 75, 192–97, 275
"Walk like a human being," 112
Watanabe Sensei, Yasutoshi "Moon,"
   11–12, 15, 60
Watson, Andrew, 269–70
Watts, Alan, 34
*Way of Aikido, The* (Leonard),
   282–83
*Way of Harmony, The* (podcast),
   283
*waza* (techniques), 68, 110, 181–82,
   253, 257
Witt, Bill, 37, 62, 73, 276
Wright, Peter, 185–87

Yamaguchi, Seigo, 110
Yin/Yang symbol, 142
Yoder, Elaine, 216–18, 297
yoga practice, 12, 13

*zanshin* (sustained energetic
   connection), 235
zone of resonance, 135

# Books of Related Interest

**The Hidden Power of Aikido**
Transcending Conflict and Cultivating Inner Peace
*by Susan Perry, Ph.D.*
*Forewords by John Stevens and John Perry*

**The Art of Mastery**
Principles of Effective Interaction
*by Peter Ralston*

**Aikido and Words of Power**
The Sacred Sounds of Kototama
*by William Gleason*

**Embodying the Mystery**
Somatic Wisdom for Emotional, Energetic,
and Spiritual Awakening
*by Richard Strozzi-Heckler*

**The Writer Who Inhabits Your Body**
Somatic Practices to Enhance Creativity and Inspiration
*by Renée Gregorio*

**Qigong Teachings of a Taoist Immortal**
The Eight Essential Exercises of Master Li Ching-yun
*by Stuart Alve Olson*

**Shaolin Qi Gong**
Energy in Motion
*by Shi Xinggui*

**The Spiritual Practices of the Ninja**
Mastering the Four Gates to Freedom
*by Ross Heaven*

INNER TRADITIONS • BEAR & COMPANY
P.O. Box 388 • Rochester, VT 05767
1-800-246-8648 • www.InnerTraditions.com

Or contact your local bookseller